FISHING ACROSS AMERICA

FISHING ACROSS AMERICA

Luke Ovgard

Copyright © 2023 Luke Ovgard
All rights reserved. No part of this book may be reproduced in any form or by any electronic means, including information storage and retrieval systems, without written permission from the author, except by reviewers, who may quote brief passages in a review.

ISBN: 979898781
ISBN 13: 9798987811511

Edited by Emily Hanson and Zach Alley.

Cover designed by Ella Bocchi.

Visit www.caughtovgard.com to read free content.

Subscribe to the author's weekly column, CaughtOvgard, at www.patreon.com/CaughtOvgard.

5 4 2 1

Dedicated to my dad for giving me a love of fishing, to Cam Wogan for inspiring me to start a fishing journal in eighth grade, to my first editor, Steve Matthies, for teaching me how to write for an audience, to Gerry O'Brien for letting me start my column, to my longest-running editor, Holly Owens, for shaping me as a writer, to Holly Dillemuth for encouraging me to syndicate my column, to Matt Miller for guiding me through the daunting process of publication, to my mom for reading this book before anyone else, and to everyone I've fished with along the way.

TABLE OF CONTENTS

Foreword
Preface
Introduction

PART 1 — THE RUT
Chapter 1: The Email
Chapter 2: Second Chance

PART 2 — THE PLAN
Chapter 3: Decisions
Chapter 4: Buildup

PART 3 — THE TRIP
Chapter 5: Pit Stops
Chapter 6: Desert Lakes
Chapter 7: The Old Country
Chapter 8: Middle America
Chapter 9: Coffee
Chapter 10: The Wedding
Chapter 11: Trash and Treasures
Chapter 12: Disneywhirled
Chapter 13: Water ... Without Fish?
Chapter 14: Marco? Hoplo!
Chapter 15: The International Incident
Chapter 16: Miami Vices
Chapter 17: Pride and Joy
Chapter 18: Tropical Storm Casey
Chapter 19: A Really Bad Day
Chapter 20: Shark Weak
Chapter 21: The Conch Republic
Chapter 22: Snakeheads
Chapter 23: The Pursuit of Happy
Chapter 24: The 324th of July
Chapter 25: Housekeeping and Sweepers
Chapter 26: Real Unicorns
Chapter 27: B-A-N-A-N-A-S
Chapter 28: Worms
Chapter 29: Twenty-Five
Chapter 30: ICAST
Chapter 31: Meet Your Heroes

Chapter 32: Telling Time
Chapter 33: Faith in the Unseen
Chapter 34: The Florida Panhandle
Chapter 35: Sweet Home Alabama
Chapter 36: Shelton's Clothing
Chapter 37: Babysitting Done Right
Chapter 38: Staying Mobile
Chapter 39: Pier Commercialism
Chapter 40: Photos, Pirates, Pearls
Chapter 41: Judge Not, Lest Ye Be Wrong
Chapter 42: Apple of My Eye
Chapter 43: The Ozarks
Chapter 44: 40 Days and 40 Nights
Chapter 45: Time as a Force of Change
Chapter 46: Five Decades of Cultural References
Chapter 47: Heaven and Hell
Chapter 48: Bad Decisions
Chapter 49: The Elephant in the Room
Chapter 50: The Last Day

PART 4 — THE RETURN
Chapter 51: Coping
Chapter 52: The Bitter(sweet) End

Acknowledgements

FOREWORD

When people think of greatness they often liken it to a sports star like Babe Ruth or a war hero like Audie Murphy. The average person wants to be anything other than average.

True greatness is hard to define, but everyone knows it when they see it. No one sees the hard work and the long exhausting climb it takes to get to the top. They want the payoff. They want the big payoffs.

To the average person, work is the thing they reluctantly roll out of bed to do on a daily basis. Following someone else's grind isn't their idea of greatness.

Greatness in the world of fishing usually runs parallel with winning large sums of money by besting competitors in a defined amount of time or chasing world records of renowned species.

To the novice angler, catching an average-size fish isn't the stuff of legend or even worth remembering. To that person I introduce: "Luke Ovgard: The World's Greatest Average Fisherman."

The pursuit of fishes 200-plus days a year without competition, without financial gain in the balance, or without the allure of trophy-size fish would be seen as crazy to most.

To Luke, that's the goal.

He certainly doesn't catch the biggest fish.

He doesn't catch the most fish.

He rarely catches fishes you would have any interest in under normal circumstances, but his quest isn't quite normal. He doesn't fish to accumulate wealth. He doesn't fish out of a boat that looks like a floating billboard to advertise products no one needs.

What he does is what the sport was intended to be in its purest form. He fishes for the internal accomplishment of man versus nature.

To him, every fish is a trophy no matter the size or species.

In this book you won't find the pursuit of conventional greatness. What you will find is an average guy in the pursuit of average fishes across an array of species most of us never even knew existed. This is something any one of us could potentially accomplish, but we won't.

This is a book about Luke Ovgard and his utter love and obsession with catching fish.

When was the last time you loved something so much you put all of your time, money, and effort into it knowing the world around you wouldn't care about the results? This book is motivation in its purest form: the internal pursuit of greatness.

— Marcus Moss || Friend of the Author

PREFACE

Before I talk about how I manage my depression by fishing, or I jump into my personal history, or tell one of the most epic yet surprisingly relatable travel stories you've ever read, I need to provide you, dear reader, with quick lessons in world history and science. I am, after all, a teacher.

Throughout this book, I'll be talking about fishes. A lot of fishes. Those fishes all have names and to avoid confusion, I use their specific names because a trout is not just a trout. A trout is a *specific kind* of trout. It seems awkward to interject this here, but awkwardness seems to follow me around, so I want to talk about the two names every fish has: a common name and a scientific name. Here goes.

Every species on planet Earth has a common name. This is the simple, easy-to-remember name in an everyday, spoken language. Americans, Brits, Indians, South Africans, Australians, Jamaicans, Kiwis, Singaporeans, Canadians, Liberians and any other native English speakers will recognize "Domestic Dog" or "Domestic Cat" or "Human" or "Goldfish" as common names for four of the world's most plentiful species of vertebrates (animals with backbones).

Virtually every language in the world has a common name for dogs and cats and humans and goldfish. In fact, most fishes, birds, reptiles, amphibians, mammals, fungi, plants and even bacteria generally have common names, although not every species has a common name in every language. It wouldn't make sense for a small lizard endemic (meaning found only in a given area) to a patch of the Sahara Desert to have a Farsi or Korean or Navajo common name, even though the Persians and Koreans and Navajo likely have general names for "lizards" as well as specific Farsi and Korean and

Navajo common names for specific species of lizards common in areas where those respective languages are spoken.

You with me so far? Good.

Generally, when the term *common name* is used, it is referring to the English common name of the species and not Farsi or Korean or Navajo common names. Yes, this is rooted in imperialism, but arguably the greatest benefit of imperialism is shared language. Though all bear a multitude of sins, world empires centered in Egypt, Babylon, Persia, Greece, Rome and Mongolia all spread their respective language: humanity's most essential tool.

Though most of today's historians argue that Genghis Khan's was the final world empire in the traditional sense, many subsequent empires boasted a larger total population, stronger economic influence, and/or more military might. Still, only one empire in history officially controlled more lands or a higher percentage of the world population than that of the Mongols.

As humanity spread to all corners of the world and settled in more than 50 million square miles of earth's land area, the ability for a true, contiguous world empire like Khan's faded away, but the British did manage to create a disjunct empire that spanned nearly one-quarter of the world's land area and one-quarter of its total human population and included territory in almost every time zone. Had the Mongols conquered the world in the late 18th or early 19th Century, we would likely be speaking Mongolian and have it serve as the basis for common names, but time was on the side of the British.

Given the peak of British influence coming so recently in world history (just prior to World War I) and the fact that Britain passed the torch of global dominance to an English-speaking United States and its worldwide pseudo-empire without any notable lapse in leadership, it's no wonder English is so prevalent in the world today.

English is widely recognized as lingua franca today, that is, the most dominant language on Earth, but it has only held that title for a few hundred years, beginning with Victorian England's domination of the world, bolstered by American reconstruction of Europe and Asia in the aftermath of World War II, and solidified by "The American Century" that saw the United States develop into the largest economic power since the dawn of man. Thus, English common names.

For *scientific names*, we must go back to the dawn of man. The Biblical creation story prominently features the first humans, Adam and Eve, naming the other animals. The ancient Greeks attempted to develop classification systems for living things. Ancient Chinese and Indus Valley civilizations separated specific animals by name as did New World civilizations in the Andes and Yucatan. Islamic and Jewish scholars routinely wrote of the animals populating the lands and discussed which were clean and unclean. Alas, no system was comprehensive or even attempted to be comprehensive for all life until the modern era. Feudalism and other draconian systems of government across much of Europe and Asia stifled progress for centuries, or something like modern taxonomy might have developed sooner.

One of those systems was the Catholic Church. Though it had many failings, the Medieval Catholic Church also provided several great services to the world at large. Along with Muslim clerics, Jewish rabbis, and Buddhist monks, the Medieval Catholic monks and priests were arguably the most highly-educated individuals of their day. Though their research was often restricted by prevailing Church doctrine, they did preserve and (to a limited degree) expand upon writings of the ancients that would later serve as the foundation for work by many modern thinkers.

Not only that, but those monks kept ancient Greek and Latin alive as the dominant languages of the intelligentsia at a time when Europe was rapidly diverging into the linguistic and cultural miasma it is today. Over time, and probably due to the legacy of Roman rule, it was Latin and not Greek that predominated the intellectual landscape. Without Latin tying a common thread from its diligent benefactors in the Holy Roman Empire, the Russian Tsardom, the Spanish Empire, the Kingdom of France, the Ottoman Empire, the Kingdom of Sweden, and the many fractured city states, duchies, and serfdoms of Eastern and Central Europe would likely not have had the running start towards modernity the Protestant Reformation provided.

As Martin Luther opened the doors of scientific exploration to those Europeans not entrenched in the clergy in 1517, Latin (not Luther's native German) carried the torch from that point forward. Some 200 years later, when Swedish botanist Carl Linnaeus developed his system of classifying all living things, a system we know today as "taxonomy," he did so not in Swedish, but in Latin. In addition to dividing up all living things into Kingdom, Phylum, Class, Order, Family, Genus, and Species for cataloging and research purposes, Linnaeus developed what would become known as "binomial nomenclature," or the use of a two-part scientific name.

The scientific name is a Latin name generally assigned to a particular species when it is described as a unique species. Every living thing from obscure bacteria to Bactrian Camels has a scientific name. Scientific names are always two words with the first word representing the Genus and the second indicating the Species. For the Bactrian Camel, it is *Camelus bactrianus* but would usually be written with the common name first, a comma, and then the scientific name written in italics: Bactrian Camel, *Camelus bactrianus*. Subspecies get a third Latin word following the first two, but that is largely beyond the scope of this book.

Even exalted humanity has a scientific name. Human beings are the only surviving species in our genus, *Homo*, and there is some debate over which other species (if any) once joined us there. Regardless, surviving people have an English common name of Human and a scientific name of *Homo sapiens*, derived from the Latin "to think". We write this as Human, *Homo sapiens*.

Sapience describes beings with the ability to think, the capacity for intelligence, the ability to acquire wisdom. Humans are the only confirmed sapient beings on earth. *Sentience*, on the other hand, is often confused with — and incorrectly used in place of — *sapience* to describe extraterrestrial life in Science Fiction. Sentience merely describes a being with consciousness, the capacity for sensation, and a subjective experience (like a cat, a dog, or a goldfish) — it says nothing of intelligence, rationality, or wisdom that we humans possess. Though there is some debate here, as well, the consensus is most living things are *sentient*, while only humans are *sapient*.

As a sapient Human, *Homo sapiens*, I try to catch, photograph, and release (arguably) sentient fishes. In this book, when I first mention a species of fish, I'll list its common name with a comma and then its scientific name in italics. I'll typically only use the scientific name with that first mention but proceed with only the common name thereafter, as I'm not a scientist; I just play one on paper sometimes. I'll also mention the scientific name with every new species I catch, even if I'd previously mentioned it.

Oh, and I already missed a fish in this book. I mentioned the Goldfish, *Carassius auratus*, without mentioning its scientific name that first time, so there ya go. I won't forget from here on out; my memory is at least as good as that of a Goldfish. Since I mentioned a Domestic Dog, *Canis lupus familiaris* (subspecies included to separate Spot and Fido from the Gray Wolf, *Canis lupus*) and Domestic Cat, *Felis catus*, I'll include those here, too, but this is not a book about pets or birds or lizards, so when I mention a gull or a feral cat or an alligator, I won't list its scientific name like I will when I mention a fish because this is a book about fish. Well, fishes.

One more thing: when I refer to a single fish, I mean one fish, a single specimen. Fish refers to one trout or one salmon or one bass. These are not specific species as listed, so notice how trout and salmon and bass are not capitalized and don't include scientific names here? When I refer to a group of fish of the same species, such as a school of trout or salmon or bass, fish is still the right word; however, when I refer to two or more species of fish in any amount, I will use fishes.

Again, a single trout (species not specified) is a fish. A single Rainbow Trout, *Oncorhynchus mykiss* is a fish. A school of Rainbow Trout is also fish. A school of trout and salmon and bass (an unlikely mix in nature) are fishes. I'm done talking about science and history and nomenclature, so whether you wanted to or not, you just got schooled. Like a fish. School is out, so let's get to the story of a summer vacation unlike any other.

INTRODUCTION

Do they still call it a "midlife crisis" if you're 28?
Well, it's the only way I can describe my life during most of 2018 and 2019.

Depression has shaped my life for as long as I can remember, but I think high school is when I finally had a name for the general malaise, apathy, and inexplicable sadness that hovered over me like a dark cloud. Sadly, just like most Western men battling depression, I refused to seek formal treatment out of misguided machismo, fear of public opinion, and a fundamentally American notion of self-reliance.

Instead of seeking counseling or medication or telling anyone about my struggles, I tried all of the home remedies: eating well, maintaining a schedule, practicing good sleep hygiene, avoiding drugs and alcohol, exercising regularly, and throwing myself into my work and my social life. It stayed the demons and kept me from self-harm or suicide, but it didn't make me happy. Not even close.

Only one thing ever did that: Self-medication.

Self-medication has long been a part of my family, and I continued the trend. My paternal grandfather died of smoking-related complications before I was ever born. My maternal grandfather lived well into his 90s but wasted much of his life as a drunk who only defeated alcoholism in his 60s after finding Jesus.

I never adopted either vice, learning from their mistakes and knowing that my genetic bent toward addiction paired with perennial depression probably would've pushed me to suicide if I ever reached for the bottle.

Instead, I chose another, healthier vice they both shared: fishing.

The dopamine release when you catch a fish is palpable. Paired with exercise, sunlight, adrenaline, and the choice of solitude or socialization on the water, fishing is the ultimate remedy for depression, a consummate and holistic win for your psyche. Long before I was diagnosed with depression and began receiving treatment, I realized nothing defeated the darkness quite like tricking trout with a shiny piece of metal or tuft of feathers.

Troutcomes

Long before I knew anything of science or history or depression and was just beginning to experiment with human language, my dad took me fishing. He first took me trout fishing when I was just a baby, putting me in a baby backpack while he wet waded Southern and Central Oregon's trout streams in pursuit of Brook Trout, *Salvelinus fontinalis* and Bull Trout, *Salvelinus confluentus* and Rainbow Trout. He remembers me drooling on his neck as he waded through beaver ponds and frigid riffles in the heat of summer, so I came by it honestly.

My earliest memory, at 3 years old, is catching a fish at Howard Prairie Reservoir between Ashland and my native Klamath Falls. Dad told me how to work a spinning reel, but in the heat of the moment, I forgot and just started walking backwards up the hill with the rod in my hands until I'd pulled the hatchery Rainbow onto the shore.

That trout was the first of thousands to come. I didn't catch anything on purpose but trout (and the odd head cold) until I was 13 years old, at which point I sightfished some Bluegill, *Lepomis macrochirus* in a pond behind my brother's baseball game using grasshoppers I caught in the tall grass on the bank.

Not long after, shortly before turning 14, I realized fishing wasn't just my hobby; it was my purpose.

I realized this on a trip with my Dad, my brother Jake (11), and some family friends, the Wogans. Cam Wogan (my dad's longtime friend) mentioned he'd started a hunting and fishing journal to track his outings, and he found it incredibly helpful. I was taken with the idea and recorded that very trip in a notebook I bought with money earned mowing lawns and refereeing soccer games.

That first notebook, which I named "Luke Ovgard's Sportsman's Journal" was the first of six handwritten journals I would fill up with hunting and fishing trips throughout the years before going digital, and that Sportsman's Journal marked the first time I ever wrote about something by choice. In it, I recorded dates, locations, conditions, species encountered, bad fish puns, and anything else I could fit into my stories that nobody but me ever read. That very first entry included notations about the fish we chased most often: wild native Redband Trout, *Oncorhynchus mykiss newberryi*. I caught a few that day in a small tributary to the Klamath River called Spencer Creek.

Redbands stole my heart and helped forge my passion into an obsession in the years that followed as I evolved from small fishes in small streams to big fishes in rivers and lakes. Though fishing was still my passion, I was involved in every extracurricular at my tiny school, and I didn't have a car until my senior year, so fishing took a backseat in my teens to sports, music, and other extracurriculars.

When I finally got that car and opted not to play a spring sport but instead get a job to pay for gas and fishing tackle, my world opened up in a way the Little Mermaid couldn't even imagine. With every spare moment and every spare dollar, I was fishing.

In college, I further expanded my trout fishing exploits, targeting trophy trout, but I also got into bass, crappie, sunfish, and even saltwater fishing. Casting lures and sitting on bait expanded to flyfishing, trolling, jigging, surfcasting, topwater fishing, and everything else I could afford. By the time I'd graduated college, I was a multispecies angler.

Most of the iconic fishing books paint a romanticized tale of flyfishing for trout: a gentleman's obsession with chasing noble trout in clear waters unmarred by the masses as they perfect the arts of flytying, casting, and dressing for America's most erudite pastime that requires neither sailboat nor horse.

There's nothing wrong with flyfishing. There's a market for it, and the flyfishing purists and their disciples have long kept their classic fishing novels at the top of the genre. I flyfish myself on occasion.

I love trout, and wild Redbands remain my favorite fish, but trout fishing wasn't enough to keep the clouds away.

Strangely enough, after starting counseling and low-dose medication to combat my depression just prior to COVID-19 isolation, I was making progress. Unfortunately, the upending of my life and my routine with nowhere to go when I awoke sent me spiraling again. Fishing kept me sane and functional, but at the height of the Coronapocalypse, I'd lie in bed after waking for hours, with no motivation to get up and nowhere to go.

It was painful, and it made me realize one thing: fishing is not the only thing essential to my happiness; travel is the other piece of the puzzle.

Wanderlust

My family didn't have a lot of money as I was growing up. We really only traveled for sports. After my dad endured some serious health problems and a land deal failed, years of being underwater finally forced my parents to declare bankruptcy. Wondering if we could afford to send me to our team basketball camp a few hours away was stressful enough, so real travel was the last thing on my mind.

I didn't fly on a plane until I was 21 years old, and about 20 minutes after takeoff, I jumped out of it.

Skydiving was, to-date, the single most enjoyable non-fishing experience of my life, and while it provided a rush, it would be two more years before I got on a plane that actually landed with me on it.

Shortly after skydiving, I watched a movie called *The Big Year* in which the main character, an everyman birdwatcher played by Jack Black, travels around the country and tries to observe as many birds as he can in 12 months. I was fascinated by the premise, but having never flown on a commercial flight, I filed it somewhere at the back of my mind.

At 23, after graduating from college, I finally hopped on a plane and went to an insurance conference in Denver, Colorado for my day job. It was the furthest I'd ever been from home, and apart from skydiving that one time, my first flight. On that trip, I realized that after five years, insurance wasn't the field for me. I gave my bosses advanced notice when I returned, thanking them for being so incredible for so long.

Within a few months, I'd signed up for the Law School Admissions Test (LSAT), gotten my practice score to the point where it was higher than the average admitted student at my dream school, Stanford Law — albeit not high enough for many scholarships — and prepared to become an environmental lawyer.

Honestly, I had doubts about whether that was actually the right career for me. Getting saddled with debt to go work 60- or 70-hour weeks in a big city didn't leave a lot of time for fishing or travel, but I pressed forward, albeit riddled with uncertainty.

A month before my scheduled test date, a friend from college, David Clarke, invited me to come visit him in Auckland, New Zealand. Uncertain of my future and lukewarm with regards to law school, I threw caution and responsibility to the wind, embraced the wanderlust, and flew out the day I was scheduled to take the LSAT.

I figured if my heart was still in it when I returned, I'd reschedule.

The trout fishing in New Zealand was a far cry from what I'd grown up with, and I was disappointed. We caught fewer and smaller trout than I could at home, so David and I spent most of our days kayaking the Tasman Sea, fishing for anything we could catch, which was mostly Australasian Snapper, *Chrysophrys auratus*.

When I arrived in New Zealand, I'd caught 50 species of fishes in my lifetime. I added 10 new species in a month down under, realizing just how much of the fishing world I was missing out on. At some point while living among the Kiwis, I was unwittingly primed to become a Species Hunter.

The variety and taste of the unknown that fishing for the unfamiliar provided was just as exciting as hooking into a 28-inch trout, and I returned to the States with a new appreciation for the fishes around me.

David's mom is an attorney (the Kiwis call them barristers), and in talking with her, I realized I didn't want to be an environmental lawyer, after all.

Out of insurance but still holding on to a part-time sports writing gig for the local newspaper and also working for their IT desk, I returned to the States with no real plan.

I ended up in education, but writing became my passion second only to fishing. I diverged from sports and published my first fishing column in 2015. It found moderate success, running in papers all over the Western United States — the largest of which was *The Seattle Times*. Emboldened by the fact that people actually wanted to read what I wrote about fishing (and the other topics weaved throughout my writing under the guise of fishing), I started a blog: www.caughtovgard.com.

In the years that followed, I traveled and fished incessantly, chasing the unknown to slake my wanderlust and help me find that elusive contentment.

I joined the Air National Guard around this time, which I hoped might let me travel more. Travel came with the uniform, and I was able to visit Alabama for Officer Training School and Texas for Tech School in subsequent summers, fishing along the way.

Upon my return from Texas in the Fall of 2017, I'd learned of the formal Species Hunting community, a group of like-minded individuals whose goal in life was to catch as many species as possible, in the same vein as birdwatching or Pokémon, but with fishes.

When I officially joined this body of anglers, I signed the obligatory blood oath and brought with me 105 species. Despite an established regional writing career, I was pretty insignificant in the face of people with more than 10 times as many species, but I was glad to be a part of this newfound fraternity.

#SpeciesQuest

The world of Species Hunting goes by many names: Species Hunting, Species Fishing, Lifelist Fishing, Lifelisting, etc., but since I started my blog in 2013 and before I even knew Species Hunting was a thing, I've called it my #SpeciesQuest. In effect, it's trying to catch as many species of fishes as possible.

Growing up, I fished for trout more than everything else combined, but trout fishing was limited by the seasons and weather conditions to a few months of fishing time.

Over time, I began broadening my horizons and chasing other species as the enjoyment of fishing became a passion. That passion became an obsession. Eventually, the temperate climate I lived in and my love for the Pokémon games and their "Gotta catch 'em all" message made me a Species Hunter. That is, an angler who tries to catch as many species of fishes as possible.

Tenets

Like any good cult, Species Hunting has evolved its own set of rules, established by the people who partake in the sport, with precedence given to those individuals who have found the most success or have the most tenure. The Tenets of Species Hunting are as follows:

1. Every species has value. There are no "trash fishes" out there. Every fish has worth if only for that first-time catch, called a "Lifer" by most. I personally hate the term Lifer, so I usually say "New Species" instead. It's the counterculture Oregonian in me, I suppose.

2. Science matters. Species Hunters generally tend to value the science of fishing, of knowing what species reside where and how those species fit into the larger ecosystem. This inquisitive nature tends to make Species Hunters better anglers overall. If you know what little fishes trout or bass are feeding on, you can target them more effectively, right?

3. Species hunters don't eat their young. The species hunting community is more tightly knit than almost any other angling community. As a trout angler, I'm unlikely to give you GPS coordinates of where I caught my latest 28-incher. As a Species Hunter, I'll tell you exactly where I was standing when I caught that species you're currently chasing — most of the time. I even track this in a Fishing Map, which you can learn how to build on my blog under the "How To" section. Bloggers — SMH.

4. Species Hunters are social. There are a number of social constructs out there for Species Hunters, and I'm part of Facebook groups, online communities such as specieshunters.com, and there are always Instagram and Fishbrain (follow me @LukeOvgard).

5. Be honest. Most Species Hunters only count fishes they legally hooked in the mouth on hook and line. Others allow snagging fishes where legal. Still others might include catching fishes by hand, spearing or shooting them or even using a net. However you caught a fish, the community encourages you to be clear how you caught it and to never lie — even if the sport of fishing, as a whole, is one that tends toward exaggeration.

Follow these rules, and you will be welcomed into Species Hunting. Start following my #SpeciesQuest from the beginning on my blog, www.caughtovgard.com, if you want, but for now just start at Species #255 with this book.

The Trip
With #SpeciesQuest in full swing, travel for fishing was mostly limited to summers. I still traveled, making up for lost time, but fishing was secondary. Oh how my priorities were skewed in those days.

My depression peaked (or troughed, I guess) after returning from my second trip to Europe early in 2019.

My family eventually recovered financially from the dire straits of my childhood, and when my brothers and I were all grown, we took our first family vacation requiring a flight to get there. It was a new experience for all of us. The Ovgard Family went to visit its youngest member, Gabe, who was studying abroad in Vienna. He never learned her name, but he enjoyed the experience.

I took to travel quickly and holistically. The same small-town kid who hadn't flown on a plane until age 23 subsequently visited 33 states and 12 countries in the five years prior to the events of this book

I loved Europe, but when I returned home, I felt like my life had gone from vibrant color to black and white. I came home to the town where I'd spent 28 years of my life and now found myself in that mid-life crisis decades too soon, a mid-life crisis that I hoped had come well before the middle of my life, or I was doomed to die before 60.

Treading water was doing nothing for my mental health, so I tried other avenues and kept busy.

Inexplicably, I remembered *The Big Year,* that movie based on the book by Mark Obmascik of the same name in which an avid birder travels the world trying to catch sight of as many bird species as possible in one year, and it spoke to me.

The trout-obsessed part of me notwithstanding, I had evolved as an angler, and I was ready for all the world could throw at me; I wanted a "Big Year" of my own. I couldn't quit my job and live off savings and loans from my parents as the protagonist in that story had done, but I could make the most of the summers I had off as a teacher, and that's what I planned for — despite a lot of obstacles threatening to derail all of those plans.

Expectations

Anglers are as varied as the fishes they chase, and though I love flyfishing for trout, the world of fishing is much too large to stop there. This book is not focused on the isolated niche of flyfishing for trout that is foreign to those who don't live within that realm.

Most anglers in the United States don't live near blue ribbon trout streams with these fragile gamefish, and it's not right to perpetuate the elitism that assumes everyone is so privileged.

This book is about fishing in all its flavors collected into the trip of a lifetime. Sure, I chased trout in pristine mountain streams, but I also chased everything from minnows in dirty water under highway bridges to sharks in the sand flats of the Florida Keys. The healing nature of the unknown and the stunning variety of experiences you will read about in *Fishing Across America* will appeal to every human being — whether or not you fish.

This book has the simple premise of a story unlike any you've ever read, a taste of adventure in the midst of the ordinary, and it offers so much of that.

As I traveled across the country, I found myself dodging gators, poachers, sharks, snakes, venomous insects, and my own internal turmoil as I endeavored to catch more fish species entirely within the borders of the United States in a period of six weeks than anyone before me, an adaptation of the "Fishing Big Year" record.

It's not a record printed anywhere or even held in esteem by most anglers. Heck, if we're being honest, most anglers don't even know *Species Hunting* exists. Regardless, the episodic tale is one that all readers will appreciate, regardless of the role fishing plays in their lives.

For those outsiders who picked up this book, I think you'll be glad you did so. For those still on the fence, maybe the numbers will convince you.

I'm dropping numbers because numbers tell a story. Here's the story contained in this book:

46 Days
13,668.8 Miles
122 Fishing Stops
19 States
2,019 Fish
211 Species
147 New Species

Crazily, yes, I caught 2,019 fishes on my trip in the summer of 2019. Initially, I was shooting to break 1,000. Then, as the final days drew to a close, 2,000. It was only in the days immediately after my return home, as I began plugging my notes into a spreadsheet, that I realized I'd hit that number.

Coincidence? Nope.

Miracle.

So miraculous that I actually played with the idea of titling this book *The Summer of 2019* but that felt like it would be better suited for a bittersweet romantic tale. I guess this is a bittersweet romantic tale, but not in the traditional sense. No, *Fishing Across America* was apropos.

This was a trip measured by the fishes I caught, the states I experienced, the coffee shops I visited every morning, the people I stayed with, the hours of music, and the audiobooks I listened to along the way. It was an adventure all its own that stretched the bounds of what is traditionally written in the "Fishing" genre. Brace yourself; you're about to be CaughtOvgard.

PART 1
THE RUT

Chapter 1
The Email

April 8, 2019

"The journey of a thousand miles begins with a single step."
Lao Tzu || Chinese Philosopher

That may be true, but the journey of 13,668.8 miles began with a single email.
Like most people, Monday is definitely not my favorite day of the week, but that particular Monday — April 8, 2019 — was promising.
I'd resolved to try something different the night before, and after so much routine, different was healthy. I was up and out of the house early. Arriving at work well before I needed to be there, I got to preparing for the week's classes.
My energy level was unsurprisingly higher than that of my first-period students, though I can't blame them. My third-period seniors were working on their Senior Capstone Presentations, which, despite routinely checking to see if anyone needed help or advice, left me relatively unoccupied that morning.
I checked my school email.
Nothing.
I checked my personal email.
There was junk email from credit card companies, a thank-you email from one of my editors, Holly Owens, for sending that week's column early that week, and a billing receipt.
Oh. One more email.

It was from Fishbrain, the world's largest fishing app and social media platform that had chosen me to be a member of its Pro Staff nearly two years before.

This move had briefly made me think about making fishing (my all-consuming passion), into a career before dismissing the idea on the grounds that it could corrupt my love into something else if I depended upon it for a paycheck.

The email was from Hanna Grevelius, the woman who served as point person for the Pro Staff at Fishbrain, and it read:

"Hi Luke,

"Hope you are well!

"Remember ICAST last year? I heard it was a great time, and I am excited to say that I will be going this year. It will be my first time attending ICAST. I was just at a similar event in Sweden a few weeks ago, and it was so much fun. Firstly, I wanted to check if you would want to attend again this year? We would love to have you there!

"Secondly (since I am new to organizing this) I wanted to ask if you remember how we worked out the payments for you last year, what costs did Fishbrain pay for you? Thank you for helping me out.

"I truuuly hope you're able to join us at ICAST!

Cheers,
Hanna"

ICAST, the International Convention of Allied Sportfishing Trades, had brought me to Florida the year before. It was my second trip to Florida, but given my first trip was just an evening of fishing and trying not to become a statistic in the sketchiest waterfront stretch of Pensacola, ICAST had made Florida feel wonderful.

Incredible fishing, obviously, had been the highlight, but I'd also been able to meet one of my childhood heroes, the "Great American Fisherman" Roland Martin. I sat next to Roland's son, who happens to be the most famous angler on YouTube, Scott Martin, at breakfast, and even met April Vokey, the Canadian queen of salmonids (trout, char, and salmon). April followed me on Fishbrain later that day, but I played it cool and only got a little giddy.

I'd seen the scope of the fishing industry, with the hundred or more booths splayed out in the Orange County Convention Center.

Although Orlando's food scene was underwhelming, to put it nicely, it had still been an incredible trip.

My reverie brought on by the email was interrupted when a hand shot up, and I had to put my thoughts on hold. Class wound down, and the bell rang.

Without a second thought, I skipped my three-minute window between classes to run to the bathroom and replied to Hanna's email with a resounding "Yes!" noting that I was planning to be in Tampa for my cousin Austin Crawford's wedding a few weeks before anyway.

My analytical mind began running in UPS Mode as I began to consider the logistics of my summer. Brown couldn't do anything for me though; I'd have to plan this myself.

Austin and Darian's wedding was June 20, 2019, in Tampa.

ICAST was July 10-12, 2019, in Orlando.

These locations are just 90 miles apart. That didn't concern me. What did was the fact the events were three weeks apart — 17 days to be exact, I calculated, thankful I had the right amount of fingers and toes for the task despite several close calls throughout the years.

I could fly down twice. At first, I just assumed I would. Then I began looking at flights and quickly realized that two flights and two rental cars would put me in the neighborhood of $2,000. Ordinarily, this would've been fine, but given that this email came just a few weeks before my closing date, and the older house I was buying was going to swallow some money during renovations, I was a little more cost-conscious than I normally would be.

Then it hit me: I could drive. It wouldn't be my first cross-country road trip.

Two years before, I'd driven down to Montgomery, Alabama, for Air Force Commissioned Officer Training (COT). Though that school had been a six-week stretch of stress and rampant diarrhea, it let me see a lot of the country. The year after that, I'd driven to San Antonio for Health Services Administration (HSA), my Tech School. I loved that six-week span as much as I hated COT, and it was at that time that I was sure my decision to join the military had been the right one. The one weekend I donned the uniform every month as a Medical Services Corps (MSC) Officer in the Oregon Air National Guard was a nice change of pace from teaching, and it allowed me to serve my country and make a little extra money while working toward a second pension.

Both road trips (even the one for COT, which had been fairly miserable apart from the bookends of travel) had hit "refresh" on my life, and I'd returned with a new outlook on the mundane, appreciating my hometown much more than before I'd embarked. I wondered if this tentative trip to Florida might do the same for me.

"God, I need this," I half-prayed, half-worried to myself.

Both road trips had allowed a week or so of travel and fun on the way down to work, but this road trip would only have three days of work (ICAST), and a few days for the wedding and festivities afterward. With three weeks between the two events, and maybe a week or so of drive time each way, that meant this road trip would be at least five weeks in length.

This road trip wouldn't be a means to an end (military training); it would be an adventure.

Like, a real adventure — not the horribly misappropriated verb girls put in captions on social media posts and in dating app profiles referring to a day hike up a well-worn trail or rafting a tamed stretch of river with a cooler full of light beer and White Claw.

Those are not adventures, mind you.

According to the powers at Google, an adventure is definitionally "to engage in hazardous and exciting activity, especially the exploration of unknown territory or to put (something, especially money or one's life) at risk." This five-plus-week road trip would certainly be an adventure. I'd be traveling to places unknown through at least a dozen states, and five weeks on the road would certainly put my money at risk. Little did I know, it would also put my life at risk a few times, so I proceeded blindly.

The only problem? Even with an aggressive pace, it would take four days to drive from Klamath Falls, Oregon, to Tampa, Florida. Totally doable, except that the wedding was June 20, and the "Last Day for Teachers" printed on our District Calendar — a calendar I was contractually bound to — was June 18.

Profanity.

Chapter 2
Second Chance

April 15, 2019

"When we are no longer able to change a situation,
we are challenged to change ourselves."
Viktor Frankl || Austrian Psychiatrist
From *Man's Search for Meaning*

My school is a great place to work. It really is. The quality of the teachers and support staff also makes it a great school. It consistently has one of the highest graduation rates in the state of Oregon, and it was ranked as one of *U.S. News*' Top High Schools in 2018.

Further, I really like what I do, but I had some tensions with my former admins until the latest regime took over, and it became smooth sailing. At the time the idea of a road trip hit me, things were moving forward, though. I think I'd finally mended fences with my boss. We were in a good place, but I wasn't sure if we were "use one of my two Personal Days to miss the last day of the year," good.

I explained the situation in earnest to my boss. I could fly twice and spend a load of money, or I could drive once, hit the wedding and the conference and probably spend the same amount, but certainly have a better experience.

My principal, Mr. Jack Lee, didn't say no.

He said he'd have to check with Human Resources, and I accepted his willingness to ask.

The week passed by on hold. I didn't want to get my hopes up, so I didn't start planning.

The following week, I checked in. He told me to plan on it, and he'd take any heat if it arose. I thanked him profusely, and I was glad to see what this kindness on his part meant for our working future together — even if we'd had a variety of past issues. I could leave after school got out June 15 or wait and leave early the next morning.

I had a departure date!

With that out of the way, my next obstacle was to get permission to reschedule my July Drill Weekend for August. Most Drill Weekends are Saturday and Sunday, and July was no different. Basically, for Drill, you just go and work your military job for two days in service to your mission.

The Medical Group Commander, then Lieutenant Colonel Edwin Tuhy, allowed one Excusal per year, and though I hadn't actually requested an Excusal that year, a teaching obligation had caused me to work a Friday/Saturday instead of Saturday/Sunday a few months prior. I'd had another Friday/Saturday accommodation for August Drill due to a teaching conference. I wondered if that would matter. I mean, I wouldn't actually be missing any other Drill days, but rules are rules.

Fortunately, what my military position lacks in adrenaline-pumping excitement, it more than makes up for in quality personnel, leadership, and a desire to make its members the best they can be.

My supervisor at the time, then Captain Joel Ainsworth, gave me the green light, but passed it up the chain to Lieutenant Colonel Rich Long, who oversaw our area.

Fingers crossed, I got the green light from Lt. Col. Long. It progressed up to Lt. Col. Tuhy, and I again got the green light.

I was approved to make up my July Drill in August.

My Friday/Saturday August Drill would take place Aug. 2-3, so I had a return date!

My trip would span June 15 to Aug. 1.

Two of my careers' logistics were squared away, and I'd submitted my column and magazine articles from the road each week in the two previous trips. Though less than ideal, it was doable. I just wish I had a working laptop. I could revisit that, though.

Even though Klamath Falls had grown stale, work hadn't.

Maybe this trip would even help with that gnawing sameness that I'd grown tired of in nearly 30 years' time.

"Could this get me out of the rut?" I wondered, as I drifted off to dreamless sleep.

PART 2
THE PLAN

Chapter 3
Decisions

May & June, 2019

"A good plan, violently executed now, is better
than a perfect plan next week."
General George S. Patton || United States Army

Organization and planning are two of my natural talents. While I don't necessarily enjoy all forms of these Type A rituals, at times, some can be quite enjoyable. Planning for the weeks-long epic fishing trip of a lifetime would qualify as enjoyable.

There's no shortage of legwork that a trip of this magnitude entails, especially considering I'm not wealthy. I would have to come up with some creative solutions to solve the money problem.

Add in the fact that in recent years, my fishing focus has shifted from "catching lots of fishes or catching big fishes" to "catching as many new species as possible," and that breadth of focus requires careful planning. Not porcupine reproduction careful, but you get the point.

(Pause for laughter).

Barring the wedding and the conference, it would be a fishing trip that could last from June 15 to Aug. 1, assuming I used every day possible. That required planning.

Route
Mentally, I broke down my trip.
The drive down would take about 50 hours. Leaving after school Friday, June 15 would only get me so far, and I'd be tired, so I opted

to leave early Saturday, June 16. That left me four days to drive those 50 hours.

Between the wedding and the conference, I had 17 days to fill. I could stay in Florida or leave Florida and come back, but I had to be in Orlando the night of July 9 to be ready for ICAST. Should I stay in Florida or detour up into Georgia, Alabama, or the Carolinas? Just staying in Florida seemed easiest, so I would.

I opted to start the slow route home July 13. This would give me 20 days to get back to Oregon, but I left my return route open-ended and planned to finalize it later. It would prove to be incredibly stressful, but (spoiler alert) I didn't die.

Small Decisions

Big decisions made, I had to consider logistics. Such trivialities as lodging, food, my car, what gear to bring, how to store bait, and whether or not I should get bangs all vied for my attention.

After struggling with these problems and which one(s) to attack first, I finally decided to take it day by day. I planned to pick where I fished, where I slept, and then more or less wing meals, bait, ice, gas, and other daily necessities on the fly. To make that strategy viable, I needed to establish a routine. I created a template, and after revising it half a dozen times, arrived at something that could work.

Using the Notes app (yes, really) on my phone, I began planning the trip. For every piece that fell into place, two more holes opened up. This would be a lot of work, I quickly realized, but it had to be worth it, right.

Right?!

In writing this book, I debated back-and-forth with myself about how (or even whether) to include the places I stayed, the food I ate, the gear I used, the licenses I had to buy, and of course, the places I fished.

When I first wrote this book, each element was its own chapter at the beginning, starting right here. I think the 30 pages or so of what broke down to packing lists and clever dad jokes add value to the reader, but not enough to the story to include them here. Instead, I'll give you some highlights here. Reach out to me directly if you want that sort of mind-numbing detail.

Hopefully you enjoy that strategy and encourage your friends to buy my book. If not, well, writing this book made the trip a tax write-off, so I still consider it a win.

Chapter 4
Buildup

May & June, 2019

"Far and away the best prize that life has to offer is the chance to work hard at work worth doing."
Theodore Roosevelt || 26th President of the United States

The weeks leading up to my trip were among the best of my life but some of the most difficult. In addition to the mountain of prep work I was doing for my trip, I was still teaching full-time, doing days on base for my National Guard position, preparing for my upcoming Guard fitness test, trying to write six weeks' worth of columns for the time I'd be gone, and renovating my house. It was a lot, but it was a great feeling to accomplish so much, and being busy makes it difficult to be lonely or sad, so my depression was held in check.

I was firing on all cylinders, and though I could scarcely wait for the trip, I was appreciating everything else in my life more than I had in a long time. I did some of my best teaching, wrote some of my favorite columns, and performed as well in my military uniform as ever before.

It was a high point that spanned almost a month, and it included me getting back into shape. I've never let myself get fat, but when I'm out of shape, I tend to just waste away. My brothers once jokingly drew a straight line and asked me what it was. I replied "A line," to a chorus of laughter and then Jake, barely able to contain himself, said "No, it's you turned sideways."

He wasn't too far off. There was a time when I was in great shape, but I'd lifted weights exactly one time between the year I graduated college (2013) and the time I took this trip (2019).

As I prepped for the test, I still didn't go back to the gym, but I started lots of body weight exercises and stepped up my cardio regimen, ultimately setting my personal record (PR) for the 1.5-mile run that is part of the Air Force Fitness Test with a time of 8:41. It was a neck-and-neck race where I won at the finish line. During my time in the military up to that point, I'd been in half a dozen fitness test runs and 5K races. I'd never finished below second place, but I'd also never come anywhere close to running a mile and a half in less than nine minutes, so I was feeling pretty sure of myself when I finally broke that barrier.

My confidence extended to the basketball court, where I had some of my best days ever playing basketball in open gyms. My most realistic comparator in the NBA has always been Dennis Rodman because of my outlandish hairstyles and close, personal friendship with Kim Jong Un. JK. It's because I'm exponentially more likely to grab 20 boards in a game than score 20 points. I was scoring quite a bit during this time. It was an open gym, mind you, so the stakes were remarkably low, but I still managed to feel proud of myself after most open gyms that month, which isn't always the case.

In fact, I felt great all-around, physically, and it didn't stop there.

Relationally, I was able to spend more time with my family, and my parents both put in a lot of time helping me to renovate my newly purchased home. Mom did a ton of cleaning to get it sparkling, Dad painted the interior to perfection, and I ripped out the old carpet in preparation for the laminate flooring.

It took about a month, and we all worked on the yard, removing garbage, cutting trees, and making its curb appeal rise ever-so-slightly. I slowly furnished it and prepared it for a summer of income generation on Airbnb that made my whole cross-country trip possible. Today, there are more than 200 competitor Airbnbs in my market, but at the time, there were five, so it was a sure thing. Not anymore.

Getting my own place also conditioned me to being alone all the time. A few months prior, I would've struggled to be alone so much, but the combination of my productivity and having something so great to look forward to kept me strong. Emotionally, my depression lifted for a time, and despite some stress at work, I was able to enjoy the end of the year, spurred on by some incredible fishing that helped me get a handful of new species and experience some excellent trout fishing.

I caught my third-largest Brown Trout, *Salmo trutta* while fishing with my friend Mark Doolittle, a fishing mentor who taught me how to flyfish and helped me master fishing our local lake from a boat.

This led to me joining another friend, T.J. Orton, for a fishing trip we'd long talked about but never made. It was a productive day in which we both caught fish, but after taking a break from flyfishing and trying out some trolling, I picked up something I'd been working toward my entire life: a 30-inch wild, native Redband Trout.

I'd come close on numerous occasions, including several fish within a quarter-inch of the mark, but I had to catch nearly 2,000 of those fish before the conditions of the moment and a little of God's providence gave me what I'd been after for so long. Even better? T.J. is a phenomenal photographer with a camera capable of doing that fish justice, and he got half a dozen great pictures in between fully submerged respites for the massive trout in my custom RSNets King model net, which allowed it to recover in between the 5- or 10-second photo sessions before we released the magnificent beast.

I never laid it flat because of the adrenaline, but while holding it, bent, in my wet hands against the wet gunwale-mounted tape measure, it broke 31 inches. Flat, it would've easily added another half inch.

I caught that fish a few weeks before my trip, and it slated my thirst for fishing, as I tried to plan for every contingency.

Even still, I was afraid. Afraid I was going to forget something essential. The planner in me obsessed and prepared and anticipated, and you know what? I did forget some stuff, but I made due. I adapted. I didn't let fear of failure keep me from making my best attempt, and in the end, the admittedly daunting undertaking of traveling across the country for a month and a half would help me grow more than I ever imagined.

PART 3
THE TRIP

Chapter 5
Pit Stops

June 15, 2019

Day 1
Origin: Klamath Falls, Oregon
Destination: Ely, Nevada

"There is something uniquely American about the motel:
It speaks to the transient nature of America itself, one enabled
and encouraged by our roads and highways."
Hanya Yanagihara || American Author

    Strange how some of the most extraordinary things begin with the ordinary. The morning of Saturday, June 15, 2019, I awoke like any other. I hopped in the shower, as I do every morning, steaming the sleep from my eyes and the rheuminess from my joints. My routines: putting in my contacts, brushing my teeth, shaving (every three days or so), eating breakfast, drinking coffee, and going to the bathroom. It all felt like any other day. Given my excitement, I did it with an unfamiliar fervor. My toothpaste was just a little mintier, my coffee just a little more rich and flavorful, and any hint of tiredness only fleeting.
    I had loaded up my car in the days leading up to Saturday, so I didn't have much to pack. With my phone, charger, keys, and all the perishable food loaded into the cooler, I was ready. This was it. Though I'd purchased my house, the renovations had taken long enough that I opted not to move in before I left, so I stayed with my

parents. I hugged them as I said goodbye; Mom cried, and I promised to be careful.

It was at least the 20th trip one week or longer I'd taken in the years since high school, but being the last of the Ovgard Boys in Klamath Falls since my brothers Jake and Gabe had both moved away, I was the only bastion between my parents, an empty nest, and the slow decline into cat collection. So I smiled through the extra seconds of the hug and parted with a "Love ya!" as they waved, understandably emotional, and I drove off.

Author's Note: my parents now have three cats in place of the three boys they raised.

Oregon

My car has a built-in seatbelt alarm that sounds if the seat detects a certain weight without a fastened seat belt. It lasts for 15 seconds, but it feels like an eternity. That's what she sai— never mind. The first 15 seconds of my road trip were corrupted by the shrill beeping registered by the cooler in my passenger seat. It would repeat every time I turned on my car for the next six weeks, and it quickly grated on my nerves.

The road rolled out in front of my car as I made my way east. I hadn't planned any stops to fish in Oregon, but when, after more than 100 miles of driving, I came across a small creek forming a pool on the side of the highway, I couldn't resist. Well, in all honesty, I needed to pee, and I was trying to be efficient.

This area happened to be within range of the Northern Roach, *Hesperoleucus mitrulus*, a species I'd tried in vain to catch on several occasions. Though its range is limited to a handful of tributary streams in the Goose Lake Basin and the Upper Pit River system, it is (allegedly) plentiful in that range.

Suuuuuure.

Further complicating things, it is a "micro," a fish targeted in the ever-growing subset of the angling world with a technique called "microfishing." Microfishing is a Japanese technique originally invented to target the Japanese bitterling, a small fish most Americans would dismiss as a "minnow" out of hand. While technically correct — bitterling are Cyprinids (Old World minnows) by definition — it takes a special angler to appreciate microfishing. Of note is the fact that the Japanese competition is to catch the *smallest* bitterling possible, with top honors usually going to the angler with a fish that can fit on a small coin.

Then again, this subset of the sport is especially accessible because micros flourish in waters everywhere. Fresh and saltwater, urban and rural, tiny stream and massive river alike all hold micros.

Kids love microfishing because it's visually stimulating, usually fairly productive, and the fishes are tiny and totes adorbs.

A large number of female friends and past romantic interests I've taken fishing have universally told me they enjoy microfishing because the fishes are so adorable. They might be projecting their true feelings about me onto "the fish," which is likely, but no man has ever regretted taking a woman at the literal meaning of her words, so I'd be a fool to stop that trend now. After all, women don't have subtext. Microfishing does.

Microfishing doesn't mean catching small fishes merely because you fail to catch large ones; it means targeting tiny fishes (typically those that don't top six inches in length) intentionally using equally tiny gear.

For a Species Hunter, someone trying to catch as many species of fishes as possible before they die, microfishing is a necessity because so many fishes scattered around God's green earth are tiny. In the same stream where you catch trout, there are probably native sculpins, dace, chubs, or darters just waiting to be appreciated. In the average water, it's a safe bet that roughly half of all available species are micros, so getting into microfishing means catching more species.

When I officially identified myself as a Species Hunter and started joining Facebook groups also identified as such, in December 2017, I had already caught 105 species. I didn't even know the Species Hunting or Lifelisting cult even existed. I'd been a die-hard fisherman for some 15 years at that point, but I was simply expanding my horizons, actively trying to catch new fishes instead of just actively trying to catch a specific fish with sport value.

In the year and a half that followed, I increased that number from 105 to 255, with 70 of my 142 new species during that time being micros. Math says that's almost half of them.

So microfishing had obviously become a staple in my fishing endeavors, much to the dismay of naysayers embittered that I (and many others like me) could enjoy catching something roughly the size of their p—

Never mind.

I just slap a bumper sticker on the side of their oversized Ford, Chevy, or Dodge Compensator that reads "No, it's AVERAGE!" and happily go on to catch tiny fishes while they get skunked waiting for that big fish to finally bite.

The Northern Roach was just one of these tiny fishes that I'd found particularly challenging.

Once during the early winter (the worst time to chase micros, mind you), I'd seen a single roach but been unable to get it to bite.

Like Los Angeles' iconic yet unofficial animal of the same name, this roach seemed to scatter at the slightest hint of light.

So I struck out during the winter.

Later that spring, I'd met with my friends Steve Wozniak and Marta Bulaich in hopes of chasing (among other things) this small fish. Both creeks we'd tried were moving way too fast and just a little too dirty to be considered seriously, but enough about my dating prospects.

To answer your burning question, yes, I know Steve Wozniak. We've fished together several times, and that makes me a pretty big deal, right?

Yes, he does actually use an iPhone, and I don't know how close he and Steve Jobs were before Jobs' passing because I haven't asked.

I don't know why that would matter because it's not the Steve Wozniak you're thinking of. This guy was an executive for a tech company, but it wasn't Apple.

This Steve Wozniak is most famous for being the first person to catch 1,000 species of fish, a feat he accomplished in 2010. I remember reading the article and thinking how cool it was. I happened to "meet" Steve via email in 2016 and then actually got to fish with him for the first time in 2018.

We've since stayed in contact and fished together several more times, and I've been able to help contribute in some small way to his own #SpeciesQuest that has become the worldwide standard. In close to a decade since, his number has climbed, and he has since eclipsed the 2,000-species mark. He has become a mentor and is an incredibly valuable resource for me, personally.

That Northern Roach trip was, in fact, the only time we'd struck out on a main target together, so it stood out in my mind and made me all the more eager to remedy the situation. I got my chance at redemption just hours into my summer trip — completely unexpectedly.

This fish, native to the Pit River system, provided an ideal pit stop. If you missed the pun, please try to keep up. The small, roadside creek had a pool just large enough for me to see all of the little micros darting this way and that. They didn't scatter in my presence or that of the daylight, so I was skeptical they were roaches, but it didn't stop me.

I quickly caught one, wet my hands (a necessity when handling all fishes but especially micros), and snapped a few quick pictures of the totes adorbs Leucicid.

My micro pictures are above average. Weird flex, I know, but it's true.

Here's how I do it. After wetting my hands, I gingerly grab the fish. I lay it flat in my left hand and gently pinch its left pectoral fin between the knuckles of two fingers to hold it in place. From there, I submerge it an inch or so underwater because most micros won't extend their fins unless underwater, and identification of micros often requires clear pictures of fins to allow for the counting of rays, spines, and other frustratingly minute details that would give an accountant far too much pleasure.

A photo tank (basically a clear plastic or glass box actually intended to be a container, vase, or collectible display case of some sort) is an option. You fill it with water and place a small fish in to get better photographs without harming it while showing fins all splayed out, but it's inconvenient and markedly slower than using your hand. Though I caught several roach (roaches?) in no time, nothing else came out to play.

Gently, I held the fish just under the water and snapped my #SpeciesQuest photo, the picture I'd add to my Instagram Story and ultimately, to my blog.

I had my first new species of the trip on my first pit stop and my one and only Pit stop.

Species #255 — Northern Roach (*Hesperoleucus mitrulus*).

My goal for the trip was 100 new species. With about 45 days planned, I needed to get 2.2 new species per day. And yes, micros are small, but they count as a whole species — not 0.2 — so I was almost halfway to my goal for the first day, and I hadn't even left Oregon yet.

Crap.

I hadn't even left Oregon yet! I had like 12 hours of driving to do, and I'd only accomplished two, so I hopped back in the car. As I passed through the empty desert and canyonlands of the Oregon Outback, I realized something: given the limited range of this species, the necessity for micro hooks that were only recently made available in the United States, and the remoteness of its limited habitat, I was probably the first one to ever catch one with hook and line. Disclaimer: since no one gives a flying ... fish.

You should know that since I don't use cast nets, seines, handheld nets, or anything else to catch fish, just assume I mean that I caught every fish on hook and line from here on out; the only other fishes I come into contact with are the kind I order at restaurants. As for my claim, there are not many species left in the United States with that potential, those that have never been caught, so that was even better. Granted, I'd been the "First to Catch" a handful of other species before, but this was the first species of my trip, and it was also a "First to Catch" — not a bad start!

Nevada

I'm probably not the first person to think this, but Nevada was a string of disappointments.

Driving U.S. Highway 140 East from Klamath Falls will take you through Lakeview and then down into Nevada. Just as you start to appreciate the natural beauty that has been fenced and parceled but otherwise undisturbed by humanity, you'll come to a border town called Denio. There is almost nothing here. The tiny restaurant that at various times has also provided lodging and fuel had temporarily stopped the latter and spiraled me into denial. Or is it Denio?

IDK.

Though I had enough gas to get to the nearest gas station some forgettable number of miles away, I didn't like it. The vast nothingness of Nevada is intimidating, and I'd never want to run out of gas in the middle of nowhere. I knew from experience the combination of frustration, embarrassment, and desolation that wells up inside you when that happens. Well, not from experience because I'm too responsible. It's never happened to me before.

Confident in the trip ahead of me, I gassed myself up.

Then, I gassed up, by myself. Unlike Oregon, Nevada doesn't prohibit pumping your own gas, so you have to risk contracting some hideous disease by handling the gas pump and breathing the fumes yourself. That aspect of traveling outside the best state in the Union always grosses me out. Add my aversion to pumping gas to the list of hopeless Oregonisms in this book.

I covered the pump handle with a shopping bag, a habit I'd adapted after traveling to Central Europe where every gas station provides disposable plastic gloves at their impeccably clean gas stations that serve impressively good coffee and pastries and even hot breakfasts markedly better than those served in most American chain restaurants. Okay, I'll lay off the chains.

I wasn't in Europe, though. I was in Nevada.

In that moment I realized how privileged I was to have been born in Oregon. Nevada was a far cry from Austria, Germany, and Slovenia, but it does have Guppies.

At least, it is *supposed* to have Guppies.

Microfishing haters will appreciate the fact that the first two fishes I targeted on this trip were a minnow and a Guppy, the two names commonly used by laymen to describe small fishes — whether or not those small fishes are actual minnows (fishes in the families Cyprinidae or Leucicidae) or Guppies (*Poecilia reticulata*).

Musing to myself and no one else because I was smack-dab in the desolation of north-central Nevada, I pulled over at a small, roadside spring I'd found data mining the United States Geological Survey Non-Indigenous Aquatic Species (USGS NAS) collection data available online.

The USGS has conducted sampling of various water bodies in the United States since 1873. Yes, when the Union contained only 37 states and before the telephone had been invented, biologists were going out and looking to see what fishes had been introduced outside of their native range. It's pretty incredible, and though those insanely early samplings are limited, they increased in frequency in the 146 years leading up to the events in this book.

All of this data is stored at the public's fingertips in two basic forms: online and for download. Though you can search the database online, in a fairly pictorial search function by state, species, or drainage, it can be tedious.

Instead, I downloaded it as a spreadsheet and spent hours and hours pouring over nearly half a million rows of data to find many of the stops for my trip.

I am not exaggerating.

This spreadsheet, which you can download as a .CSV file and adapt for use in Microsoft Excel or Google Sheets, is 20 MB of text only. No macros, pictures, links. Purely 20 MB of text. At the time I wrote this, said spreadsheet numbered 368,274 rows of data. That is, one row for every invasive species recorded in a given sampling. So if USGS went to a small pond in central California and found Bluegill, Largemouth Bass, and Channel Catfish, *Ictalurus punctatus*, they would produce three rows of data for that one sampling. You tracking? USGS is.

Still, with 10 columns worth of data in those 368,274 rows, we're looking at 3.68 million cells. That's not a small amount of text to cycle through. Given the scale of the file, even standard sorts take up to several minutes, so it's slow going, but thankfully I had nothing but time in the months leading up to my trip, and there were a lot of fishes I needed to catch, ranging from shiners to sharks, and USGS data promised to help with at least some of them.

Since the USGS doesn't discriminate against small fishes, my first use of USGS data on the trip led me to chase after a tiny fish famously used as a euphemism for all small fish: the Guppy.

Several times over the past decade, biologists have sampled guppies here, and I figured that this aggressive livebearer (a group of small fishes in the order Cyprinidontiformes that give birth to live young instead of laying eggs like most fishes) would be an easy mark.

Turns out I was the easy mark.

The spring was underwhelming. Not only was it spewing from a pipe at just a few cubic feet per second (CFS), there was no real spring pool. Instead, the flow downsized into a narrow ditch, thoroughly overgrown by all manner of desert brush and noxious weeds. There was little bank to speak of, and what existed was thick clay mud that grappled at my flip flops.

Begrudgingly, I realized it was not conducive to fishing, but I plowed ahead anyway, desperate for another new species that day. I could see fat livebearers that I identified as Guppies. I spent well over an hour scratching up my legs, covering my feet in the foul-smelling mud, and serving as an all-you-can-eat buffet for mosquitoes and horseflies before I finally landed one of the chunky livebearers.

Aquarium Guppies can be vivid and covered in a wide array of colors and patterns, but wild Guppies look almost identical to Western Mosquitofish, *Gambusia affinis,* a livebearer common (and largely native) throughout the Southern and Western United States.

So I snapped a picture and ambled back to the car, confident I'd tallied another new species.

Washing myself like countless "Burners" had before me in the roadside spring pump, I returned damp to the car to eat my lunch of peanut butter crackers, an apple, and a pouch of tuna because if Capri Sun taught me anything, it's that pouches make you look cooler than cans.

It was only minutes later that I would look up the description on page 442 of my *Peterson's Guide to Freshwater Fishes of North America* that would be a staple on this trip.

"... red or blue blotches in fins" — check.

"Gray body; slightly outlined scales; 6 or 7 dorsal rays" — check one, two, three.

"Similar to Western (*G. affinis*) and Eastern Mosquitofish, *Gambusia holbrooki* ... but *lacks* black teardrop" — dammit.

The conspicuous black spot indicated it was just another Western Mosquitofish. The hardest-to-catch mosquitofish I'd ever landed, mind you, but still just a mosquitofish — a fish planted all over to keep populations of its namesake insect (and favorite snack) in check.

I cried an appropriate amount of time as I headed toward Great Basin National Park near Ely that had brought me out to the middle of nowhere in the first place. I'd planned to get a Guppy, hit up Great Basin National Park, then detour up to a nearby hot spring in Utah. The "Guppy" that was actually a Western Mosquitofish ruined all that.

My fishing was over for the day, but at least I could take in the majestic portrait of the high desert before trying to sleep in my car, right? Great Basin National Park did not disappoint, but it had been a long day.

I made my way back to Ely along U.S. Route 50, deemed "The Loneliest Road in America," and wondered if a solo road trip of this magnitude was wise.

That remained to be seen, but I was beat. After all, I'd driven 702 miles that day. The filthy mess I'd become warranted a shower. Pilot or Love's or whatever truck stop they had charged $12 for a shower. Showering morning and night meant I could have a decent at-best night in my car that I'd soon try to forget for $24 (coincidentally almost the exact sales pitch used by prostitutes in this part of Nevada), or I could rent a room at the punny Deser-Est Motel for $45 per night.

Obviously, I opted for the latter.

Though I'd wasted precious cargo space by bringing a sleeping bag and pillow along and intended to use them, my resolve faltered the very first night.

After moving all of my gear to one side of the car, I collapsed one seat and an outstretched sleeping pad fit perfectly. I topped it with a sleeping bag and crammed my 6-foot, 2-inch frame into the narrow space. If the United States Postal Service taught us anything, it's that the government can keep select elements of Americana alive long past their natural life with enough public support.

No. Wait. It taught us that "If it fits, it ships."

I fit. Barely. It was tighter than the body of your favorite Instagram fitness model.

Then I started sweating. This just wouldn't work. Not really. Ely, Nevada, would be one of my coolest overnights as I made my way south, and it was too hot. Unfortunately, that meant my trip costs would go up dramatically. Even staying at cheaper motels costing around $60 per night, including tax, that totaled $3,000 for 50 nights. Three grand wasn't possible on my budget, so I'd have to figure something out.

Regardless, I was on the road! I was doing it. Day 1 was over, and I'd caught two species — only one of them was new. Granted, I was fishing the desertiest region of the West, and it was notably difficult fishing, but it was bound to get easier.

"It's all downhill from here, right?"

At least, that's what I told myself. I just wish I'd believed it.

Chapter 6
Desert Lakes

June 16, 2019

Day 2
Origin: Ely, Nevada
Destination: Rock Springs, Wyoming

"Imagine if we made one thing better at work than it was today and one thing better at home than it was today. Imagine we did that every day. The power of that in mass? Idealistic, but possible."
Colonel Retired Jeff Smith || United States Air Force

Ely, Nevada, sits at 6,437 feet above sea level.
Rock Springs, Wyoming, sits at 6,388 feet above sea level. So technically, it was downhill from my first day on the road, a full 49 feet down. In reality, Day 2 of my trip would prove to be arguably the worst. Not downhill but an uphill struggle.
It began with me driving the short distance from Ely, Nevada, to Utah.
Uneventful, and without Audible in my life, it would've been downright boring. All in all, audiobooks were a major part of this trip, and I finished two books in the first two days given the long, long hours in the car. The night before, I'd finished the fourth book in the *Undying Mercenaries* Series, a book by B.V. Larson about near-future human mercenaries capable of being recreated, cloned really, after death with a strange alien machine. The fourth iteration, *Machine World*, was an interesting read and kept me alive with the casual tone and perfect blend of action and humor. The series is a

bit trope-y, but still entertaining. At least, still entertaining through four books — not sure I'll make it through all 11.

As I drove north and cut into the desert toward Blue Lake, a smattering of hot springs primarily in Utah but right on the border with Nevada, I finished the classic *Childhood's End*, by Arthur C. Clarke. This book is about a future in which humans are visited by aliens that look stereotypically like the devil — a fun coincidence I'll explore later — who collectively help bring humanity utopia — at least for a while.

It was a very interesting take, and as I wrapped up the final lines, I turned from an improved, graded gravel road onto a less improved gravel road given to the washboard ravages of rain and snow just in time to hear a different voice over the car speakers. The standardized narration in formal masculine bass said, "Audible hopes you have enjoyed this program."

I did. Normally, that single line serves as my note of completion, indicating that it's time to start another book, cue up some music, or just take a break. Given the poor quality of the road, I opted for the latter.

Less than a quarter mile onto the road, I knew what Parkinson's sufferers deal with on some very small level, and I couldn't take it. The shaking permeated my entire body. Had I decided to listen to another book, I wouldn't have been able to hear it anyway thanks to the panicked chattering of my car on the moguls.

Fortunately, a less improved two-track paralleled the high berm along the south side of the road. I scooted onto that, and it was relatively smooth sailing from there.

I alternated between at least 30 minutes of teeth-chattering gravel roads and the powdered sugar two track when it was available, and I only stopped to photograph a large rattlesnake while saying "Crikey!" in my only-slightly-cringey Australian accent. Minutes after my impromptu Steve Irwin tribute, I'd arrived at Blue Lake.

Blue Lake

Blue Lake itself is a large geothermal hot spring with a nearly 10-acre footprint. It dips as deep as 60 feet at full pool and is popular with divers, swimmers, and anglers who enjoy playing chicken with meningitis in the lake's eerily warm but not-quite-hot waters.

Given Blue Lake's renown, it is also very heavily pressured.

When I pulled up, I was at one of half a dozen smaller pools in the vicinity of Blue Lake, and I immediately started fishing. I was alone, but not for long.

Now, for the better part of a decade, I'd walk up to any water containing panfish and toss in a specific worm-tipped jig I'd grown to love. This discontinued ice fishing jig is called the "Bergie Worm Jr." by Uncle Josh. When they discontinued the product maybe 10 years ago, I called the factory and bought 250 packages of them. At the time, the $750 purchase nearly bankrupted me, but in the successive years, that sacrifice paid off. Besides, it only took me 75 nights of selling my body to pay off that debt. Worth it.

Excluding tanago hooks for micros and sabiki rigs (also called herring jigs — basically a pretied line with several small hooks attached to it), I've caught more species of fishes and more fishes in total on these jigs than on anything else. And like that one time in college I agreed to race my Division I track star brother (Jake) in the 100 meters, it's not even close. In that scenario, he was the Bergie Worm Jr., and I was, well, I was not.

For this trip, I loaded up the last dozen or so Bergie Worm Jr. packages I had left and brought them along. I had no intention of losing them all, but I knew it was possible, and I wanted to be ready. I'd had no intention of losing every woman I've ever dated, but here we are.

These lures are champs and capable of catching hundreds of fishes in a day before the thin wire hook eventually breaks. My single best day fishing — a day I fished from dawn to dark, breaking only for lunch and to answer nature's calls — is owed to a Bergie Worm Jr.

Well, two actually.

I caught 318 fishes that day, mostly Bluegills with some bass, crappie, and trout thrown in there. The first jig lasted almost 300 fishes before that wire hook, bent and straightened one too many times, finally broke.

Its effectiveness did not diminish over time or by location, so I was ready to fish Blue Lake and its surrounding ponds. I tied one onto my ultralight and tipped it with a quarter-inch piece of red worm.

It appealed to the Nile Tilapia, *Oreochromis niloticus*, I caught on my very first cast. Though not a new species, I was impressed with how easy this tilapia was to entice compared to others I'd struggled with in parts of Arizona, Texas, and Florida.

As I reeled in the tilapia, a couple of locals showed up. Instead of fishing any of the other pools nearby within 100 yards of the parking lot, they set up about 15 feet from me. They clearly had no idea what they were doing and asked if they could keep what I caught. I agreed to give them tilapia because the invasive menace is everywhere.

They took it happily, as I questioned its table value from such a likely polluted and definitely popular swimming hole.

To each their own, I guess.

The redneck menace bugged me, but it was the bugs that proved to be the real pests, and as I slapped and slapped at my legs, arms, and face, I realized I'd been there almost 15 minutes without anything to show for it but tilapia.

Fortunately, *Childhood's End* and its devilish aliens proved prophetic, and I reeled in a pale white-and-orange fish I quickly identified as a Red Devil Cichlid.

Species #256 — Red Devil Cichlid (*Amphilophus labiatus*).

Red Devils proved somewhat common, and I quickly hooked another. After unhooking the lil' devil, I set my rod down, the baited jig happening to fall into the pond at the water's edge. When I picked up the rod, I set the hook on whatever was nibbling and quickly found myself with another new species. It is a fish commonly called the "African Jewelfish" or "African Jewel Cichlid," but that doesn't describe a species. That describes a genus of at least half a dozen species native to Africa and common in aquaria.

For some reason, when USGS first did its sampling, it lumped all African Jewelfish together as one species and has maintained that tradition since. There are some simple ways to distinguish them by paying attention to the two or three spots on their side.

Amazingly, I caught three separate species at the first stop.

Species #257 — African Jewelfish (*Hemichromis bimaculatus*).
Species #258 — Blood-Red Jewel Cichlid (*Hemichromis lifalili*).
Species #259 — Jewel Cichlid (*Hemichromis guttatus*).

These would be the first of 44 "African Jewelfish" of widely variable appearance I caught in various locations, taking pictures and begrudgingly counting as a single species until someone from the North American Native Fishes Association (NANFA), explained everything to me and identified my fish.

So four species at the second stop? Not bad.

I continued to catch tilapia there. It was stupid easy for the size of the fish, and I counted my blessings as I pulled in each of the 13 Nile Tilapia. The local flavor also counted their blessings, as I kept most of them for their passive suicide attempt — I mean, fish fry.

That said, I wasn't really after tilapia; I was after a species found here and nowhere else in the United States: the Giraffe Cichlid, *Nimbochromis venustus*.

Giraffe Cichlids live up to their name. Their incredibly conspicuous form includes a neck nearly a foot long which they use to feed on shoreline vegetation from the water while breathing from a vestigial lung. Giraffe Cichlids can be easily spotted grazing on the shore where present. It's an incredibly unique adaptation for a fish, and if you're incredulous, then you should be because I made that all up.

I suppose the blue-black patterning on them sort of resembles a giraffe, but they're really just an ordinary cichlid. Except for the fact that they are not ordinary.

On several occasions, Giraffe Cichlids had been recorded in Blue Lake by USGS, and several anglers had recently posted pictures of those they'd caught there. It seemed like a sure thing, which is probably why it evaded me.

In total, I spent about four hours at Blue Lake and the surrounding ponds. I hopped around from pond to pond, fishing every spring pool and even Blue Lake itself.

Neither did I see a Giraffe Cichlid nor did I catch one. I caught 34 fishes in total, but only the five species already addressed. Even with a play-by-play from my friend Chris Moore of Arizona, who'd fished there in the past few weeks and told me where to go, I managed to miss a giraffe.

It's hard to be disappointed after getting four new species and catching that many fish, but I had a long drive back along Satan's Driveway (not its actual name, but I hereby formally submit it for consideration) and then across hundreds of miles of highway to Salt Lake City. A pit stop to clean the filthy mud from my feet was all it took to keep me on track.

Salt Lake

I love Salt Lake City. I find the scenery, culinary scene, coffee (yes, really), and general aesthetic of the area to be very pleasant.

Just a little south of SLC, Provo is another worthwhile stop. The lakeside city is basically a fully realized version of my hometown, Klamath Falls, if Klamath Falls were to get Google Fiber and a multimillion-dollar infusion of capital for radical transformation and modernization. But my trip through was not about enjoying the city; it was about hitting three or four stops on my way east to Rock Springs, Wyoming.

My first stop was supposed to hold several species I hadn't caught, but from my research, I could tell access would be a problem.

Though mining has been slowed dramatically in the 21st century, Utah still has a very active mining industry. Utah also has an active sporting community centered on hunting, fishing, and other outdoor activities that rely on such novelties as decent water quality and a lack of industrial pollutants just lying around. The state doesn't have the same environmental management ethos as most of its Western neighbors and tends to prioritize industry over conservation, but it still understands that outdoor recreation is an industry and takes steps to protect this vital source of revenue.

Maybe not the best means, but it gets to an acceptable end. Utah's policy includes dealing with the aftermath of mining.

My first stop was at a tailing pond, basically an enclosed waterway used to store pollutants and runoff from mining facilities to keep it as inert as possible to limit soil and water contamination.

Strangely enough, tailing ponds aren't always entirely toxic and given that some are fed by water from other sources, some even hold fish.

The spot I was fishing was one such location.

After parking alongside the highway, I hopped a gate and began walking toward the water. A pallid gravel road paralleled what was obviously the water, but thick grass quite a bit taller than me blocked access. I ended up walking almost half a mile down the road, ultimately coming into some heavy industrial buildings.

Fortunately, it was Sunday, and I never saw a soul to kick me out or arrest me for light trespassing.

Unfortunately, the fish I was after is tiny, and when I finally did make it to the water, the clarity was so terrible there wasn't a prayer of really microfishing.

Carp sipped bugs off the surface here and there, but I was neither equipped properly to chase carp nor interested in doing so with such an ambitious schedule that day, so I high-tailed it away from the tailing pond, and proceeded to the first of several public access points of the Jordan River since I try to limit my trespassing while fishing.

The first was blown out. The river was high, muddy, and though I tried fishing for half an hour, even a 1-ounce weight wouldn't keep my bait down in the way conditions were keeping my spirits down.

The next stop was a little better, but after an hour of fishing under the bridge where I'd seen numerous Utah Suckers, *Catostomus ardens* recorded on Fishbrain, I was still coming up short.

My rut continued on into the evening, as I stopped in for some Indian food. Rarely is Indian food bad in my opinion. Like Mexican food in the Southwest, Indian food is pretty much a safe bet anywhere there's civilization.

There's an exception to every rule, though, and I found it that night. I was disappointed almost as much by the food as I had been by the day's fishing. So I plugged on, passing the Flaming Gorge on the Utah/Wyoming border with hungry eyes as I wound my way into the town of Green River. I'd hoped to spend an hour sight fishing for sculpins with a headlamp, a technique I hadn't invented but certainly pioneered and then mastered years before.

Even when you know what you're doing, fish aren't guaranteed. This river was also blown out and despite the frigid temperatures I knew sculpins thrive in, visibility was nil.

Dejected, I drove the rest of the way to my destination, finishing the day's drive with just 468 miles logged as I pulled into Rock Springs, Wyoming, where I'd booked a motel, absent-mindedly hearing them say they didn't have air conditioning but not really registering what that meant as I filled out the paperwork. It was summer, and it should've been hot, but when you travel far enough north, high enough in elevation, and far enough inland to experience the negative downswing of continentality, it turns out you don't need A/C.

Continentality (one of the few things I remember from college Geography class), is basically the principle that the further you travel from the coasts, the more variable temperatures are. It's why Seattle, Washington, averages a daily temperature from 45 to 75 degrees Fahrenheit (a range of 30 degrees) whereas Bismarck, North Dakota, averages from -10 to 85 (a range of 95 degrees), despite the fact that they are at almost the same latitude. In short, it meant I didn't need A/C because in the T-shirt, shorts, and flip-flops I usually travel in during the summer, I was cold when I got there that night.

Even though some cigarette-wielding, scantily-clad women in the motel parking lot made their best effort to change this fact, I had nothing to warm me up that night except a chance to dive into my family history: Rock Springs, Wyoming is the place where my grandparents first met as part of a large group of Slovenian immigrants who settled the area more than one hundred years earlier.

Chapter 7
The Old Country

June 17, 2019

Day 3
Origin: Rock Springs, Wyoming
Destination: Omaha, Nebraska

"Velike ribe male žro." Slovenian Proverb, very roughly translated to: "Men are like fish; the big ones devour the small."

My maternal great-grandparents emigrated to the United States around the turn of the 20th century. I'm routinely asked "Where did they come from?" and that's a difficult question.

Given that Europe's map east of Prague and Milan shifted faster than its fashions for most of the 19th and 20th centuries, the question has a complicated answer.

Culturally and linguistically, my great-grandparents were Slovenes, a people group that had existed for centuries and maintained a unique cultural identity without ever having its own country. At the time my great-grandparents emigrated to the United States, they had been living in the Austro-Hungarian Empire, in part of a geographic region that is today inside of Slovenia. So nationally, they were Austrian.

They fled the political unrest that was building in the "South Slavic" region of the Empire to the United States. They joined the other Slovenians heading en masse to the United States during the 1880s until the start of World War I in the largest wave of Slovenian emigration to-date.

Those who remained in the Old Country didn't accept the status quo. Citizens of what is now Slovenia, in addition to modern-day Croatia, Bosnia and Herzegovina, Serbia, and Montenegro all held national resentments toward their Austrian overlords. It was this collective unrest that ultimately led to the group of Serbs and Bosnians who worked together to successfully assassinate Archduke Ferdinand, heir to the throne of the Austro-Hungarian Empire, which would trigger World War I in 1914 and lead to the creation of a still less-than-ideal "Southern Slavic State" called Yugoslavia in the aftermath of The Great War. Yugoslavia would last for decades.

As the long-rusted Iron Curtain began to disintegrate, so too did the Slavic proxy for the Soviets with no "official" ties to Moscow.

Yugoslavia began to crumble in 1989. Slovenia voted to declare independence in 1990 — the year I was born — but wouldn't officially become its own nation until June of 1991.

Many wars would follow, but when Slovenia and Croatia became independent nations in 1991, their freedom foretold the doom of Yugoslavia, a state that would survive just a year longer before dissolving entirely. After nearly 50 years of Communist rule by the greater powers, Bosnia and Herzegovina, Croatia, Kosovo, Montenegro, North Macedonia, Serbia, and Slovenia were all free.

It would take several more wars, territorial disputes (i.e., Kosovo), and name changes as recent as 2019 (i.e., North Macedonia), but the small fishes of the proverb would be free to swim in the directions they chose without fear of being gobbled up.

Rock Springs

Though most Slovenian emigrants settled in the United States, specifically Ohio, a small group headed to the middle of the least populous state in the Union: Wyoming. My great-grandparents ended up in Rock Springs, Wyoming. My great-grandfather was the sheriff, and at various times arrested such famed outlaws as the Sundance Kid (of hipster film festival fame).

Though technically the "good guy," my great-grandfather was actually a terrible human being who drank like a fish and routinely abused his wife and children. When my grandfather was 19, he married my grandmother (17), and they moved west to Oregon, settling in Klamath Falls and leaving much of their past behind them.

Despite the dark and sordid history of his time in Rock Springs, my grandpa still told me stories about it. Holding the horses of outlaws and lawmen alike for a nickel while they drank at the local tavern, hunting and fishing, and generally living in the inhospitable wilds of Wyoming. He passed away years ago, and he would have been 108 if he were still alive when I rolled into the city where he met and married my grandma.

I'd passed through Rock Springs very briefly on a road trip in 2018, but this time I spent a few hours there, walking the train tracks downtown and appreciating what the little city had to offer. Not a whole lot, as it turns out — especially in terms of fishing. I'd hoped to find a Northern Plains Killifish, *Fundulus kansae* or a Plains Topminnow, *Fundulus sciadicus*, but the pond hopping and limited creek fishing turned up nothing, so I grabbed a cup of coffee by the train station, checked out an impressive street art memorial to the Chinese-American workers that built most of the nearby railroad and were subsequently slaughtered for it. Unlike that same railroad, I headed east from Rock Springs.

The drive across Wyoming is pretty desolate, and this is coming from a guy who had driven "The Loneliest Road in America" just days before. There are several stretches with 60 or 80 miles between civilization of any kind, and I-80 stretches further than a supple yoga instructor. The one advantage would be that it has a generous speed limit, and the roads are lightly trafficked, but every time (okay, all three times), I've taken it east through Wyoming, it has been an endless chain of road work driving all six cars on the empty road between stops into a single, diverted lane. Inevitably, a truck moving 30 miles per hour — or worse, a cop — will slow traffic to a crawl.

There is an Internet conspiracy that Wyoming is not real but rather a carefully crafted lie by the government. If my incredibly boring drives through the least populous state are any indication, I'll bet this rumor began when someone drove through Wyoming and just forgot about it. I almost did.

Nebraska

I drove through Wyoming into a marginally less desolate state: Nebraska. Again hoping for the Plains Topminnow or Northern Plains Killifish, I had marked a chain of small ponds that appeared to be connected to a creek, very accessible, and just off the Interstate.

Oh how wrong I was.

When I arrived at an oversized gravel parking lot, I found myself staring at a large, fenced area with an open gate. There were industrial buildings and trucks going in and out.

I found neither "No Trespassing" nor "Authorized Vehicles Only" signs, so I drove through. It quickly became obvious that something sketchy was happening. It had the vibe of a major drug distribution center, and as I ambled along the poorly maintained roads, I began thinking I should turn around.

As I got out of the car to look at the overgrown ponds, a gunshot rang out, and I was soaked in a cold sweat.

What a way to die.

The pain in my leg suddenly announced itself, and I thought "Huh. Being shot doesn't hurt as much as I thought it would."

Horrified, I looked down as I quickly tried to get back into my car for cover. A single black spot above a trickle of blood peeled my eyes wide, but upon closer inspection, I saw the black spot had wings. It was a massive horsefly, and it was sucking my blood with fervor.

The timing was at once immaculate and cruel, like so much modern European engineering. The bug had bitten at precisely the moment I heard the shot, and my mind filled in the blanks. I crushed the bloodsucking bastard with so much happiness, words can barely express it. I wasn't shot!

"Cracccccckkkkkkkkhhhhhhh!"

Yet.

"Cracccccckkkkkkkkhhhhhhh!"

I needed to get down.

Another shot rang out, and I saw two guys in a beat-up SUV peel out maybe 200 yards distant. I thought they were coming for me until I saw a deer bound away. They were shooting at the deer. Funny, I've never heard of a late June deer season.

"Oh, (profanity not suitable for print)," I whispered aloud.

They looked extremely guilty, but I was a little nervous these poachers were going to shoot me. I pretended not to notice them until the ginger redneck behind the wheel hopped out, the exertion of his felony causing his skin to match his red hair.

"Crap," I said under my breath.

"This here is private property," he said, flashing a badge that was clearly fake and appeared to be printed with "FBI: Female Body Inspector" but refusing to identify himself or keep the badge up long enough for me to scrutinize it.

Visions of my kidneys being removed and shipped in cold storage flashed before my eyes. I swallowed hard.

"I'm sorry," I managed. "I was just looking for a place to fish."

His unblinking, featureless face reddened further as he put a hand on the rusty revolver (again, not a real cop) on his hip holster.

"Well you can't (his twang actually spit out 'caint' but...) be here."

I stood there, motionless, as he stepped toward me.

He was shaking and twitching in the way only habitual users of hard drugs can manage, and I was unnerved. His eyes hardened, and he made a motion to grab the revolver out of the holster.

Before he could react, I lunged for his eyes, gouging them out with surprising precision. He screamed in pain as the passenger emerged, sawed-off shotgun in tow. I grabbed the pistol from the holster and put down the other poacher with two shots to the chest.

The bleeding man on the ground moaned "Whhhyyyyy?"

The wind changed, and it snapped me from my waking nightmare. I shuddered at the violent turn my daydream had taken.

"Well?" he repeated, obviously repeating something he'd said while I was blanking out.

"Huh?" I inquired intelligently.

"Why don't you just leave," the ginger repeated.

"No problem. Have a good one," I said, driving out the gate praying all the while they wouldn't shoot me in the back.

They didn't, and I headed down the road to a place where the parking lot was not fenced.

I was shaking a little, but I managed not to vomit or pee that much, instead focusing on the water available to me across the large parking lot maybe 500 yards away. It was a disgusting soup of dirty pond water, and I quickly caught some small Largemouth Bass and Bluegill. As I went to snap a picture of one adorable little micro bass that was my first fish in Nebraska, I heard a car peel out of the parking lot.

It was the "cops" I'd encountered moments before. I was still on edge, and I dropped my phone into something equal parts liquid and gel pooled on a piece of plastic near the waterline. Gagging and very nearly vomiting for real this time, I grabbed it out and washed off the milky liquid-gel in the pond to get the chunks off.

I dry heaved.

Thankfully, my Lifeproof case held up, but I was horrified to see some indescribably filthy biological substance on my phone even after rinsing. I wrapped it in one of the old rags I always tuck into my waistband to wipe my hands when fishing with bait and drove to the nearest gas station to clean my phone.

A full minute under the running water of the sink followed by a bath in rubbing alcohol and then another minute of washing, and I was satisfied that the filth was removed.

Whatever *Breaking Bad*-type operation I'd bumped into had me shooketh (that's slang for "shaken," for those older than 25 because apparently using the wrong verb tense and adding letters to words is cool).

Daily horror behind me, I drove under the highway arch to the river I'd been given as a place to chase Shovelnose Sturgeon. Like most flowing water I'd encountered on the trip thus far and the hairstyles of an increasing number of elderly women as I made my way further south, it was blown out.

Calling it a night, I drove on to Omaha, fighting heavy traffic en route to "The Gateway to the West" for the College World Series.

I wanted a fairly healthy meal, so I opted for Japanese.

Fighting exhaustion, I powered down a pork belly bao, seaweed salad, and some excellent ramen before staggering out of the restaurant. Eschewing my car and trying to limit lodging costs, I'd embraced Couchsurfing, and tonight would be my first stay.

I was an early adopter of Airbnb. It was founded in 2008, and I stayed in my first Airbnb during the summer of 2010. That trip had let me check out a house rented with friends in the Seattle suburbs and a basement apartment in Vancouver, British Columbia. I'd avoided rape and murder and saved some money, so I was satisfied.

Unlike Airbnb, I was not an early adopter of Couchsurfing — even though it's basically Airbnb for free — and actually predates it by four years. When I finally heard about it from a friend, I was intrigued, and it sounded like a way to avoid some nights in my car without splurging for a roach motel.

Here's how it works: essentially, people offer up their couch, spare bedroom, or floor for you to sleep in or on. It's very European in spirit, and admittedly, it made me hesitant, but if it meant not sleeping in my car, I figured I'd risk getting watched while I slept.

Knowing I may not be able to rely on the kindness of strangers every night, and also wanting the chance to strut around naked from time to time without being urged to do so by a Couchsurfing host (there are a lot of nudists on the platform, so always double-check), I shifted my plans from sleeping in the car about half the time to Couchsurfing half of the time. This, I hoped, would allow me to save money on lodging and spend money on stuff that actually mattered to me, such as food and fishing opportunities.

Still, this was my first Couchsurfing experience, so I had no idea what to expect.

Slowly, I made my way to the house. I was staying with Ashley, who had told me to just walk up and knock when I arrived. I did so, despite the darkened house, and she opened up with a smile.

After a quick walk-through tour of the place, in which she offered me free access to the kitchen, introduced me to her kids (who were sharing a room tonight after forfeiting one room to me), she told me about her job as a Terrorism Auditor for PayPal. I was intrigued, but it was too late for meaningful conversation, so I showered and called it a night as I fell asleep on the little bed in her daughter's unicorn-themed room, wondering if I'd be trusting enough to let a stranger into my house with little kids.

I battled for uneasy sleep all night.

I was up, showered, and out of the house before they went to school, and my first Couchsurfing experience went better than I'd expected. At least, I assume it did, but you can't really tell if someone watched you sleep, right?

Before leaving home, I decided I'd leave a thank-you card and a $5 Starbucks gift card for every person who let me Couchsurf with them. I had a box of thank-yous and a stack of gift cards in my center console.

I left the card on the pillow, stripped the sheets and slipped into the quiet morning.

Chapter 8
Middle America

June 18, 2019

Day 4
Origin: Omaha, Nebraska
Destination: Nashville, Tennessee

"We must accept finite disappointment,
but never lose infinite hope."
Dr. Martin Luther King, Jr. || American Civil Rights Leader

In my rush to get on the road, I wasn't able to conduct my morning routine. Basically, Irritable Bowel Syndrome (IBS) dictates my life for about the first two hours I'm awake. TMI, I know, but I usually have to make two trips to the bathroom during the first hour I'm awake almost without fail.

Anyhow, I went from my Couchsurfing stay toward TD Ameritrade Park, just to say I saw the College World Series. On my way there, the gripping urgency in my descending colon sent me scrambling to find the nearest Starbucks. Though their coffee isn't the best, they almost always have a clean, private bathroom. Given my condition, the privacy and sink next to the toilet collectively make Starbucks my favorite pit stop. Without going into any more detail than that, urgency, frequency, and pain associated with the condition all have an impact on my mood at times. When I wake up and know it's going to be a "bad day," it often contributes to the depression I battle on the regular.

For the first three days of my trip, I hadn't experienced it, but today, the limited sleep, long drive the previous day, disappointing fishing, and intestinal issues had me in a dark place.

When I found out the highway was flooded near Kansas City, and I'd have to take an hour-and-a-half detour through Des Moines, I was downright dejected, but what happened next was nothing short of miraculous.

Though I've had all sorts of struggles, the one constant in my life has always been my Christian faith. My relationship with Jesus Christ is far from perfect, and I'm not the best Christian, but Christianity requires understanding your imperfections and the need for help as you pursue a living relationship with Jesus.

Whether you have faith or not, try to understand the comfort it can be to people and the comfort it has brought to me and countless others.

Faith (called religion by some) has been shown to increase life expectancy in many studies, but namely a comprehensive longevity study by the journal *Social Psychological and Personality Science* that found it to be one of the most consistent ways to increase the human lifespan.

In my life, it certainly helps me cling to something when everything else feels bleak.

Some may attribute it to coincidence, but in my darkest times, something has always snapped me out of it and kept me from making irreversible choices. I believe it's God. Regardless, something — or someone — snapped me out of my funk that day, too.

A guy I follow on Instagram, Casey Shanaberger, messaged me, asking if I'd be coming through Iowa. I told him I would now, and he suggested we meet up to fish for a little bit.

It proved to be just what I needed.

We met at an urban creek and after exchanging pleasantries, began microfishing, and I quickly caught a Bigmouth Shiner.

Species #260 — Bigmouth Shiner (*Notropis dorsalis*).

They were abundant, and the large school kept to the shallow, rocky run, swaying around our submerged legs like mosaic snakes in response to the current at our looming presence. While Casey looked for darters, I continued trying to catch the dozens of micros in the creek. Bigmouth Shiners predominated, but eventually I got another new species, the Bluntnose Minnow.

Species #261 — Bluntnose Minnow (*Pimephales notatus*).

With two new species right off the bat with Casey, the College World Series proved worthwhile. I'd told him I only had like an hour to fish, given that my detour extended my already 10-plus-hour drive to more than 12, and I wanted to cover my bases. When you're catching fish, soaking up the sun, and coming out of a depressive state, it's tough to walk away.

We waded upstream and down, and though we saw Johnny Darters, *Etheostoma nigrum* and Fantail Darters, *Etheostoma flabellare*, they wouldn't play.

Passing under a graffiti-splashed bridge, we came to a slow-moving pool and tossed in. I set my micro sabiki into the deepest part of the pool, optimistic about a sculpin or large darter, loosened the drag, and we used tenkara rods to play with micros.

Tenkara is a form of flyfishing originating in Japan that uses ultralight, collapsible rods with a length of line tied to the tip. At the end of the line is fly that is repeatedly drifted through a stretch of stream to catch small, native trout.

At least, that's how you're supposed to use tenkara rods. I mostly use mine for microfishing. Paired with micro sabikis, I'm basically a walking Japanophile.

The micro sabikis I use are a game-changer. I got them from a Japanese contact I met at ICAST in 2018 named Mauro Macias. He works for Sasame, and though Sasame's products aren't yet available for retail in the United States, he shipped me some as a favor. The small hooks cover the water column an inch or two apart and are incredibly productive for micros — especially Cyprinids or Leucicids (that is, Old World or New World minnows, respectively). Unfortunately, they aren't as easy to fish with as larger, saltwater sabikis. First, the line is very light, so if a little bass, trout, or sunfish takes your bait, consider that hook (and maybe the whole rig) lost. Second, the hooks are tiny, sharp, and easy to snag into your flesh, clothing, or one another. This is especially common when you hook small sunfish that flop like their life depends on it. Sometimes, it does — especially if they ruin one of my priceless little rigs. Third, the sabikis have a light weight at the bottom, and if you happen to hook a larger fish and that weight gets dragged between two rocks, it's over. I've lost several nicer fishes this way. Finally, they're not conducive to travel. Steve Wozniak, who first showed them to me years ago, told me they're basically disposable because of how difficult they are to transport once opened. Ordinarily, that wouldn't be a problem, but given that I only get a handful every year from my contact, they're invaluable.

Regardless of the struggles they present the angler afflicted with wanderlust, they're incredibly effective, and sometimes I use them in a risky manner.

You're here for the fishing stories. In blind fishing, you just toss out a worm (or small piece of worm in this case), and hope for the best. Alas, only small sunfish obliged us on our tenkara rods. With time running short, we began to head back downstream. I picked up my blind rod and felt weight. Realizing it was much larger than a sculpin, I was careful not to over-stress the threadlike line.

It stayed on long enough for us to see it was a small redhorse (a type of sucker), and though we called it a Shorthead Redhorse, *Moxostoma macrolepidotum* (a species I caught several times in Canada), there's no way to be sure. Still, I'd managed two new species on that stop, gotten to meet an "Insta Friend" in person, and soaked up enough sun to part the clouds in my mind as Casey and I parted ways.

Mizzou

My brother, Jake, is kind of ornery. He's a social butterfly and quite funny, but often at the expense of other people. I've been his victim as often as anyone else, but I've learned to laugh at myself publicly and cry about it later, only when I'm alone. Nonetheless, his charisma ensures that he can make fun of you in a way that is good-natured enough to make you laugh at yourself. It's a strange phenomenon, but people still like him. He calls it "Jaking" instead of "Joking" which probably helps.

Though I'm probably his favorite victim, his former roommate, Caileigh Smith, comes in second.

Caileigh is now a podiatrist on the West Coast, but she did her undergrad at the University of Missouri, affectionately called "Mizzou" because the best abbreviated names also change two letters in the shortened version, obviously.

After hearing a million stories about Mizzou from Caileigh while Jake teased her, I happened to see a Mizzou student post about some fishes (namely Redfin Shiner, *Lythrurus umbratilis*) they'd caught in a creek on campus.

Since I was pazzing through Columbia, Mizzouri, anyway, I had planned to stop.

The shoreline was overgrown and choked with extremely thick vegetation, but the creek itself was wide, shallow enough to wade comfortably, and had enough flow to support a diverse biomazz.

Twice, I drove over that bridge, looking for a place to park. Twice, I failed.

The grass was thick and tall, coming right up to the pavement. There was no shoulder, no pull-outs, and apart from a faculty parking lot about a quarter mile away, it looked hopeless. It was summer, and the parking lot was only sparsely filled in, so, like the one time I bought sushi at a convenience store, I threw caution to the wind and decided to go for it.

With my tenkara rod and a pair of spinning rods in tow, I busted brush down the slope and began fishing under the bridge. Knowing I still had more than six hours to drive and three more planned stops, I set my phone's timer for 30 minutes, put my flip-flops in my hand, and jumped into the water.

In seconds, I'd found fish. There were micros and larger fishes alike, but I decided to start with what looked easier: the micros.

Indecision plagued me as I tried to decide if I wanted to start with my tenkara and its single-hook presentation or fish multiple hooks with the micro sabiki. I opted for the latter.

On my first cast, I hooked into something larger. I was optimistic when I saw the deep-bodied golden fish, thinking I'd tied into a redhorse, River Carpsucker, *Carpiodes carpio*, or buffalo (another type of sucker) of some kind. Sadly, it was just a palm-sized Common Carp, *Cyprinus carpio* — the smallest one I'd ever caught by at least two pounds.

The wait for a new species wasn't long, though. My next cast yielded a bright, golden fish that I quickly identified as what I thought was a Common Shiner.

Species #262 — Common Shiner (*Luxilus cornutus*).

For the next ten minutes, I struggled. Time was short, and I could feel myself roasting in the sun as I realized I hadn't put on sunscreen, and I couldn't really immerse myself in the fishing. Fortunately, there were enough fishes that it didn't matter, and I quickly caught the next species, Sand Shiner.

Species #263 — Sand Shiner (*Notropis stramineus*).

Then I caught four more. They were persistent once I got into the school, and believe it or not, the Sand Shiners were all residing over a sandy bottom.

Though I never found my Redfin Shiner, I did notice a big, colorful shiner I thought might be a Redfin. I caught it, and the gorgeous light blue fish with red fins, a purple-pink head, and pink and blue vertical stripes behind the gill plate were their own reward. It looked like it had been in an industrial cotton candy accident. I called it a Redfin Shiner and then called it a day, heading back to the car.

I posted my catches to the NANFA Facebook Forum and drove on. Within minutes, my Redfin Shiner ID would be corrected. I was only a "fin" off of the correct answer. It was a Red Shiner, *Cyprinella lutrensis* — not a Redfin Shiner.

I'd already caught Red Shiners, but never a spawning male colored up like this one. Like humans, Cyprinids and Leucicids (minnows) show what is called sexual dimorphism, meaning both genders have distinguishing physical characteristics. This is common in many fish species, but spawning Cyprinids and Leucicids can be especially telling. Female Red Shiners are bright silver with almost no other coloration whereas males look like someone painted them using only colors available in Easter decorations.

So Caleigh, Mizzou was okay. I've obviously been to better places, but it was pretty cool, I guezz.

Carlyle Dam

My next stop should have produced something big or new. Instead, no matter what I tried, I caught lots of White Bass, *Morone chrysops*. It was a spot several friends had mentioned as a must-stop location, and so it went on my list.

There is a small but vocal sect of the Species Hunting community that believes fishing with a guide, going on a charter boat, or sharing spots with fellow anglers is sacrilegious. Obviously they're entitled to their opinion, but most anglers are not wealthy enough to possess the time and money necessary to blaze every trail on our own.

Instead, we share spots or find them by scouring the USGS NAS, Fishbrain, iNaturalist, or a host of other online resources, but those tried-and-true spots provided by friends are usually the best bets. Roughly 30% of the spots I fished on this trip came from family, friends, and acquaintances, people who told me where to go and for what. Most of them panned out, too.

Carlyle Dam was not one of them.

The remaining spots came from data mining or just randomly stopping at places I thought "looked fishy," or happened to be visible from my pit stop on the side of the highway.

Carlyle was so hyped that I didn't exactly know what to target. There were a dozen or so fishes there I hadn't caught, ranging from the diminutive to the river monsters. Instead of focusing on one, I brought something for everyone as I ambled down the grassy banks to the tailwater of the dam.

Without a doubt, it was comical for those watching me make my way down to the dam carrying half a dozen rods, all rigged in different ways. I used worms, sabiki rigs, curlytail grubs, Rapalas, spoons, spinners, cut bait, live bait, and desperate prayers.

You know those people who have a weird obsession with their gear? Like, they have an entire room of their house dedicated to it and obviously own more than they could ever possibly use? The terrible sort of people who could've given that money to charity or paid off some student loans or done something better with that money? Well I'm one of those people.

A lot of anglers say this, but few go so far as to buy dozens of identical gear bags, standardize the basic fishing tools inside and then specialize them by species or type of fishing. Perhaps some do, but do you know anyone else who paid to get monogrammed names on each gear bag? I paid someone to sow white block letters in all caps spelling out the type of gear it contained therein: TROUT, BASS, PANFISH, BOTTOMFISHING, SHARKS and more than a dozen other names. Yes, it's a sickness. No, I didn't take them all with me on this road trip.

I brought a shark rod, three medium-light rods for all-purpose fishing, an ultralight, a medium rod for flinging lures to gamefish and a pair of tenkara rods for microfishing. My gear included small and large lures, some light jigs, an array of hooks and weights, light leader, and loads of sabikis, a pre-tied five- or six-hook rig designed to catch bait in saltwater that has become the darling of Species Hunters everywhere for its versatility.

With the exception of the shark rod and a tenkara, I brought every rod in my car with me to fish below that damn dam and still failed to catch anything new, forcing me to lug all that gear for nothing.

Daylight was running out, and I still had a few hours of driving until I made it to Nashville.

I'd planned to fish a park across state lines, and I'd even purchased an Indiana license for the stop, but ended up burning it when I realized I didn't have enough time for the detour. Like that multi-level marketing thing I did in college, it cost me $9 I'll never get back.

I had finally caught a few fishes over a pound, but if that's your best consolation as an angler, consider golf. Acknowledging the graying light, I took a quick sink bath in the disgusting public bathroom, packed up all 348 rods I'd brought down to the water, and began driving the final hours to Nashville.

Nashville

Nashville had impressed me on my first visit, and I vowed to spend more time there in the future. Alas, this might as well have been former President Bill Clinton's wedding vows for how well it was honored.

I arrived in Nashville around 10 p.m. After scarfing down a piece of pizza (that's all that was open and quick nearby), I arrived at Raj's place, where I would be Couchsurfing that night. Raj was incredibly friendly and gave me a tour of his palatial home, which, amazingly enough, turned out to be just one half of the largest duplex this side of Texas. It had at least six bedrooms, three bathrooms, massive common areas, and a partially-covered rooftop patio overlooking the city. It was impressive, to say the least. He was tired, and I was, too, so I thanked him, and we called it a night. I had a nice room and bathroom to myself, and as I climbed the stairs and walked down a hallway that was conservatively 100 feet long, I looked forward to a really restful sleep.

Chapter 9
Coffee

June 19, 2019

Day 5
Origin: Nashville, Tennessee
Destination: Tampa, Florida

"May your coffee kick in before reality does."
Unknown || From Pinterest

We've established the importance of coffee. Not only do I (sometimes) need it to start my engine in the morning, but each sip of delicious coffee is an experience. Frankly, I love the taste and aroma alike. Balancing the two senses for the perfect cup can be tough, but when done properly, it is exquisite.

Like wine, coffee can be described as nutty, chocolatey, syrupy, fragrant, mellow, charred, buttery, toasty, and rich. Coffee is compared to honey, fruits, chocolate, nuts, wine, flowers, vegetables, and grains.

A well-chosen cup of coffee, I've found, rarely disappoints. The last leg of my journey down to Florida had arrived, and coffee would once again come through.

Just as the suave Neal Caffrey from television's *White Collar*, "I never say no to good coffee."

I definitely try to look for a local coffee roaster for that good coffee, but I'll settle for Starbucks if I must. Starbucks is not the best coffee — not even close — but it is consistently palatable enough, and I will break my "No Fast Food" rule if no better coffee options exist.

Though I'd awoken early, I expected my host, Raj, to be awake. I showered, packed up, and made my way downstairs, but he wasn't stirring, and I didn't want to wake him, so I left the thank-you card on the counter and went out for breakfast.

Though Nashville's Germantown neighborhood is rustic, post-industrial, and full of historic wood-and-brick buildings, it was the prevalent street art that stood out. One particular postmodern portrait of a little boy with half a dozen skin tones and the word "HARMONY" emblazoned in gold was especially powerful. The artist had signed @CREATIV_TY, and I marveled at the modernity of the world in which we live — a social media handle but not a name. I snapped a quick picture and walked into the Red Bicycle.

The nutty cup of java with citrus overtones was top-tier, but it wasn't that particular coffee that cemented the day in my mind. Nor was it the pretty good breakfast I ate there. Instead, it was the unique decor of the coffee shop that included exposed brick, industrial metal pipework, and a collection of furnishings that were almost Classic Americana and Turn-of-the-Century Italy at the same time. Nebulous as that is, it was memorable.

As I headed out of Nashville, it was a sign reading "Welcome to Coffee County" in rural Tennessee that perked me right up. It meant I was close to my first destination, a spot Martini Arostegui had shared with me that held Flame Chub, *Hemitremia flammea*.

Despite sounding like a very unpleasant STI, Flame Chub is actually a relatively uncommon fish he'd found to be common in this particular spot.

I parked at a little convenience store, crossed the country road with a couple of rods, a photo tank, some worms, and a few bemused looks from the local flavor passing by. Sometimes I wonder what others think of me when I fish places like this, but then I remember that I just don't care.

It was a small stream with adequate flow, but certainly too small to hold any monster fish. This place whispered similarities to a lazy trout stream but wasn't quite right to draw anglers in. That was fine with me, and I took advantage of my solitude on the creek to maximize my haul. When Martini had said these fish were easy, he wasn't kidding. They were so thick, I caught a dozen of the silvery little fish tinged with red-orange before I caught anything else.

Species #264 — Flame Chub (*Hemitremia flammea*).

Streams like this one have a variety of habitats: slow, deeper pools, fast runs, lots of flow and aeration, and a mix of sand, dirt, rock, and weedy bottoms. Though Flame Chub was the dominant species here, I also caught Creek Chub, *Semotilus atromaculatus*, Green Sunfish, *Lepomis cyanellus*, and five Striped Shiners, *Luxilus chrysocephalus*, the latter being another new species.

Species #265 — Striped Shiner (*Luxilus chrysocephalus*).

After that, I spent way too long trying to get a tiny darter to bite. Darters are in the Percidae family, closely related to Yellow Perch, *Perca flavescens*, Sauger, *Sander canadensis* and Walleye, *Sander vitreus*. In North America, there are more darter species (at least 300 species by the latest estimates) than any other group of freshwater fishes save Leucicids (minnows, which also include more than 300 species).

Alas, apart from a female Rainbow Darter, *Etheostoma caeruleum*, I couldn't get anything to bite. Having caught the all-too-common Rainbow Darters before, I wasn't too impressed. Failing to get the less common species of darters left a bit of a bitter taste in my mouth, but overall, Coffee County had produced, and I had no heartburn from the stop whatsoever because I knew that if I came back for the darters with a headlamp at night, as I preferred to do, I'd catch them easily. I'd let the idea percolate and come back some day.

Georgia
I had a long drive ahead, so I hopped back into the car and made for Tampa, my penultimate destination.

En route, I fished a park where I'd failed to hook up in the past. Though the park was undergoing construction, I just drove through the heavy equipment as if I belonged there, parked my car past the epicenter of work and headed into the woods before anyone could complain. White privilege is real.

Seconds after arriving, I noticed a couple aggressively making out on the bridge just upstream of where I was fishing. Georgia's air was already hot and heavy, but this couple was single-handedly — well, quadruple-handedly — making it worse. Occasionally, they'd steal glances my way as if the little exhibitionist show was as much for my benefit as their own. I tried to avoid it at first, but it continued. He wanted me to know he was a stud, so I smiled and nodded once to validate him. Once I looked away from their softcore performance, I didn't have to look far to see fish.

At first, I only caught the usual suspects: sunfish and shiners. Then I noticed the small, pike-like fish hovering just under the surface like an overdue argument. They darted and zipped around in powerful bursts, resting almost motionless with bent frames and flowing fins calmly working overtime to keep the fish stationary. Turns out the guy on the bridge wasn't the only stud nearby; these were studfish. Spooky or aggressive — there is no halfway mark for fishes in the Fundulidae family, but these proved to be the latter. I caught fish after fish, knowing all the while I'd lucked into some incredibly handsome and virile specimens of Southern Studfish.

Species #266 — Southern Studfish (*Fundulus stellifer*).

I did my best Katy Perry impression. "Hey, hey, hey," I said as two of them hit my micro sabiki at the same time. My outburst caused the lovers on the bridge to look up, and this time the woman smiled at me before returning to her work. Absolutely shameless.

Nothing else new or exciting showed itself, save for a few moves the still standing lovers on the bridge proffered, so I waded upstream, underneath the bridge upon which the two lovers tried to go as far as the law allows in a public space this side of Amsterdam.

Briefly, a hogsucker (a small sucker with intense coloration) did take my bait, but apparently it could've taken notes on how best to use its mouth from the pair on the bridge because its commitment to my bait was half-hearted. Time was running out, so I climbed out of the water, declined a threesome, hopped back into the car, and drove the last few hours to Florida.

Welcome to Florida
Now three cups of coffee deep for the day, I learned my brother, Gabe, and his fiancé Rylee (now wife) had flown into Orlando — not Tampa.

"But the wedding is in Tampa," I said.

"I know," Gabe said.

I read between the lines.

Knowing this young couple needed to pinch pennies for their own wedding as much as the couple at the park needed to pinch one another's unmentionables in public, I volunteered to pick them up.

My car was loaded to the brim, so I was a little concerned about how we'd fit everyone and everything in it, but a little spontaneity never hurt ... well, why not roll the dice? You're probably guessing where this is going, and for once, assuming the worst consequences for one of my impulsive decisions would be inaccurate.

I made it to Orlando, and though we had to wait almost an hour at the most, well, quintessentially Florida rental car agency you can imagine while he dropped off the rental they'd used the day before, we made it safely to Tampa.

Exhausted and unaccustomed to being awake after midnight, I hit the bed hard just minutes after a shower. I could see the hairs and what appeared to be blood stains on the sheets. I'd recently been making an effort to be more positive, and this looked like an opportunity to be Hepatitis B positive.

Tempted as I was, I avoided that side of the bed, too tired to care now that the day's coffee, coffee, iced coffee, and Coffee County had worn off, I drifted off to sleep.

Chapter 10
The Wedding

June 20, 2019

Day 6
Origin: Tampa, Florida
Destination: St. Petersburg, Florida

Amy: "I have always wanted to go to Florida."
Jonah: "Like, the Florida from the news?"
Amy: "If you ignore all the people, it's basically Hawaii."
Amy Dubanowski, Jonah Simms || From *Superstore*

I've been to Italy, and while I was impressed with neither the quantity of garbage found floating in the Italian Adriatic nor the hole-in-the-floor toilets at several upscale Venetian restaurants, the food was pretty great. You know where else you can find disgusting water quality and poorly maintained bathrooms? Yup. Florida.

Florida, however, does not have the greatest food. Having spent more than four months there fishing throughout the years and traveling around the entire state, I've been largely unimpressed with most of the top-rated restaurants on Yelp!

Nowhere I've traveled has the caliber of food measured up to the food here in the Pacific Northwest. Only parts of Slovenia, Austria, and Germany have the caliber of coffee we have in Cascadia, but they fall behind in their respective food scenes.

The crown jewel of the PNW, from a culinary perspective (and virtually nothing else), is Portland.

Portland, though most well-known for underemployed wealthy White Millennials, anarchists, drugs, homelessness, rabid soccer fans, Antifa, and an extra dose of strangeness is also home to the best food scene on the planet, a fact for which it was awarded in 2018. The rest of the state doesn't slouch either, and it's grown me up to be a bit of a food snob and a definite coffee snob. This means several things, but for starters it makes me avoid fast food and chain restaurants like the plague. These are fine for people who don't know any better, but once you've lived in Oregon, you can't bear such plebeian fare. In fact, most of the time I'd rather skip a meal than eat fast food or dine at (most) chain restaurants (like a peasant).

The Pacific Northwest is the Food Mecca of the world, so I'm a bit spoiled, but rare is the Washington-, Oregon-, or Northern California-caliber restaurant outside the region, and they are especially lacking in Florida. After dozens of subpar dining experiences spread across the entire state, I just assumed all food in Florida more or less sucked.

That all changed the day of the wedding after a morning on the beach.

We spent the morning playing in the surf, tanning (well, burning) our grotesquely pale bodies, playing Spikeball (people stand around a tiny trampoline and take turns spiking the ball off of it) and waiting around for the wedding that evening.

It was casual, lowkey, and we enjoyed ourselves.

After a few hours of beach bumming, I got bored and went fishing. Using the only bait I had, red worms, I cast a truncated sabiki into the surf. Almost immediately, I caught a fish. Then another.

I then tried to get my brothers to give it a go, but they didn't have the patience and quickly returned to their other activities. In 30 minutes or so, I landed six Gulf Kingcroaker, *Menticirrhus littoralis*. The small croakers were plentiful, and though I was hoping for something more exciting, larger, or simply new, the croakers marked my first fish of the trip in Florida.

Eschewing the beach for air conditioning, we showered, changed, and split up to grab lunch. Jake found an Italian deli that looked promising. The scene was unique and very much European. The unassuming deli had a counter where you could order sandwiches, pizzas, calzones, and salad, as well as an espresso bar, several coolers full of beverages, some Italian dry goods, and a pastry case loaded with uniquely Italian creations.

I opted for a sandwich and a pastry I couldn't pronounce. The pastry was roughly triangular with accordion-style construction of crispy layered crust adjoined by a chewy center and stuffed with an almond-pistachio filling. It was dusted with what looked like powdered sugar but had to have been cocaine because it was absolutely addictive.

I devoured it in an uncomfortably intimate moment where I'm sure I made all sorts of off-putting noises as I relished each and every unique bite. It paired nicely with the iced Americano, and I looked forward to the sandwich.

It didn't disappoint.

Almost certainly, it was the best lunch I've ever had in Florida and perhaps the best pastry of my life.

Part of why I love traveling around to fish is to experience the bountiful array of foods the world has to offer. I prioritize trip spending this way, too. In fact, I've spent $40 or more on dinner more times than I've spent $80 or more on lodging, and it's not even close. I'd rather spend $40 or $50 or even $100 on an incredible dining experience than pay more than the bare minimum for a place to sleep. Why? Well I'm only conscious for one of those two experiences.

For small trips of two or three days or even a week long, that's fine. For trips measured in weeks or even months like this one, my inner gourmand would have to tone it down, take a cold shower, and settle for less than — but not all the time.

No, in that moment, I enjoyed the entire dining experience.

If you've ever seen *Parks and Recreation*, you'll know Ron Swanson. The character is hilariously entertaining and apart from dozens of other quirky personality traits, he takes a picture of himself with every steak he's ever eaten at his favorite restaurant, Mulligan's Steakhouse, and keeps it in a scrapbook. Now, we laugh, but those of us Millennials who post pictures of every incredible meal on Instagram really aren't far off, are we? I photograph most of my top-notch meals and put them on my Instagram Story to remind people I was born in the '90s. I'd already eaten the first pastry, but the second one went into my digital scrapbook of sorts, and despite the acid in the coffee and the sandwich, I found myself feeling just a little more basic than before.

Wedding

We returned from the restaurant and prepared for the wedding as a group, taking our time to get dressed and enjoying one another's company. When it came time for wedding pictures, we made our way downstairs, wandered out to the beach, and started posing.

It just so happened that a film crew was shooting for the reality TV show *Floribama Shore*, which is likely as terrible as it sounds, but

I wouldn't know. Given that my IQ is above 100, I don't watch reality television and relish the chance to mock those who do. Whether we're talking *Survivor, The Bachelor/The Bachelorette*, or anything else equally egregious to human intelligence, reality television is so far removed from actual reality that it's a perennial stain on American society. Will I ever watch reality TV? Hard pass.

If you watch it, I'm not judging you. Well, I am, but pretend I'm not if that makes you vote me off the reality TV island and out of the rose ceremony.

The reality we were living (a beach wedding in Florida) was pretty great, so why reach for another? Then again, weddings rank just a few places above reality television on "Luke's List of Dislikes," so I was admittedly skeptical. Of course I was going — Austin is one of the cousins I'm closest with — but I wasn't expecting much. In spite of the fact that I'm a hopeless romantic, or maybe because of that fact, I've never liked weddings. The contrite formality between guests, my crippling fear of public dancing, and the constant reminders that I'm single never fail to strike a dissonant chord in me (even while those around me celebrate).

But this wedding? This was great.

It started with some music. We were lined up on the ramp leading down to the beach. The small band of guests was seated, and we slowly made our way up to the front in pairs, barefoot and fancy free. The ceremony progressed quickly.

When the time came for Jake, Austin's Best Man, to provide the ring, he dropped it. This cut through any tension with a knife, drew a few laughs, and made us feel less self-conscious about sweating bullets in the still-too-hot evening sun.

Austin and Darian shared their first kiss as a married couple; we clapped and started taking pictures.

Despite the lightweight linen pants and white shirt, I was soaked in sweat. It was bloody hot.

We raided the lifeguard station for cold water, towels, and red booty shorts. We then proceeded with pictures before making our way back to a banquet room off the lobby for the reception.

Jake made an emotional toast, and Darian's sister, Kaylee, followed him up.

We enjoyed a pleasant conversation, flavorful food, and even though I was sitting by some folks I barely knew, I couldn't complain. I finally bumped into some folks I knew, and I was able to talk with Austin's younger brother, Mason, and Kaylee's husband, Gary Robinson, whom I often played basketball with back home.

We were living in harmony. Then, everything changed when the Fire Nation attacked. And by "Fire Nation attacked" I mean the music started playing.

"No, God, No!" echoed Michael Scott's words in my mind.

My desperate attempts to escape through reality into the world of *Avatar: The Last Airbender* or *The Office* failed miserably. Cold terror gripped my colon like a vice. They were dancing. Dancing!

Little in life scares me, and I basically have just three fears.

There are two parallel fears: I either end up alone or end up with the wrong person, and both eventualities are equally chilling. One at least means I don't die a virgin, I guess, but that's a small consolation.

Despite the dancing, I stayed and talked, knowing full-well that if I didn't escape soon, I'd end up getting dragged onto the dance floor. That couldn't happen. I took a break to walk out on the patio, drank iced tea like it was going out of style, and subsequently went to the bathroom like a man with a much older, much larger prostate.

Hours after the ceremony, people were still dancing.

I decided to sneak out for an hour to go fishing, so I grabbed my tenkara rod and went out in hopes of catching a small needlefish, a saltwater gar-like fish that has long eluded me in the Gulf of Mexico. Since my wedding apparel was already casual, I just traded dress shoes for flip-flops, shed my shirt, and snuck out into the blackness wearing nothing but slacks and sandals to the water maybe 100 yards from the dreaded dancefloor.

The needlefish were there. And here. And over there. Unfortunately, I couldn't hook one. I tried in vain to catch some sort of small baitfish, perhaps silversides or mullet, but it was dark enough, and the angle was poor enough that even with my headlamp, I couldn't identify the roiling silver mass.

Apart from a micro Pinfish, *Lagodon rhomboides,* I caught nothing.

I put my shirt back on, stowed my fishing gear and returned to the wedding maybe an hour later. Nobody had noticed my absence in the gyrating fray; however, now that I was visible, they noticed me and the others averse to dancing.

One at a time, they began calling people out to join them on the dance floor, chanting each poor sap's name and then using a simulated fishing pole to hook and reel them in. Though I appreciated the motion, I certainly didn't like what it meant.

I could see the writing on the wall. I kept my eyes glued to my phone and tried to stay motionless, but the herd spotted me. I could feel their invasive stares. My body, already sweaty from Essence of

Florida, was instantly soaked with a cold sweat when they started chanting my name.

I was mortified. There was no chance of escape. Suddenly, I knew what a gut-hooked fish must feel like. That clawing dread that slowly rips you apart from the inside, knowing the end is near. I'll spare you the gory details, but I did eventually go out on the dance floor — begrudgingly. They made me do a little dance in the middle of the circle that I immediately repressed the memory of. I danced for enough time to look the part before retreating, once again, to the margins of the room.

Sobbing uncontrollably inside, I managed to put on a brave face and pretend like I hadn't just been assaulted and raped emotionally by the collective will of the people.

Dancing. In. Public. The horror!

I suppose it was for a good cause, though. Austin and Darian had been dating for years prior to the wedding. Darian Grigsby (whom we always called "Grigs" for short) had quickly fallen into the group. She was a great fit for Austin, and we all approved. Now, in their moment of triumph, I realized that we'd have to come up with a new nickname for Grigs, given that she was now a Crawford.

Though the dancing left me shaken, I was mollified by my love for Austin and Darian.

The night wound down, and we said our goodnights and goodbyes, headed to the roof for a chance to relax briefly, and the happy couple went off alone to become even happier. We stood on the roof of the tower, surveyed the Florida night and then decided to call it a day. I was beat, and when we made it back to our Airbnb shortly thereafter, I hit the pillow with a vengeance.

The wedding was over, but a long weekend of festivities was just beginning. As my conscious thoughts were edged by darkness, I envisioned myself at a press conference, telling the world of my plans for the next few days. After fishing and heading to Orlando the next day, there was only one thing in the books: "I'm going to Disney World!"

Chapter 11
Trash and Treasure

June 21, 2019

Day 7
Origin: St. Petersburg, Florida
Destination: Kissimmee, Florida

"As a songwriter, the only thing I do is make jewelry for the inside of people's minds."
Tom Waits || American Musician

Our final night at the Tampa Airbnb was anticlimactic. We went to bed late and when I woke up, everyone else was still fast asleep. I suppose if ever sleeping in was justified, it was today. It was June 21, the Summer Solstice, and the longest day of the year. There was literally more daylight to burn. Being the senior person at the house meant I would be the only one up for a while. I whipped out my phone, checked Yelp! for a local coffee shop and ended up at a "kombucha and kava bar" that had an espresso machine. Coffee isn't as big in the South as it is back home. In fact, there's almost no coffee culture there. These people think Dunkin' Donuts is prime coffee. I just ... sigh. So I was left with few options.

I got drinks for Jake, Gabe and Rylee. Inexplicably, the coffee shop didn't have cream, so I picked up a quart of half and half and some fruit from the grocery store nearby, returning home with the spoils.

The crew had risen from the dead and begun packing.

Our plan was to make our way to Orlando, well, Kissimmee actually, to the Airbnb we'd booked for the next few days. I hadn't really gotten to fish any of my intended stops in Tampa, though, so I arranged for the fam to get rides, loaded my car with their luggage, and went on my merry way, looking to soak up the riches of the longest day of the year.

Trash
There is a resort called Isla Del Sol in Tampa Bay. That's "Island of the Sun" for those who took French or German or Klingon in high school. What better place to enjoy the sun's longest tenure of the year, right?

I was turned onto it by a friend, and though the signs everywhere said "No Parking," I generally give zero effs when it comes to signage that gets in the way of my fishing, and I have a string of parking and speeding tickets to prove it. I parked, grabbed some bait and proceeded onto the docks.

Hardhead Catfish, *Ariopsis felis,* quickly bit, but nothing else would cooperate. I saw Atlantic Tarpon, *Megalops atlanticus* and Jack Crevalle, *Caranx hippos* up to 30 or 40 pounds, dozens of Common Snook, *Centropomus undecimalis* and Sheepshead, *Archosargus probatocephalus* on every piling, but they wouldn't play. After two hours of sweating profusely and sweating my lack of success, I moved on.

Parking ticket? Nope.

Treasure
Isla Del Sol had been trash.

Granted, one man's trash is another man's wife. No. Wait. That's not how it goes. One man's trash is another man's *treasure*, and my next stop would prove to be as good as Isla Del Sol had been bad — a veritable treasure trove. After making no fewer than seven U-Turns on my way to a decent parking area, I finally grabbed my rods and did what God intended.

I was fishing at the base of a highway bridge, and the area had a wide range of habitats to choose from. One side butted up against the mangroves, transitioned to a jagged rocky bottom, followed a seawall to the pilings, morphed to a sandy bottom, and then wrapped back around the other side of the bridge's base to more mangroves. Though I wasn't sure where to start fishing, I knew I should be using my Sasame micro sabiki.

Boy howdy.

Riches beyond my wildest dreams in the form of silver, gold, and jewels all came out to play in short order as I listened to a handful of the same songs on loop via Spotify, trying to justify the subscription cost.

Goldspotted Killifish were my primary target at this stop, but the first fish to play were the silversides that attacked in droves. The brilliant, chromatic fish with bright silver stripes lived up to their name, and the anal fin origin in front of the dorsal fin, canary yellow fins, and presence in saltwater helped identify them as Tidewater Silversides.

Species #267 — Tidewater Silverside (*Menidia peninsulae*).

Ten of the polished metallic baitfish experimented with hooks that day, despite warnings from their parents and schools.

I had silver!

Moving from under the bridge and relinquishing the sweet, sweet shade it provided, I swung over to the sandy area near the seawall. In short order, I added gold! The small pupfish behaved so aggressively that it was hard to believe they weren't tiny super-predators.

The first Goldspotted Killifish I caught, a somewhat bland female, got me jumping up and down like a child because (1) they're super-awesome little micros with a beautiful pattern and (2) it was probably my top micro target of the trip.

Species #268 — Goldspotted Killifish (*Floridichthys carpio*).

The first male stole 15 minutes of my life as I took photos of it in my photo tank from every possible angle. Somehow, a rainbow shone through the glass onto the already-stunning fish, and my soul swooned at its majesty. In traditional anime fashion, my eyes became giant cartoon hearts as I finished the photo shoot.

Goldspotted Killifish were aggressive and very prevalent on the flat, sandy bottom up against the seawall, but as I moved into the shallows below the mangroves, I noticed fish that were long, thin, and certainly something different.

As it turned out, they were Longnose Killifish, *Fundulus similis*. I'd caught a few in Corpus Christi, Texas, the prior year, so they weren't new, but they were a pleasant surprise. I added one to the photo tank.

I crossed the highway like a wayward gator, albeit slightly less leathery, earning a few dirty looks and invoking the wrath of one driver who actually sped up to try and hit me. Frogger enactment over, I finally made it to the side where I'd parked. Two old guys were already fishing. They were obviously after bigger stuff, so I asked if I could microfish right next to them.

The obligatory "What the hell is microfishing?" question came next, but they were actually pretty entertained with it as the three of us tried our best to get heat stroke that afternoon.

A school of small fish held close to the shore, hovering midway in the water column. I was hoping for Gulf Killifish, *Fundulus grandis* or Marsh Killifish, *Fundulus confluentus*. They were the former, and I caught the first of 40 that day on my very first drop.

Species #269 — Gulf Killifish *(Fundulus grandis)*.

With the micro sabiki, it was stupid easy. I was able to look down and catch two or three fishes on every drop — mostly Gulf and Goldspotted Killifish — but I quickly started catching other species, too.

Perhaps the biggest surprise was the pile of African Jewelfish, the same fish I first caught in Utah earlier this trip. This was straight-up saltwater, but they were there in numbers. I caught Pinfish, saw what were either Frillfin Goby, *Bathygobius soporator* or Notchtongue Goby, *Bathygobius curacao*, that wouldn't bite, and then set my sights on catching a needlefish. This was a species I'd seen everywhere in the Gulf of Mexico but had never been able to catch. I'd had hits and even briefly hooked a few but never landed one. I fought the insecurity welling up inside me but lost out, deciding I would catch one or die trying. Leaving my micro sabiki on, I removed the weight and began sight-fishing to the handful of needlefish patrolling the surface. It took awhile, and I did a few laps of the bridge before I finally hooked up with one. Carefully, I battled the fish in. It completely tangled and destroyed my micro sabiki struggling to get free, but I'd finally done it! I had my first needlefish.

Species #270 — Redfin Needlefish *(Strongylura notata)*.

The toothy little rail of a fish was hooked fairly with one hook, but the line had wrapped around its jaws during its death roll, ensuring I would be able to land it. Unfortunately, this also ensured it was a pain to unhook — for both of us. Managing to slice my fingers on its razor-sharp maw only twice was a feat I'm still proud of. Needles in Florida waters are something you don't want to penetrate your skin, so I'm fortunate I didn't contract something horrible.

I took detailed pictures of its fins to show the reddish edge and then took my #SpeciesQuest shot of the fish facing to the right. Most scientific photos of fishes face the subject to the left, but when I first started taking photos of my catch with a disposable camera some 15 years ago, I chose to face them to the right because it felt natural to hold fishes in my left hand and use the dexterity of my dominant hand to take the picture. I kept it going to prevent people from stealing them without crediting me. I realize it's out of the norm; that's the point.

Since there were no Sharps containers nearby in which to dispose of it, I let the needlefish go.

I continued catching fish after fish, and even though my live and cut bait rods didn't get any business, my micro setup did. My next species was, like every other fish I caught that day, one that I sight-fished. I could see a larger group of silvery fish that weren't quite micros. They weren't ready biters, but they eventually latched on to my bait, and I had another new species, the American Silver Perch.

Species #271 — American Silver Perch *(Bairdiella chrysoura)*.

This fish is in the croaker/drum family, Sciaenidae, and many of the species in that family look very similar. I got clear pictures and then caught five more perch before getting a small, bonus Spotted Seatrout, *Cynoscion nebulosus* to bite.

The new species counter rolled to a stop for the day, but I would continue fishing until I was given the all-clear to head to Orlando, finishing with 109 fishes in just six hours. Gold, Silver, and Jewels.

I was all smiles as I pulled up to the Airbnb in Kissimmee (just outside of Orlando) that night. The group was wrapping up a session in the pool as I arrived, and I joined in time to get settled into the game room where I was staying.

The sleeping pad and sleeping bag I'd carried with me across the country were finally validated as I spread them out on the sectional and staked my claim. We lounged around for much longer than I was expecting, and so I made a loop around the ponds behind the townhomes. I didn't see anything exciting, so I didn't fish, but I enjoyed watching baby ducks as our 8 p.m. dinner time approached at an injured crawl. When dinner was finally served, and we chowed down on Italian at a restaurant I'd eaten at once before, I was one happy boy. With the "Happiest Place on Earth" just hours away, it could only get better.

Chapter 12
Disneywhirled

June 22, 2019

Day 8
Origin: Kissimmee, Florida
Destination: Orlando, Florida

"Standing in a two-hour line makes people worry
that they're not living in a Democratic nation."
David Sedaris || American Humorist || From *Santaland Diaries*

Which one sounds familiar?
"The Happiest Place on Earth."
"Where Dreams Come True."
"What Will You Celebrate?"
No matter what slogan you grew up with, the message is the same. Disney has long touted itself as having a monopoly on fun and once-in-a-lifetime experiences.

Perhaps their most famous advertising campaign, "I'm going to Disneyland/Disney World," has since become the standard of celebration the world over since its inception in the 1980s at a dinner party. It became familiar to the public during a Super Bowl commercial, but it was born into an event with less glamor than the biggest television event of the year: a dinner party. Then-CEO Michael Eisner and his wife, Jane Eisner, were having dinner with George Lucas (creator of *Star Wars*, which Disney now owns) and Dick Rutan and Jeana Yeager, the first couple to fly around the world without stopping.

This who's who of dinner parties was relatively uneventful, as the story goes, but left a lasting legacy. Initially recorded in Michael Eisner's memoir and later reported in a 2016 article by ABC News, the dinner conversation had stalled. To fill the silence, Michael asked Dick and Jeana "Well, now that you've accomplished the pinnacle of your aspirations, what could you possibly do next?"

Jeana replied, reportedly without hesitation, "I'm going to Disneyland!"

Realizing the potential, Jane said "You know, that's a good slogan."

It debuted in a Super Bowl commercial soon after, and the rest is history.

Today, no celebration at the peak of personal accomplishment is complete without the magic of Disney. As such, Darian and Austin had planned to spend some time at Disney World to aid in celebrating their own personal peak accomplishment: marriage.

Darian had worked at Disney World through a college internship program and had become intimately familiar with the inner workings of Disney that only the most dedicated patrons ever learn from the outside — and only after hundreds of hours and thousands of dollars' worth of churros, chocolate, pretzels, and nonalcoholic mint juleps.

We'd been invited to join the festivities. This meant that I'd be going on a honeymoon with newlyweds, and strangely enough, not for the first time. Years before, I'd gone fishing with my childhood best friend Ben Blanchard and his new wife, Autumn. Granted, their honeymoon had been a month long, and they'd spent a ton of time alone together, but it made for a great story about me, the ultimate third wheel.

I even wrote one of my earliest fishing columns on the trip back in 2015, which I've shared here to show you how not much has changed.

"Third-wheeling along the Oregon coast," originally published Jan. 30, 2015:

In 1988, the United States government outlawed the production and sale of three-wheeled ATVs, commonly known as 'three-wheelers' because the third wheel made the vehicles incredibly awkward and unsafe. Two years later, I was born. I grew up blissfully unaware of the ban on three-wheeled vehicles, routinely spending time with my coupled friends and making an awkward triad.

Triad was also the name of my high school, but that's just a coincidence. I think.

As I got older, I became aware of when it was okay to third-wheel with my friends and when it was not. First dates? No.

You've been dating for months and you're now sitting at a basketball game? Yes. Oh. You're going to propose at this basketball game? That's awesome! Don't worry, I didn't blow the surprise. Retroactive congratulations, Shawn and Maddie Elliott!

Understandably, most of my friends desired alone time with their significant other, so I tried to give them space.

We all grew older, and before I knew it, it was 2014.

My best friend, Benjamin Blanchard, was engaged and planning his wedding. The timing of the wedding meant our annual fall fishing trip to the Oregon Coast — tradition since graduating high school six years earlier — was off the table.

I'm not going to lie, I was a little disappointed. Still, I was happy for my friend, and I absolutely understood. Then, he surprised me by saying that he and his then fiancé (now wife), Autumn, wanted us to take our fishing trip, with her, during one of the days of their nearly month-long honeymoon.

Not one to turn down a fishing trip, I immediately agreed.

December rolled around, and we made plans to meet up in Lincoln City where they were staying. I started my weekend with a few days in Portland before heading to the coast. Ben, Autumn, and I met briefly the night before to catch up in their beachside vacation rental, where they were spending their honeymoon, before I retired to their floor.

Kidding. I retired to the offsite motel room they'd generously rented for me.

The next day started off brisk and cold as we drove to nearby Depoe Bay, the world's smallest navigable harbor. We climbed onto the charter boat and got to know some of our fellow passengers.

Once everyone else on the boat discovered that Ben and Autumn were honeymooners, everyone congratulated them.

When people learned I was third-wheeling their honeymoon, we had a few laughs, one weird look from an older gentleman who thought we might've been a trio of lovers, but finally a comment from the captain, who said "Wow. That's an honor."

Indeed it was. As we reeled in fish after fish, Autumn battled seasickness with a remarkably positive attitude. Considering the fact that we were adrift in the middle of the ocean during mid-December, it was unseasonably warm. My phone listed the weather in the 50s by mid-morning.

The fishing was productive, too, even though both Ben and Autumn out-fished me. In total, we landed more than 40 fish, representing a variety of species. Black Rockfish, *Sebastes melanops,* Blue Rockfish, *Sebastes mystinus* and Yellowtail Rockfish, *Sebastes flavidus* made up the majority of our catch, but we also landed several vividly orange, then threatened Canary Rockfish, *Sebastes pinniger,* several Lingcod, *Ophiodon elongatus* and I even caught a species I'd never caught before: a Widow Rockfish, *Sebastes entomelas.*

They survived the first stormy seas their marriage would see (pun intended), and we had a great time together. They never called me a third wheel, and though some of you might, I'll counter with this: apart from the steering column, boats don't have wheels.

Entertaining, right? Well, my editor at the time, Gerry O'Brien, thought so, noting that catching a Widow Rockfish on a honeymoon could be darkly funny. It was just the third fishing column I ever wrote, and it was the one that served as a tipping point to make way for my weekly column to start soon after, which, in turn, eventually led to this book.

My third-wheeling in Orlando was different, though. It wasn't just the two lovebirds and me.

Sure, Mickey and Minnie (Austin and Darian) were there with Goofy (me, obviously), but Donald, Daisy, Pluto, and a dozen other characters were along for the ride, or at least, along for the rides. Our goal was to hit as many rides as possible and visit all four parks: Animal Kingdom, Hollywood Studios, Epcot, and Magic Kingdom (in that order) in a single day.

It was ambitious, but so is dating for a serious relationship in your 20s, and it worked out for them!

We hit all four parks, but we ended up riding very few attractions due to a number of complications. It was an enterprising goal that would have made for an incredible experience if we'd spaced it out a bit more. It certainly wasn't the first overscheduled Disney trip in history, but it was mine. Maybe it was too much of a good thing? I'm getting ahead of myself. I can't spoil the magic. I'll walk you through each park as if it were a feature film. After all, drawing things out as much as possible in an effort to monetize them is the Disney way. So I'll tell this fairly straightforward story in four parts, and you tell me if this sounds like "The Happiest Place on Earth" when all is said and done.

Animal Kingdom

We were plagued by misfortune from the beginning. We'd arrived right at the time the gates were supposed to open — at least, the time the gates open on a normal day. Little did we know that our chosen Disney day had been one where the park opened an hour early.

Huh.

If you didn't already feel like an ant in the roiling activity of a Disney Park, arriving late and then making a beeline for the newest ride in the park will guarantee you do. Our first stop, at the newly opened *Avatar:* Flight of Passage ride began well enough. Nobody got sick and nobody got heat stroke despite the punishing early morning sun that harkened a horribly hot day to come.

The only real downside? We waited more than three hours to ride the ride.

The six-minute duration of the ride was enjoyable, but is six minutes really worth the wait? Tune in once I'm married to see what my wife says after our honeymoon. Spoiler alert: I probably won't be inviting anyone other than my wife along for my own honeymoon.

Regardless, in this case, I didn't think six minutes was worth the wait.

Avatar: Flight of Passage was like Disneyland's Soaring California but while sitting on a less comfortable seat shaped like a crotch-rocket without wheels.

Honestly, I don't remember doing anything else at Animal Kingdom. I mean, we probably did, but I just remember getting separated from Austin and Darian and their wealth of knowledge. I then split off with my brothers, Rylee, and our friend Christian Wood, and together we proceeded to do everything wrong. From failing to get Fast Passes to hitting popular rides during peak times and waiting for hours on end to eating during peak meal times to letting ourselves get a little dehydrated, we made all of the bad decisions. This was only Park No. 1. We had three parks' worth of bad decisions to go.

I should have been happy to be at Animal Kingdom. As a kid, this would have been my favorite park for sure, but as an adult struggling to climb out of that rut, a few days on the road hadn't yet cleansed my palate and cleared my mind of the stresses and pains of everyday life. All the waiting and the fast-paced itinerary created an expectation to cram as much fun into a narrow window as we could. It just felt forced.

But with a name like Luke, the Force will always play a role in my life, and the Force was front-and-center at Hollywood Studios.

Hollywood Studios

Animal Kingdom was new enough, but Hollywood Studios even more so.

When Darth Vader marched a contingent of stormtroopers in full gear down the street, my first thought was "Awesome." My second thought was "It's 90 degrees out, and he's used to the Dark Side, which is probably cooler."

I stopped thinking at that point.

Our party survived the encounter without being Force Choked, so we called that a win. Impressively, only one person in the party made a "Look Luke! It's your dad" joke, so at least it wasn't a wasted opportunity.

Speaking of wasted opportunities, we passed on several rides to hit up the two most-acclaimed rides at Hollywood Studios: Rock 'N Roller Coaster and Tower of Terror.

As was becoming the trend, we timed both wrong, opting to ride the Tower of Terror at the hottest part of the day. The uphill line zigged and zagged all the way back to the starting point, and we were enduring abject misery, but at least we had company. Misery allegedly loves that.

Don't get me wrong; I love roller coasters and thrill rides. Not enough to wait hours for one, but I really do enjoy them. For this reason, I'm more about Six Flags than Disney, but I still enjoy the latter in ideal conditions. These were far from ideal. It was a grueling sauna. My feet were sore, my back ached, and I was done in the sweltering heat with nobody to flip me over.

Jake, Gabe, Christian and I cooked slowly.

Worse still, Rylee gets insanely sick on roller coasters (a lingering side effect of a severe concussion she had in high school), which meant she was stuck waiting outside the ride. It was shaded (sort of), but we felt bad nonetheless.

I'm not one to complain (I lie, midway through a chapter-length complaint), but it was too long. Time was as stagnant as the dank Florida air, so I couldn't tell you exactly how long we waited, but it was long enough that I took three bathroom breaks.

Of course, three bathroom breaks didn't stop me from peeing myself on the ride after the gauntlet finally came to a close.

We did make it to the top eventually. Was it two hours? Three? That's unclear, but had I opened a 401(k) when we got in line, it would've nearly vested by the time we were strapped in.

Our particular group included Jake, Gabe, Christian and I, and we were all wearing bright colors that may have stood out a little ordinarily but made us look like strutting peacocks compared to the tour group in matching white shirts that filled the other 15 seats.

The ride itself was enjoyable, but Christian screaming at the top of his lungs like a damsel in distress and Jake and Gabe laughing uncontrollably at his reaction was worth the wait. I was beaming when it came to a stop, and the Alfred Hitchcock-but-not-Alfred Hitchcock voice said something over the intercom as we exited.

The photo was priceless. Four guys in bright colors sat in the front seat, surrounded by a sea of matching white shirts. Everyone looks terrified in the photo, including Christian, but Jake, Gabe, and I are smiling the biggest smiles imaginable. Also, my arms are straight up in the air while everyone else hangs on for dear life. This somehow makes the whole thing even better.

As long and painful as the wait was, that picture was pretty epic, and arguably the highlight of the day. It could have been the dehydration or lack of sleep, but we laughed for a long time.

Revitalized by the triple-threat of air conditioning, laughing at Christian's expense, and an adrenaline rush, we met up with Rylee and headed over to the Rock 'N Roller Coaster next. It was late 1980s- or early 1990s-themed but not in a retro sense. It simply looked like they hadn't updated the ride in 30 years, but it was still a decent roller coaster.

Having done all we wanted at Hollywood Studios, we made our way back to the car and headed to Epcot, where I must admit, things were looking up.

Epcot

The iconic giant golf ball-looking thing (actually called Spaceship Earth for no obvious reason) was the first part we noticed. We posed for a group picture in front of it, and I was reminded of Will Ferrell asking "What do I do with my hands," as we smiled. I crossed them in front of me and later regretted it.

Epcot is unique among Disney venues in that it doesn't really have rides. Its name was derived from a top executive's baby trying in vain to say the word "apricot" but, being a baby, only managing to say "Epcot." The executive liked the uniqueness of it and rolled with it. Of course, that's not true at all, which is the pits. Nonetheless, the fictitious fruity backstory of my own design helps me like Epcot more.

In reality, Epcot is an acronym that means "Experimental Prototype Community of Tomorrow" later rebranded as its own word, but my origin story is better. Regardless, Epcot is unique, and of all the parks at Disney World, it was my favorite. Probably a strange admission from a guy whose primary draw to theme parks are the rides, but it was just, well, unique.

Epcot is set up to be highly walkable, with loops and circles naturally laid out for casual strolling.

My favorite part was the World Showcase which included miniature versions of a dozen countries where the architecture was designed like the country represented therein. Interns from the "country" they worked in wore culturally appropriate clothing and served foods and drinks unique to their home culture.

I sampled a Norwegian pastry, a German sausage with mustard and sauerkraut, and a Moroccan plate lunch. It wasn't great, but everything was edible, and the experience was worthwhile to be sure. Though it wasn't a theme park in the traditional sense, or maybe *because* it wasn't a theme park in the traditional sense, I really enjoyed Epcot. Sadly, we had to leave before I could get my fill of the Experimental Prototype Community of Tomorrow.

We made our way from Epcot to the Magic Kingdom in hopes of hitting some "classic rides" and enjoying the after-dark festivities and fireworks. At this point, we'd walked about six miles. By the end of the night, we'd more than double that thanks to just how far-removed the Magic Kingdom was from the parking lot. Again, despite the experience, there was something less-than-magical about walking so much without a fishing rod in my hand.

Magic Kingdom

The Magic Kingdom is quintessential, traditional Disney. It's where you see fireworks over a castle, classic Disney characters from the iconic cartoons, and experience Disney in much the same way as it was experienced by your parents and grandparents — albeit with absurdly inflated prices.

By far, it is the most popular park at Disney World, and as such, it requires the most parking. There was a park- and parking-related pun in there, but after such a busy day, I didn't have the energy. To get to Magic Kingdom from the parking lot is a trek. Girls of Instagram might even call it an adventure.

You have to walk from the parking lot to a tram, ride a tram to a train, ride a train to another pathway and, if you happen to ride a boat ride once you make it inside Magic Kingdom, and stand near a certain iconic mouse, you'll have visited almost every possible venue in which to eat green eggs and ham.

I was tired from the trip in, but I would be exhausted for the trip out. I'll get to that, though.

During the waning hours, we managed to ride all three peaks (Splash Mountain, Thunder Mountain, Space Mountain) and got some traditional foods. I got the nonalcoholic mint julep I can never resist, one person got a funnel cake, everyone got some candy, and we all got a little closer to diabetes. We missed out on other classics like corn dogs, churros, and heat stroke, but we made it safely in and out of the drink line without anyone slipping us a Mickey.

I stopped and tried to get my mom a souvenir — she absolutely loves Tinkerbell and Groot — but failed to find anything that spoke to me, except for an annoying pull-string doll that said "I am Groot" that literally spoke to me rather than speaking to my sense of gift-giving.

By this point, my dogs were barking, and I found every excuse to sit or lean on something to stretch out my aching back, hips, quads, calves, and feet. So I stood and admired the nearest Disney princess, remembering that time years ago I talked to a girl named Ashley for a month or so on eHarmony (yeah, I actually paid for online dating for a year after college), learned she was a Disney princess at the park, and wondered how she was doing.

We lived 12 hours apart, and dating someone that far away would be absolutely crazy, right? So we never did. We parted ways amicably and wished one another a good life. I didn't see her there, and given there aren't a lot of Black Disney princesses, it appears that she's since found another gig.

Hopefully she'd found her real-life fairytale even though it looked like I might never find my own. Romantic self-pity aside, the chance to sit let me reflect for a moment.

In all the excitement, I didn't realize I hadn't been fishing. This would be one of just two days where I experienced such a tragic reality on my 46-day trip, but I'd had an almost magical time, and I couldn't complain about anything but my aching muscles in the aftermath of the 26,508 steps the Pacer app on my phone recorded that day. Given my height, that calculated out to 12.2 miles — just shy of a half-marathon. That didn't factor in standing for roughly 16 hours, either. I'm not sure what's worse: the realization that I walked a half-marathon or that people willingly choose to run twice as far for sport. I shudder. Just like those who *willingly* complete a marathon or half-marathon, I made sure you knew I did it, so I guess I do share something in common with those masochists.

In retrospect, Disney World was absolutely worth visiting, but Disneyland is a much better experience. Were I to go again, I'd limit myself to one park per day and spread it out, taking a daily break to leave the park, get a massage, and just decompress a bit. Nonetheless, it was a great experience, and it was a positive sign: I could derive at least some happiness from activities other than fishing.

Chapter 13
Water...Without Fish?

June 23, 2019

Day 9
Origin: Kissimmee, Florida
Destination: Orlando, Florida

"Always remember: your focus determines your reality."
Qui-Gonn Jin || Jedi Master || From *Star Wars: Episode I*

Chlorine.
According to Ashkan Morim and Gregory T. Guldner, two researchers who composed a work for the National Center for Biotechnology Information (NCBI) dated Sept. 14, 2019: "Gaseous chlorine is poisonous and classified as a pulmonary irritant. It has intermediate water solubility with the capability of causing acute damage to the upper and lower respiratory tract. Chlorine gas has many industrial uses, but it was also once used as a chemical weapon in World War I." Yet, we put this in swimming pools frequented by children.
Now, reasonable people understand two things after reading what I've written on this page thus far:
1. There are at least four states of matter, and the excerpt above refers to chlorine gas, while pools contain liquid chlorine. For those keeping score, gas does not equate to liquid except in the worst bouts of gastrointestinal distress.
2. The information provided thus far in the chapter doesn't tell you whether liquid chlorine is safe or not.

We know that apart from minor skin and eye irritation, liquid chlorine diluted down in water for use in swimming pools is not harmful, and its antimicrobial properties far outweigh its side effects: red eyes and itchy skin.

Chlorine is where I started, and for good reason: it sterilizes life. So an angler spending a day on the water is far from unexpected until you learn that water is full of chlorine. No fish can live in chlorinated water, and a fisherman at a waterpark would seem fruitless, right? It would seem like a waste of time fishing in the chlorinated pools full of God-knows-what, unless I told you I wasn't fishing for anything with fins. I was after something else, something deeper. I was *Fishing for Happiness* (the title of another book in the works).

I'd spent the previous day at Disney World, and I was sore, tired, and brimming with low expectations. That's why I was so CaughtOvgard by Blizzard Beach and the best theme park experience I'd ever had. I felt — get this — happiness from an activity where I wasn't fishing at all.

Expectations

It wasn't my first trip to a waterpark, and for that reason, I'd pretty thoroughly tempered my expectations. I knew it was something to do, and I knew I'd be with the group, but past experience had taught me (1) never buy gas station sushi and (2) waterparks are typically kinda gross.

I almost didn't go. I knew I'd be able to catch up with everyone else that night, and I was exhausted just thinking about standing in line again all day, but my brothers convinced me, and I'm glad they did.

It was 90 degrees outside when we arrived mid-morning, so I lathered on sunscreen, stripped down, realized how far my body had deteriorated since I gave up lifting weights some six years before, and then hopped into the line with my brothers.

The first slide was solo. We opted to kick things off with the second-largest water slide in the park, Slush Gusher. While waiting in line, I met a couple from Italy. Apparently, many of the Disney parks are staffed with foreign nationals who work at the parks, get free admission, and sometimes free lodging as well — kind of like a work abroad internship. Austin's fiancé — no, *wife* now — Darian had done this. Apparently it's available to Americans, too. Just a chance to go somewhere new, work at Disney and get to enjoy life for a bit. The exchange was pleasant. My turn arrived, and I turned and said "Ciao," with a waive. This couple wasn't the first we'd find from another country, and though the lines were short, it certainly helped pass the time.

Once we actually got to ride, my mind was no longer on pleasantries and small talk. I was wholly engrossed with the slide. The line was virtually nonexistent (at least, by Disney standards), and we had waited less than five minutes. We got to the bottom and decided to try another run on the adrenaline-generating chute.

In groups that shifted throughout the day, we enjoyed the park. Some lounged around the pool, some got snacks and drinks, others (like me) went ham on the rides. My next stop was Summit Plummet, the nearly straight-down slide with a speedometer that registers your top speed. I broke 40 miles per hour, but others got it quite a bit faster. Being tall and lean doesn't allow for the best acceleration.

The rush was palpable; I was actually shaking when I climbed out of the pool at the bottom, the adrenaline fueling my spirit and making me feel as alive as I felt when fighting a large fish or catching a new, hard-won species. Briefly, I got separated from the group and flew solo for a bit, allowing myself to thrive on the adrenaline again and again, chasing one rush with the next like a chainsmoker.

I'd been so stuck on the idea that I wouldn't have fun that I was shocked when I had fun. Well, I had a blast! Maybe focus determining reality is more than just a Jedi mind trick?

Reunited

Soon, I reunited with Gabe. Poor Rylee doesn't do well with thrill rides, so Gabe was looking for someone to hang with. As it turned out, so was I.

We hopped back in line for Slush Gusher because he'd missed the initial run with the rest of the crew.

While in line, I looked behind me and noticed a teenage girl who just sort of seemed familiar. I continued talking with Gabe. Then the realization of what my eyes had seen became real, and I turned back to make eye contact with two of my students.

Here I was 2,968 miles (according to Google Maps) from home, and I managed to bump into two of the 700 students at the school where I taught. What a small world.

As it turned out, sisters Macy and Kinsey were part of the group there for Health Occupations Students of America (HOSA) Nationals and were enjoying the park that day. The odds were astronomical, and I laughed as I said hello, introduced the two girls to my brother, and then Gabe and I were up to slide.

I went to a Disney park to realize it's a small world, after all, and I didn't even have to hear the annoying song.

We linked up with Jake, Austin and Darian, as well as Austin's mom, Nikki, and his sister, Tate. We did some group rides, races, and had a pleasant time together. After the second day on our feet in a Disney park for upwards of 12 hours, the heat and thousands of steps finally started to beat us down. People began to retreat to the shade, but a handful of us kept pounding until, at the very last, just me and Tito, my cousin Tate's boyfriend (now husband), ran the last few slides together.

I'd spent two full days without fishing, and I was ecstatic. That was new for me. Regardless, maybe it was a glimpse of some distant potential future in which I could be happy for a sustained period of time without fishing. All I needed was a world-class waterpark.

Chapter 14
Marco? Hoplo!

June 24, 2019

Day 10
Origin: Kissimmee, Florida
Destination: Marco Island, Florida

"Even good people are great at making bad decisions."
NF || American Rapper || From the Song "Nate"

After a fun-filled weekend at Disney World, the members of the wedding party had planned to go our separate ways. Within a day or two, everyone was traveling home. For most, that meant flying back to Oregon, but for me, it meant my weeks-long adventure of a lifetime was just beginning.

Though I debated with myself where to go next when planning the trip, I settled on going back to Tampa, fishing a few spots in the area, then making my way down to the Florida coast near Naples. Unfortunately, Naples is one of the most expensive places in Florida, so I opted to get an Airbnb in Marco Island, a little further south. Marco Island still isn't cheap, but neither are the women I usually date, and I like to stick to my scruples.

Reservation made, I began my trip out of Kissimmee to the homophonic song "Kiss Me" by Sixpence None the Richer because I'm a little extra and appreciate wordplay. Fourteen chapters in, you've probably gathered that. I, meanwhile, was gathering my thoughts for my first fishing spot of the day.

Tampa

Many of my fishing spots had been handed to me, but as I noted earlier in this book, some were gathered from USGS data. Regardless of origin, I compiled all 100-plus stops onto a single Google MyMaps, an incredible tool that just-so-happens to be free. MyMaps is great, but with the iOS I was using at the time, it was not possible to update MyMaps from an iPhone (it is now, though it's so clunky as to not be worth it). This meant I had to have every pin not only on the map, but its coordinates written out on my Notes as well in case I found myself trying to access the map in an area without sufficient service.

So that's exactly what I did.

Manually.

For a total of — (checks Notes) — 122 stops.

It was painstaking and reminiscent of so many tedious college projects I'd repressed into distant memory, but I hoped those joyless moments of drudgery would produce. Now that the wedding was behind me, I had weeks on the road to find out if my work would pay off.

One such spot found me parking in front of a trailer park and ambling through a bunch of flatbed trailers to a tiny, somewhat stagnant tidal stream.

Biting flies were awful, and they were feeding on the sweat pouring from my pores at an alarming rate for 9:30 in the morning. I was after Pike Killifish, *Belonesox belizanus* and Marsh Killifish, both of which had been sampled there in the past. As soon as I pulled up, I could see several small schools of Pike Killifish skimming the surface in erratic, twitchy motions reminiscent of awkward middle-schoolers at the peak of adolescence after too much caffeine and sugar. That could've just been a mental association from the acrid stench in the air, though. Regardless, these fish wanted nothing to do with me. As soon as I got within the 12 feet required to fish with my telescoping tenkara rod, they fled. I did get a few haphazard strikes and even hooked one, but failed to lift it more than a few inches above the water before it unhooked itself.

I ran back to the car and changed tactics. I removed the split shot to keep my bait on the surface and just sort of dragged it around like a miniature topwater. This elicited more strikes, but I still failed to catch fish. With a "blind rod" just left out in the middle, I hoped I might get lucky. It's sort of like a dating profile you never check: just throw it out and hope for the best.

Unlike that dating strategy, this "blind rod" actually worked, and I reeled in the largest Sheepshead Minnow, *Cyprinodon variegatus* I've ever caught. The big male was iridescent navy blue and goldenrod with obsidian accents — absolutely striking. It was also the size of a small panfish, perhaps five inches long and ridiculously fat, nearly filling my palm.

It was a nice little surprise, but it was not a Pike Killifish, so I hopped back into the car and made for my next stop: a small pond alleged to contain Redhead Cichlid, *Vieja melanurus*. Redhead Cichlids are unique. Given that most cichlids are blonde or brunette, these feisty little fellows really stand out in a crowd. That said, given their propensity for sunburn, I was a little worried that I may not be able to get one to bite during the day. My friend, Ryan Crutchfield (creator of FishMap.com), had found this location and assured me they were a slam dunk.

The residual sticky salt on my braid caught and caused a line loop, ruining my first cast. On the second, something pale and freckled smashed my jig. It was a Redhead Cichlid!

Species #272 — Redhead Cichlid *(Vieja melanurus)*.

Heck yes!

I have a few red hairs in my beard, so it's okay for me to playfully mock redheads, right? If not, then may God have mercy on my soul (which I actually have). Winking emoji.

That day, I quickly caught six of them before deciding to ride my wave of good luck to my next location in hopes of catching a species I'd spent hours and hours trying and failing to catch: a girlfriend. That seemed hopeless, so instead I targeted another catch that had always evaded me: the Brown Hoplo, *Hoplosternum littorale*.

Wilderness

While "hoplo" accurately describes my limited jumping ability (my shorter brothers, at 5'10" and 5'11" have both dunked while at just under 6'3", I haven't), it is actually the name of a small, armor-plated catfish from South America.

Like much of Florida's population, Brown Hoplos are mouthbreathers that will gulp air just like the native Bowfin, *Amia calva* and Florida Gar, *Lepisosteus platyrhincus* that often share the same waters. Since they breathe air, hoplos are quite tolerant of terrible water quality and can be found in places many fishes couldn't hope to survive.

It's crazy how empty of humanity the majority of the third-most-populous state is. I drove and drove through the dual emptiness and fullness of Florida's interior. When, at long last, I arrived at the coordinates (also provided by Ryan Crutchfield), I was alerted by the too-large gator in the small creek just downstream of the high road bridge. I opted to go upstream instead. Not because I was afraid of being mauled by a gator, but also not *not* for that reason.

I just couldn't get a hoplo to bite. I'd been told this spot was as close to a slam-dunk as any for this species, and I was despondent, left holding nothing but denial.

Moments later, I was holding da Nile — a very large Nile Tilapia, that is. God has a sense of humor.

The hoplos weren't having it, so I moved up to the road and fished from the bridge. Now, fishing for very small fish from high up on a road bridge with little or no shoulder is not a great idea, and it's never really worked for me. In fact, it reminds me of a scene from *Arrested Development*, the greatest television series of all time, in which Dr. Tobias Funkë and his wife, Lindsay Bluth-Funkë, discuss trial separation.

"Well, did it work for those people?" Lindsay asks her husband, a behavior analyst and therapist (which he combines on his business cards as "Analrapist").

"No," he replies with a chuckle.

"It never does. I mean these people somehow delude themselves into thinking it might…" he says, trailing off.

"But it might work for us!" he adds thoughtfully.

So there I was, fishing from the bridge, thinking it might work for me. I gave myself 30 minutes because making bad decisions is okay if you limit it to a set period of your life, right? That's why people eventually get over their "party phase" after college, I'm told.

Oh well. I started packing up. After a week with my family and friends and with limited success fishing, I was starting to feel the loneliness crowd the clarity out of my mind.

I still had a month left on this trip, and my mood was still far too dependent on success or failure in fishing for me to fail this early and this often. I was in Florida, and I'd only caught one new species today.

"What the eff, David Blaine? What the eff?!"

If you haven't seen that YouTube video, it's a classic. Google it.

Just as I began to slip into reverie and a vintage YouTube-fueled pity party, my final rod, the one I hadn't yet reeled in, moved. I waited. Waited. Set the hook. Optimistically, I worked in the small fish. It was a Brown Hoplo!

Species #273 — Brown Hoplo *(Hoplosternum littorale)*.

I got the picture I needed and moved on to my next spot, a picturesque little pond even more off the beaten path than the bridge had been. It involved me leaving the pavement and driving in soft, sandy-loam through a palm grove miles from the pavement in deep moondust. Fortunately, I couldn't see any clouds, and the dirt — though soft — was dry enough that I felt soaking my tires in it halfway up the rims was a reasonable risk.

Now, it features prominently in television and movies, but quicksand is both very real and not nearly as horrifying as it's made out to be — until you find yourself stuck in it. Conditions were perfect for quicksand, and in retrospect, I should've seen that driving in, but I was blinded by the possibility of catching a relatively rare killifish species called the Redface Topminnow, *Fundulus rubrifrons*. Redface Topminnow are just topminnows that exert themselves when not in great shape. Fitting, because the lake was breathtakingly beautiful. Really more of a pond than a lake, the clean (cold for Florida) pond was unspoiled if blackened with tannin.

Though Florida Bass, *Micropterus floridanus* and Bluegill were abundant, I never saw a single Redface Topminnow — nor any micro for that matter — and the only red face was mine after striking out on my third target for the day and learning firsthand about quicksand.

I just so happened to be listening to a podcast that referenced quicksand, so that's how I learned about it. Sorry if you were thinking I got stuck in it myself, though that would've made this chapter slightly more interesting.

Marco Island

When I finally made it to Marco Island, it was dark. I'd stopped for dinner, burning an hour assuming I could fish in the backyard of my destination for a wayward estuarine fish (Black Drum, *Pogonias cromis*, or some flounder species, I hoped) swimming the saltwater canals. All I caught were Hardhead Catfish, and eventually, I just grabbed the hose off the roll in the backyard and rinsed off one of my rods before heading inside. I intended to rinse them all, but defeat is tiring, it turns out, and I was asleep minutes after climbing out of the shower.

Chapter 15
The International Incident

June 25, 2019

Day 11
Origin: Marco Island, Florida
Destination: Miami, Florida

"You don't need to worry about what foreigners think about you. That's your birthright as an American."
Shirley Bennett || From *Community*

    I was a bit salty from the previous day's defeats, and so was my gear because I'd forgotten to rinse it off. Using the hose, I'd rinsed a few rods but failed to remember three or four others still in the car. Hopefully that wouldn't come back to bite me.
    I had some leftover shrimp, so I decided to start fishing the brine. A road bridge well into southwestern Florida's broken delta-coastline seemed promising. Even better, it was en route to my first stop in the Everglades. After piling up the usual suspects — Hardhead Catfish, Pinfish, and Mangrove Snapper, *Lutjanus griseus* — I got a double on my truncated sabiki. One was another Mangrove, but the other was white with horizontal yellow stripes, a pink-edged tail fin, and a large black spot.
    At the time, I was no expert at Florida saltwater fish identification. To be fair, I'm still not, but I'm much more than the novice I was then. Regardless, I tend to stay in my lane and defer to

the experts, asking friends and people whose qualifications include more than simply being in Florida for the third time. Turns out, staying in my lane was the right call. This new species was a Lane Snapper.

Species #274 —Lane Snapper *(Lutjanus synagris).*

My first purely saltwater species of the trip was on the books. I released it and headed into The Everglades.

The Everglades
Much like Washington, D.C., the Everglades is a massive expanse of land virtually useless to humans in its current state. With more than 1.5 million sprawling acres of mangroves, swamps, interlaced waterways, sawgrass, pine forest, and dense vegetation, it's no wonder hundreds of native species of fishes and wildlife call it home — not to mention the dozens of invasive species fighting Shrek for their own little slice of swamp.

One native species is the icon of the Everglades: the American Alligator. Gators are at once horrifying and awe-inspiring. The silent swamp beasts can instill terror and demand respect for anglers who happen upon them in the American South, but their interactions with humans primarily occur where worlds collide. Sometimes, these collisions are literal.

The road-killed gator was overturned and mangled, its guts half-strewn out across the stretch of sweltering blacktop unfortunate enough to play host to its final resting place. Given how unique it was, I pulled over on the shoulder of the straight, mangrove-lined road to grab a picture, and I smelled the gator before I saw it.

While gators are hardly fragrant alive, they certainly smell worse after a death that leaves them slow-cooking on the roadway in Florida summer heat. Still, the picture was worth it. I continued down the road to my first destination, paying homage to its sacrifice with one of the most reverent of social media presentations: the Instagram Story.

It was the only roadkill I'd see — surprising given how close the road is to the mangrove swamps and canals interlacing the Everglades. The Tamiami Canal runs along the primary access road through the Everglades, and it is loaded with gators (R.I.P. aforementioned lizard) and fishes. Lots of fishes. At the first stop, I immediately saw some of these fishes. I targeted what I thought was a Spotted Tilapia on a bed using a small jig tipped with an entire red worm. I didn't know it, but this exact setup would be my most effective tool for freshwater fishes in Florida. It worked, and that first success got me started using a small jig with an entire worm as my go-to presentation in fresh water for the rest of the Florida trip.

Species #275 — Spotted Tilapia *(Pelmatolapia mariae)*.

The next stop was also on the Tamiami Canal at the intersection between two canals and two roads, forming an obvious corner. Sort of like Walgreen's but rather than "the corner of happy and healthy," it was at the corner of "sweltering and humid" instead.

Nonetheless, fishes were everywhere. Below an earthen culvert crossing, Florida Gar stacked up, waiting below the pipe mouth, suspending a few inches under the surface in a small school. I caught them on Rapalas, jigs, bait, and almost everything else. Though I only landed a few, I was hooking them every cast, but their toothy, bony jaws proved as problematic for me as for any fish that found itself trapped between those jaws.

Then came the Mayan Cichlids, *Mayaheros urophthalmus* and various jewelfish, more Spotted Tilapia, and a single Spotted Sunfish, *Lepomis punctatus* — the only native species other than the gar I caught there.

No new species came out to play until I had a chance at but ultimately lost an Oscar. This would happen several more times that day, but despite losing several chances at an Oscar, I still didn't lose as many opportunities as Glenn Close (8 Oscar nominations, no wins as of March 2023). Of course, my Oscar, *Astronotus ocellatus,* is a bit easier to find.

In all, I spent several hours there (far longer than I'd planned), and I now had choices to make. I looked at the junction where I'd parked. I wasn't sure which way to go. The frenetic reality of my time crunch weighed heavily upon my psyche. I had four or five more scheduled stops and needed to arrive at my Couchsurfing stay in downtown Miami at a reasonable hour. Often, I found myself wishing I could afford to book a hotel every night to control when my fishing day ended. Oh, well.

Game time, Luke. Which way?

It was like the classic cartoons featuring an angel and demon resting on someone's shoulders. It was happening to me, but instead of an angel and demon, I had Beyoncé saying "To the left, to the left" and Matthew McConaughey telling me "All right, all right, all right." I opted for the latter because my swampy surroundings felt more McConaughey than Queen B and headed back down my intended path, cutting out the considered detour.

Linguistics

The next stop was at a place called Monroe Station. What Monroe Station is, I have no idea to this day, but it was a point of interest along the straight, unbroken sameness of the Tamiami Canal.

Southerners call sunfish "bream" or "brim" depending on the locality, and I'm pleased to say this location was brimming with fishes — some of which were brim. Mostly, though, they were Florida Gar and a collection of invasives. The only brim I did catch, a lonely Spotted Sunfish, was small and skittish in the face of the larger, more aggressive invasive species.

Finally, I found something different. An orange-and-black fish shaped like a tilapia, cichlid, or sunfish but about twice as thick (think Instagram model) that bolted out from under the weeds and hammered my jig. It struck just short and ripped off the worm, but I knew what it was: an Oscar.

Oscars have a nasty temperament, fight ferociously for their size, and if the species had been discovered 100 years later, the parallel between its personality and that of the popular *Sesame Street* character of the same name would still fit.

How it got the name, I'm not sure, but English-speaking naturalists routinely butchered non-English words. They made phonetic English versions of said words spelled entirely differently from today's versions as they incorporated them into mainstream science, history, and a number of other disciplines in the 18th, 19th, and 20th centuries. Half of our United States are named for phonetic renditions of tribes or places in Native American languages. Not to mention various and sundried French- or German-turned-English words that make for an ersatz potpourri.

Ersatz is German and means a poor substitute.

Potpourri is French and used in English to refer to a random mix.

Ersatz potpourri is also how some people might describe the water in parts of the Everglades. You're not entirely sure what's floating in it, and it's certainly aromatic, but unlike anything you'd put in a bowl in your house.

Unless, of course, you're Florida Man.

Florida Man

As a teacher, I'm constantly on the lookout for add-ins to my curriculum. A thoughtful quote, a video clip that illustrates a principle from class, or just a unique icebreaker can really go a long way to make a good lecture great. One of my favorite icebreakers is one I call "Florida Man," and I admit, it is not entirely my invention.

No, this is something one of my seventh-graders told me my first year teaching, back when I taught middle school English. He told me that if you Google "Florida Man" and add your date of birth, you get all sorts of fun headlines.

Naturally, we tried it, and it was a big hit. I saved it for future reference, and again used it for a class I taught with my friend, Bob Chambrose, wherein we produce our school magazine, *the Blue and Gold*. Given students are turned into photojournalists for a few months, it's a solid lead-in.

To date, my favorite Florida Man tale will come up if you Google "Florida Man July 30" — at least, as of me writing this. Florida Man doesn't sleep, so a better headline could've moved up Google's hierarchy since then. Just in case, I'll tell you what happened. Essentially, a guy robbed a convenience store with a small alligator and took only a 12-pack of beer. Though even Stephen King couldn't make this stuff up, it's true. As reported by the *New York Post*: "A man made a beer run into a Florida convenience store carrying a live alligator with its mouth taped shut." It's a riveting read, but essentially ends with the man taking a 12-pack of beer, packing up his portable alligator, and leaving peacefully. So Florida Man stays winning in the eyes of pop culture even if not in the eyes of the law.

I was on Florida Man's turf, and as I rounded a corner, I noticed a half-dozen people fishing in a single spot. Normally, that would drive me away because the last thing I want when fishing is other people around, but I was intrigued. Here was not one real-life Florida Man in its natural habitat, but six!

I pulled over.

Something about me must've triggered a hasty retreat because four of them just up and left. Perhaps they sensed my relative normalcy and didn't want me to feel left out? Who knows.

What I do know is that seconds after arriving, I'd found a broken baitcasting rod with a fairly nice reel. I set it aside amidst a shocking amount — a potpourri, really — of garbage and went to the water.

My first thought was "that's a peacock bass!" My second thought was "Why am I not fishing?"

One cast later, I was indignant because I hadn't hooked it, but two casts later, my pity party ended. My first peacock bass wasn't big, but I didn't care.

Species #276 — Butterfly Peacock Bass *(Cichla ocellaris)*.

I probably should've messed around with the other species there more, but I was too hung up on peacock bass. I asked one of the last remaining Florida Men to take a picture for me, and though he was a bit skeptical given the size of the fish, he obliged.

Then he told me he'd broken a rod on a peacock earlier and was planning to leave. Begrudgingly, I asked if the broken rod I'd found was his, and he said "Yes! I almost forgot." Well, there went what would've been the best baitcasting reel I'd ever owned. Ugh. Sometimes I hate having a conscience.

My consolation prize was a small pink spinning outfit nearby that nobody present claimed — whether because they were ashamed to own it or actually didn't own it, I'll never know.

In addition to five peacocks, I got more of the usual suspects, a massive Golden Topminnow, *Fundulus chrysotus* and two juvenile Hornet/Zebra Tilapia, *Heterotilapia buttikoferi* I would fail to identify correctly for almost a week.

Well, scheisse.

Germans

You know how I said German was heavily ingrained in the English language a few paragraphs back? Well it's true. You know it's true because I wrote it down, and as a high school teacher, I'm an authority figure. In reality, despite my impressive credentials noted above, or maybe regardless of them, it is true.

Not only is German language integrated into our American culture, according to the United States National Travel and Tourism Office or NTTO (don't worry; I had no idea this bureaucratic arm of the government even existed until writing this), Germans were the eighth-most abundant tourist group to the United States over the past decade, accounting for about 2.5 percent of foreign visitors to the United States in a given year.

Das gut, right?

Canada and Mexico are first and second, respectively, and the Top 10 is rounded out by the United Kingdom (3), Japan (4), China (5), South Korea (6), Brazil (7), France (9), and India (10).

Central Florida is the second-most popular tourism region in the United States (behind only New York City), and both Orlando (MCO) and Tampa (TPA) will tell you that the moment you fly in, on loop, along with instructions on how to administer first aid if bitten by a gator or Florida Man.

So the odds of running into a German tourist on my trip were probably somewhere in the neighborhood of, oh, I don't know, realistically possible.

As I stood fishing a culvert absolutely loaded with Mayan Cichlids, a lone Florida Bass, and more of those insufferable Oscars

I just kept hooking and losing, a German couple came up and started talking to me.

Now, I hate to invoke stereotypes, but Germans often rub me the wrong way, and it all started in high school, with this kid named Kevin. His last name was something long and unpronounceable for my isolated, uncultured, ethnocentric, small-town American tongue. He was one of two German exchange students in my class that year, and the girl, Anna, was a sweetheart. And kinda hot, too, if memory serves. But Kevin was a jerk.

The day I met him, while trying to make conversation, I asked "Kevin, what type of wildlife do you have in Germany?"

In his impossibly whiny German accent, he replied "Dinosaurs, mostly, you stupid American."

Huh. So it was gonna be like that, eh, Kevin?

Immediately, he took to calling me "Skywalker." I wouldn't have minded, but he told me he only called me "Skywalker" because like Luke Skywalker, I was from a small, nowhere town with nothing to offer. The only difference, he told me, was that I had "No Force and no hope."

I mean, his name was Kevin, but he should've gone by Richard because he was just an absolute dick.

Being the petulant and immature child I was, I responded by calling him "Kay-vonn" but with the same whiny, German accent he always assaulted our ears with.

During the year he was in our class, he knocked American culture, insulted us individually, and complained about getting stuck in our town. The latter point was fair; we didn't want to be stuck there, either.

After months of Kevin's antics, in a moment of supreme pettiness, I said "Kevin, you could always just go back to Germany. You know, if your people had just done that during both of the wars we beat them in, we probably wouldn't have had to beat you so badly."

Words fade, so it may not have been exactly those words, but I remember the exchange, and I remember how disgusted he looked.

Later that week, on a trip to a cross-country meet, we drove back on a cold bus with a broken heater. Kevin rolled down his window because "Germans are strong. We can take the cold."

Given that we were all post-race, sweaty cross-country runners without an ounce of fat to spare, we all asked him to close it. He replied, in typical Kevin fashion, "In a German minute."

Dumfounded, someone asked, "Kevin, what is a German minute?"

"It's whenever I want," my German nemesis replied.

It was on. I jumped across the aisle and tried to forcibly close the window. I took a few jabs to the stomach and groin, but it was cold enough to see our breath on the bus, and my sensitive parts had shrunken down enough to avoid his blows.

I overpowered him, closed the window, and he sat there stewing the rest of the night.

From then on, I think Kevin either realized he had to not be a jerk or, more likely, he just decided to try and make the most of his time there. For the rest of the year, he still called me Skywalker, and I still called him "Kay-vonn," but we mostly stayed out of each other's way.

Why did I delve into my childhood for that story? Well, because until I went to New Zealand almost five years later and befriended a number of German travelers in hostels across the North Island, like my friend Daniel Waidelich, I honestly didn't like Germans. My one and only experience with a male German had sauered all Krau— Germans — for me.

Fortunately, I overcame my German aversion over some Red Bulls with my Kiwi friend, David Clarke, and we made new friends whom I still keep in touch with. Daniel actually read this chapter and told me it was not offensive to him as a German, and I was okay printing it. Prost!

Going to Germany and Austria a few years after that and experiencing some of the intense rudeness only a German or Austrian (especially Viennese) restaurant can offer made me realize maybe Germans have the same aversion to Americans I had learned to have toward them.

That, or maybe people are just people.

When the German tourists in The Everglades pulled up to ask directions, I wasn't sure what they were saying in German, but they said something, laughed with each other, and then resumed conversing with me. They asked if they could take some pictures of me fishing, and I agreed, so long as they took a picture or two of me if I finally caught an Oscar. Turns out, international relations were all I needed. My Rapala twitched twice near an overhanging tree limb before falling victim to the blitzkrieg of a waiting Oskar. Wait, no. Oscar.

Species #277 — Oscar *(Astronotus ocellatus)*.

It would be the first of six I'd catch there, with my new German friends looking on and genuinely relishing the spectacle. I bid them "Auf Wiedersehen" as I recalled from our high school production of *The Sound of Music* and went onward to Miami.

Sorry Kevin, but despite your best efforts, you didn't ruin all of my future relations with Germans. You didn't steal all of my hope or my tomorrows because "Tomorrow Belongs to Me."

Miami

Now, there are several more stops from that day to discuss. Granted, the longest day of the year had come almost a week before, but this day was still pretty full.

I won't delve into my trip to a dog park where I saw but failed to catch a Jaguar Guapote, *Parachromis managuensis*. I won't talk about the 2.25-pound Spotted Tilapia I got or the Grass Carp, *Ctenopharyngodon idella* I briefly considered targeting in a large, urban lake in Miami. What I will talk about is how I caught two fish close to world records from the same spot on back-to-back casts.

My friend, Gerry Hansell, had given me a spot on a lake near a nice hotel. I believe he stayed there once for work, and that's how he discovered it, but if I'm butchering that story, don't worry, it won't be the last time I do that.

Anyhow, Gerry told me to walk to the shorelines and sight-fish.

Since I'd been having great luck on my ultralight, I grabbed it. It was sporting a small jig tipped with two whole red worms (like nightcrawlers but smaller and more tolerant of the Florida heat). That had worked for almost everything I'd caught in freshwater in Florida that wasn't a micro, so I figured I'd keep it going strong.

My first fish was a 3.5-pound Butterfly Peacock Bass — my largest at that point. My second fish was its mate (the males are larger in this species) that was over six pounds. I was standing on a seawall just high enough that I couldn't reach the fish to lip it, and after a stolid five-minute fight, I tried to "boat flip" it up. That's where you swing the fish into your hands. It promptly straightened out my jig.

Likely, I would've pouted about this for a while had I not almost immediately seen a massive Mayan Cichlid. I caught it, measured it, and weighed it. It was 2.5 pounds and more than twice as large as any others I'd ever seen. This prompted me to look up the world record. Dang. The record was three pounds even. After a quick pic, I released it.

Then I saw the large Hornet/Zebra Tilapia (which, you may recall, I caught earlier that day but failed to realize). It wasn't cooperative, but I finally got it to play. It, too, went 2.5 pounds with a three-pound world record (this one held by my friend, Steve Wozniak).

Species #278 — Hornet Tilapia *(Heterotilapia buttikoferi)*.

Wanting to press my luck and get the fish that actually would be a world record, I continued fishing the seawall. Just as I spotted a peacock bass that likely would've pushed seven pounds, Paul Blart's cousin appeared. He beached his little electronic ... vehicle, I guess? Seconds later, in broken English, he told me I had to leave.

Realizing he was just doing his job, I didn't press the fact that there were no signs, and I was fishing on the roadside far from the hotel, but I'd had a wonderful day, so I let him have this one. Using my final minutes of daylight, I grabbed some food and headed to the home of Jay, where I would be Couchsurfing for the next few days.

Chapter 16
Miami Vices

June 26, 2019

Day 12
Origin: Miami, Florida
Destination: Miami, Florida

"I wouldn't want to fight a man who's
brave enough to touch a fish."
Sheldon Cooper || From *Big Bang Theory*

 Fear is an interesting thing. So often we're afraid and uneasy about things that are completely harmless while something seemingly innocuous and safe that we've overlooked can be secretly harboring danger the whole time.
 Staying with randoms as I traveled across the country was a bit unnerving. Any one of them could've been a serial killer, I suppose, and I never would've known. They could've been sexual deviants who recorded me in the shower, watched me sleep, or even tried to rape me. To my knowledge, my hosts were neither rapists nor mass murderers, but some were ... eccentric.
 My Couchsurfing host, Jay, was an interesting guy. His apartment was small, and perhaps the first thing I noticed was that it didn't have a bedroom. It had rooms: a kitchen, a bathroom, and a living room, but no bedroom. He had a futon in the living room where he slept, and I got the kitchen futon.
 One wall was covered in pictures of Jay with friends and Couchsurfers. It was kinda cool. Another wall was covered in

stickers — mostly obscene and pornographic — depicting various cartoons and anime, vices that were decidedly less cool to me. Still, he turned out to be a decent guy.

He'd been fairly successful as a hotelier before the economy tanked. Since then, he spent most of his time looking for work here and there and focusing on social relationships. He was a genuinely nice person, and I'd buy him a coffee at the Starbucks down the block every day before taking off to fish. He seemed to appreciate it, and for free lodging in downtown Miami, it was the least I could do.

We parted ways that first morning, and I headed to the University of Miami to fish. Parking proved impossible, and after wasting more time than I care to admit, I acknowledged my morning had been destroyed by Hurricane U. I still had a long day ahead, so I pressed on.

My next stop was Kendall's Bait Shop, a little tackle store recommended to me by a friend. I stocked up on shrimp, dropped off a reel that had lost a slap bet with saltwater to be repaired, and then proceeded to a nearby nature preserve. The preserve had a brackish channel running out to the ocean, and I hoped it would make up for lost time.

Brack in Action

Walking any distance in Florida summer heat is miserable, but doing so through thick brush and clouds of mosquitoes is as close to a casual Hell as it gets. Add in the threat of gators, snakes, other biting insects, Florida Man, and a host of other lurking terrors, and I was never fully relaxed in Florida. Nonetheless, I made it to the water at the nature preserve I'd driven to and started fishing.

Naturally, I wasted too much time chasing needlefish I just couldn't catch, but I snapped out of that perennial trap and got off the needle more quickly than I usually do. That was progress.

Fishing shrimp on a small sabiki quickly paid off. I caught a Schoolmaster Snapper that wriggled away before I could get a picture. The picture of your catch is what locks in having caught a species in my #SpeciesQuest and in the Species Hunting world, generally, so I was frustrated. When I caught and lost a mojarra species on my next cast, handling it but not well enough to get it to stay still for a picture, I vocalized some of the profanity I've picked up over the years. Fortunately, there were schools of both species, and I promptly repeated my catches on successive casts.

Species #279 — Schoolmaster Snapper *(Lutjanus apodus)*.
Species #280 — Yellowfin Mojarra *(Gerres cinereus)*.

The Schoolmaster was an easy ID, but mojarra are famously tough to differentiate. Many species look very similar and can only be distinguished by using what are called *meristics*. Meristics is the term used to describe physical characteristics of fishes that visually distinguish them from others. Sometimes, meristics are obvious like color or unique physical shape. Other times, they are much more tedious. Mojarra meristics are often the latter. You need to look at tiny scale patterns on the top of the head, paired with very specific body length/depth measurements. That is, unless they have yellow fins. Mojarra with yellow fins are the aptly-named Yellowfin Mojarra.

Sweet.

Two species in no time was redemptive, but I would catch half a dozen more of these fishes before something else came out to play. Though I could periodically see Jack Crevalle and Great Barracuda, *Sphyraena barracuda* cruising the channel, they wanted nothing to do with my spoons, Rapalas, or swimbaits, so I went back to my shrimp. That proved the right course of action, and I quickly caught something new.

On the NANFA Facebook forum, there was some back-and-forth on the issue, but Kenneth Tse ruled out the Southern Sennet, *Sphyraena picudilla*, and identified it as a juvenile Great Barracuda.

Species #281 — Great Barracuda *(Sphyraena barracuda).*

This toothy missile is absolutely horrifying for its proclivity to occasionally jump out of the water and attack anglers with fang-like teeth. I read an iteration of "This Happened to Me" in *Outdoor Life* as a kid that gave me a lingering fear of these fish, but the fear had receded to the point where I only peed a little while handling my first barracuda. Then again, in 90-plus-degree heat with 100 percent humidity, you barely notice the extra moisture in your boxer briefs, so I'm counting it as another fear conquered.

Tidepool

Back home in Oregon, when I'm not wetting my undies in Florida for various reasons, I routinely fish tidepools. I'm used to tidepools being small holes, crevices, cutouts, and cracks in the rocky shoreline that remain full of water when the tide drops. They are harsh, craggy, heavily vegetated spaces clinging to life in extreme conditions.

The tidepool I fished later that day was a flawless public swimming hole maybe three acres in size, surrounded by white sandy beaches. Two small inlets cycled the water just enough to keep it from stagnating, but they opened to the ocean, and fishes were plentiful. At first, I played around with Goldspotted Killifish, Pinfish, Mangrove Snapper, Crested Goby, *Lophogobius cyprinoides* and juvenile mojarra of some kind.

I noticed a rock wall on the far side of the pool that had been cordoned off by orange ropes and that plastic construction latticework fencing. Naturally, the rebel in me said to go fish it. There were two smaller inlets there that kept the water flowing. A host of needlefish (eye roll) and several other species were congregated in the inflow. Almost immediately, I noticed small yellow-and-black fish darting in and out of the isolated branches likely left there for cover.

Climbing onto the seawall in flip-flops probably wasn't the best idea, but it was only five or six feet up, and I couldn't reach the fish with my tenkara rod otherwise. Without wasting any time, the little yellow-and-black fish struck my worm fleck, and I had a new species.

Species #282 — Sergeant Major *(Abudefduf saxatilis)*.

These aggressive fish out of the way, I tried for the other ones. As it turned out, there was nothing new or exciting save for the Hardhead Silversides I caught.

Species #283 — Hardhead Silverside *(Atherinomorus stipes)*.

Initially, I misidentified them as juvenile mullet, but I would later identify them as Hardhead Silverside when my friend, Tim Aldridge, posted about them on Facebook. In the interim, I managed to delete the pictures of the fish, and of all the fishes I caught during this trip, it's the only Lifer I added to the list without having a picture to show for it. Because I did have one. Promise. I also caught them the following summer and took good pictures.

I wasn't done, though.

After all, I'd caught several new fish, and those needlefish were right there, so for 20 minutes, I tried. If my life depended on catching a needlefish, I am convinced I would die. Funny, then, how when I finally did hook one a few minutes later, I actually almost died.

When I hooked that first needlefish, it was so shocking that I reacted in a graceful, arcing lurch that should've made me lose my balance but didn't. Miraculously, I stayed atop the wall. I decided to edge along the wall just a bit to move away from the snag and allow the hooked needlefish to fight, hoping it wouldn't break my ultralight line on the tenkara rod.

I swiveled my hips and took a step. Then another. When my left foot tried to take its second step, suddenly there was no wall beneath it. I'd casually walked off a cliff. Not a big cliff, mind you, but a cliff. I fell violently, smashing my hands on the wall, pounding my feet against the blessedly sandy bottom, breaking off my hard-won needlefish and smacking my head against the masonry.

You know what hit me first? The wall. It's okay. You can laugh.

You know what hit me second? The blessed realization that I wasn't dead.

I'm 6-foot-2 and change, and the wall was taller than me. Had the ground below been composed of rocks or concrete or had I slipped instead of fallen straight down, I would likely be chumming the water much more than my insanely bloody hands already were. It was a miracle! I hadn't been afraid of standing on a wall, but I should've been. Oh boy, I should've been.

My hands each lost massive chunks of skin from the palms and wrists, and I was bleeding profusely. It was mostly superficial (albeit deep), and I hadn't broken anything except my rod tip.

Looking up at the wall, I noticed half a dozen small notches cut out of the top every few feet, presumably for drainage. I'd stepped on one, and the steep angle refused to tolerate my wet flip-flop, causing me to take a tumble. It could've been so much worse than it had been, but it wasn't over yet.

Just as I'd repaired my rig (an impressive feat to accomplish with the red ultra-fine line that was hard to see on a background of generously bloodied hands), some lifeguard came over and told me I had to move. Apparently, the area was closed for safety renovations. You don't say!

Ordinarily, I would've challenged his exercise of what minimal authority he had if more species were on the table, but my body and ego had suffered enough for one outing, so I went back to the car. I put my tenkara rod on the roof of the RAV-4 while I loaded up my gear and promptly got to work on my mangled mitts.

Knowing I'm fairly accident-prone, I had packed a lot of supplies into my "portable pharmacy" that included everything from calamine lotion to eye drops to every over-the-counter drug you can legally buy and transport across state lines. Using the outdoor beach showers, a single motel soap, and a lot of antibiotic ointment, gauze, and Band-Aids, I bandaged my hands up enough to continue fishing.

After climbing into my car, I began enjoying an iced tea that had lived up to its name after a stint in my cooler. I paired it with a packet of salmon, some crackers, an apple, and some self-pity. I had one more stop planned, so I started the engine and drove there —

knowing I left some dignity behind but failing to realize what I'd left on top of my car.

Canals

As a kid, I watched countless fishing shows where some rando would take his bass boat into the canals of Miami and catch all sorts of fresh- and saltwater fish ranging from tilapia to tarpon. This would be my first chance to fish the Miami canals, and I jumped at it. Well, my hip was pretty sore from the fall, so I couldn't really jump at it and more limped at it.

This canal was loaded with fish, and I caught everything: decent peacock bass, Hornet Tilapia, Spotted Tilapia, Mayan Cichlid, and a large Florida Brown Bullhead, *Ameiurus nebulosus* (which look awesome, mind you) all came out of the fairly salty canal. One of the Mayans even got me excited when I reeled in the all-black fish. Apart from a shot at being the mascot of New Zealand's national rugby team, it was a species I'd already caught, though the first purely melanistic fish I'd landed. Later, David Parker (a NANFA contact) would help me identify it as a Red Devil Cichlid. Apparently, black is a rare morph regardless of which species it was.

Next to that melanistic cichlid was a bright-orange fish. This was the fish I was after, if I could catch one, that would be golden. It was a Midas Cichlid, and I was really excited for this sighting because many of the anglers I'd known who came down to Florida had struck out while prospecting for a Midas Cichlid. I was pretty confident, but I forced myself to pump the brakes.

If you missed the golden, prospecting, or brakes jokes already, that's forgivable, but don't miss the next Midas joke, please. These fish are notoriously picky for cichlids, and I really had to work. This particularly large Midas was lurking under a ledge below the very shore upon which I stood. I could see it, but it wouldn't bite when it could see me, so I had to mix it up and lie down on my belly to get out of sight. Drifting my worm-tipped-jig below the ledge, I decided to go by feel, to trust the Midas touch. It worked, and I set the hook.

Species #284 — Midas Cichlid *(Amphilophus citrinellus).*

My Midas Cichlid joined one each of the Hornet/Zebra Tilapia, Spotted Tilapia, and Mayan Cichlids I'd caught that all happened to be within half a pound of the respective world record. The combination of (1) my fall, (2) hours and hours of Florida sun and subsequent sweating, (3) my too-long curly hair in the insane humidity, and (4) having not eaten anything in hours made for a less-than-optimal picture of me and my Midas, proving once and for all "All that glitters is not gold."

Cuban

It was still relatively early when I got done fishing, so I decided to take a page from Tom Haverford's book (*Parks and Recreation* reference) and treat myself. I went to the Cuban District of Miami and grabbed dinner at a highly rated Cuban restaurant. The food was legit, but the restaurant nickel-and-dimed me for every iced tea refill, charged me a "sitting fee" of 18 percent on top of gratuity, and seated me outside during the hottest part of the day. Nothing makes you feel better than eating meat and mashed yucca in nearly 100-degree temps and paying a premium to do so.

I embraced the meat sweats, and, realizing it was hours before dark, made one final run to a tree farm in the middle of nowhere. There, I would catch the obligatory Mayan Cichlids and jewelfish as well as three new species.

The Pike Killifish were obvious, and though somewhat skittish, these little nightmares weren't as freaked out as the others I'd encountered. Unfortunately, I realized too late that my tenkara rod was nowhere to be found. I'd left it on the roof of my car back when I was cleaning my wounds earlier that day. Cool cool cool cool cool. The tiny pink ultralight I'd found on the roadside in The Everglades worked in a pinch, and I caught several of the monstrous little Pike Killifish.

Species #285 — Pike Killifish *(Belonesox belizanus)*.

These fish are almost too otherworldly to believe. Though called killifish, they're actually a Central American native livebearer (they give birth to live young instead of laying eggs like most fishes) released into the United States through aquaria. Imagine a killifish or topminnow that skims the water's surface except instead of a smaller, pointed head, these fish have crocodilian jaws an inch long lined with small but razor-sharp teeth. They look like a mad scientist stitched the head of a tiny crocodile to the body of a three-inch fish.

Using that same pink rod, I took off the micro presentation and switched to a jig. In short order, I landed more than 20 fish, including several Mozambique Tilapia and a single Jaguar Guapote.

Species #286 — Mozambique Tilapia *(Oreochromis mossambicus)*.
Species #287 — Jaguar Guapote *(Parachromis managuensis)*.

The Jaguar Cichlid, or Jaguar Guapote, was especially thrilling as it had long been one of my dream fish. It was small, but the protrusible, toothy mouth and its unique coloration made it a prize to be sure.

Not wanting to live any palpable fears of being alone in the sketchier reaches of the American South at night, I decided to head back after adding my eighth new species since I'd woken up that morning. Not half-bad, but I wonder how many I would've caught without my handicap?

Chapter 17
Pride and Joy

June 27, 2019

Day 13
Origin: Miami, Florida
Destination: Miami, Florida

"Please be a traveler, not a tourist. Try new things, meet new people, and look beyond what's right in front of you. Those are the keys to understanding this amazing world we live in."
Andrew Zimmern || American Chef || From *Bizarre Foods*

It was my last full day in Miami. I'd stay one more night and then head for the Florida Keys. I was ready to roll. Jay, as it turned out, was ready to talk. Again, nice guy, but I was there to fish. Part of me wanted to just up-and-leave, but he was letting me stay, saving me hundreds of dollars, and I felt I owed him this. I've always struggled to prioritize human relationships over my fishing obsession, and I just felt my conscience calling out to me to talk with him. So I did. Our five minutes stretched into almost an hour. He told me his life story, how he'd come from Mexico as a child, how he quickly and quietly worked his way into hotel management and then how he'd lost his job in the recession and struggled to get back on his feet as he battled the demons of self-doubt, loneliness, and depression. Boy, how I could relate to that latter part.

We talked about our shared struggles with depression for a bit, including how to put up the veneer to make it seem like you're fine to the people you're not that close to. His countenance improved even as we spoke. He had a job interview that day, and I was hopeful for him. Through it all, he was positive. His outlook was happy. Not just content, but happy.

I began to share my faith with him, and he wasn't that interested, so I didn't press it.

He then said "You know I'm gay, right?"

Taken aback by the dissonance of his persona as a somewhat nerdy gamer-type but trying to play it cool, I replied "Yeah. Of course," I lied.

Jay fit absolutely zero of the gay stereotypes I'd been conditioned by network television to expect, so yes, I was surprised. I was even more surprised when he asked if I was single. Not wanting to see where this was going, I said "Yeah. I just haven't found the right person." How I wish I'd said "woman" instead of "person".

He replied, "You know…" and trailed off.

Realizing my mistake, I quickly added, "It's tough to find worthwhile women where I live."

He nodded.

"For what it's worth," he said, "If you weren't straight, I'd totally date you."

Were it the first time I'd been hit on by a man, I might have been blindsided, but I took it in stride.

"Thanks, man. That's nice of you to say," I replied, sort of flattered, I guess.

"It's Miami. There is no shortage of singles. You'll find someone."

The conversation found its natural conclusion, and I wished him luck on the job interview he had. We parted ways, and I headed to a canal at the center of town that was supposed to hold Salvini Cichlid, *Cichlasoma salvini* as well as all the usual suspects.

Shopping Center

This would be the first of several shopping centers I would fish in Florida. In other parts of the country, including my home state of Oregon, a guy fishing in the parking lot draws a lot of attention — much of it negative. In Florida, it's commonplace. Though I was the only one fishing here, seemingly everyone stopped and talked to me about how they fished these canals and others like them throughout greater Miami. It was refreshing — well, not really because it was stifling hot and stuffy that day — but Florida has a lot going for it, despite the bad rap.

This particular canal stretched between a major thoroughfare that wasn't quite a highway on one side and a string of commercial properties on the other.

Despite the shoreline being at a steep angle — it was not conducive to angling while wearing flip-flops. I managed. Large peacock bass grabbed my attention first, and I spent a fair amount of time chasing them. The big female fell prey, and though I hooked the bigger male twice, I failed to land it. Saving it for later, I pressed on.

Over the next three or four hours, I walked the canal, catching plenty of fishes but failing to see a single Salvini Cichlid. Highlights included a large Jaguar Guapote and the big male peacock bass which I circled back for and finally caught. It was my first five-plus-pound pea. Eventually, I may have found Salvinis, but I walked that damn canal for a mile and failed to spot one, so I decided my time would be better spent soaking a line in the salt.

Iguanas

Since arriving in Miami a few days before, I noticed the invasive Marine Iguanas everywhere. They sat boldly sunning themselves on rocks until you got too close. Then they'd do a gyrating death dive into the water and scare the crap out of you with a splash as you watched a large green reptile just feet away from you retreat into the water.

"Not a gator. Not a gator. Not a gator," I trained myself to say even if I didn't always believe it in those fragile moments of alarm. With a few days to become accustomed to them, I got less surprised with each one I saw. Then, at my next stop, I saw King Iguana.

Brackish channels interlaced a mangrove forest just a few hundred yards from the ocean, and I was hoping to luck into a few species. Topping the list was the Mangrove Gambusia, a highly localized cousin of the mosquitofish with vivid blue eyes.

The trained eyes of a rapidly improving microfisherman didn't let me down, and I quickly sighted them. Tragically, I'd lost my tenkara rod, so catching these micros with a length of line tied to the short pink ultralight I'd found on the side of the road proved a bit of a challenge. Until it didn't.

I added Mangrove Gambusia and moved up onto the footbridge to see what else I might find.

Species #288 — Mangrove Gambusia *(Gambusia rhizophorae)*.

The iridescent sapphire-blue of this fish's eye was truly mesmerizing. Florida is absolutely loaded with beautiful fish, but this remains one of my favorites from my foray into Florida; the piercing blue stayed with me.

My own eyes were drawn from those little gambusia to a massive barracuda cruising the channel near the larger bait I'd set out. Then I saw a large, distant guitarfish. Well, it was shaped like a guitarfish. Maybe it was, dare I say, a highly endangered Smalltooth Sawfish, *Pristis pectinata*? Then a Jack Crevalle zipped by, pugnaciously. Naturally, I failed to catch any of these awesome fish. What I did catch was my first pufferfish, a Checkered Puffer that zipped out of the mangrove roots to steal some shrimp.

Species #289 — Checkered Puffer *(Sphoeroides testudineus)*.

These comical little critters inflate themselves on command by sucking in air when out of the water. It's actually awesome. Once fully inflated, they flap their fins wildly and just stare at you, irritated by the situation you've put them in and demanding you acknowledge them. I'm reminded of Russell Crowe's character in *Gladiator* yelling, "Are you not entertained?!" to the onlooking Roman crowd.

To answer your question, little puffer: yes. Yes I was.

A large Yellowfin Mojarra captured my attention as I briefly thought it might be a world record, but alas, it was not. Realizing I'd probably done about as well as I'd do in the brackish mangroves, I decided to move on to the pier. Well, "the pier" is generous. It was more of a fishing dock, and it only stuck out maybe 20 feet from shore, but it sufficed. Fishing shrimp on a sabiki again proved fruitful, and the spot yielded 19 fish, including three new species: Sand Perch, Slender Mojarra, and Mahogany Snapper.

Species #290 — Sand Perch *(Diplectrum formosum)*.
Species #291 — Slender Mojarra *(Eucinostomus jonesii)*.
Species #292 — Mahogany Snapper *(Lutjanus mahogoni)*.

The stop was otherwise uneventful until I was almost back to the car. Traversing the dirt path that wended its way through the thick mangroves, something big, green, and just over four feet long popped out of the underbrush and started running toward me. Given that the 25-pound beast was easily twice the size of any other iguana I'd seen, I mentally went back to gator, and my fight-flight-freeze instinct kicked in.

"Eff," I remember saying. Yeah, seriously. I tend to substitute less offensive words for actual profanity in practice, but I'm not sure it makes me sound more intelligent.

I lowered my rods to form a sort of palisade and shook like a mangrove leaf. I'm not sure if this scared the big lizard away or if it had just decided it wasn't about to play chicken with a man, but it veered off course and ran right by me, diving back through the brush and culminating the encounter with a terrifying splash. It was just an iguana, but my eyes had failed to convey that information to my trembling hands and pounding heart.

Many authors don't wanna talk about their fears and underlying problems, but iguana talk them out.

In retrospect, I wondered how Floridians might combat the explosion of invasive iguanas. In my research, I saw all manner of proposed controls, but the one that stood out most in my mind is eating them. Some companies and dozens of individuals have begun doing so already.

In the Caribbean, where Marine Iguanas are native, they're referred to as "pollo de los árboles" or the "chicken of the trees." I know what you're thinking, but don't count it out. Gator is my favorite meat, and iguana is compared favorably to gator.

It is completely legal to catch and kill iguanas in Florida, and those who eat them use nets, traps, and snares primarily, though some folks shoot them where safe and legal.

Honestly, a part of me regrets not killing and eating an iguana when I was down there. I absolutely love to eat gator, rattlesnake is decent, and iguanas are just another reptile. Since marine iguanas arguably eat a more appetizing diet than the mice and rats and bugs snakes devour, I have to believe iguana would be even better than rattlesnake. Not only that, but the very same type of iguanas found roaming feral in Florida sell for upward of $50 per pound at specialty online meat markets. Next time I'm in Florida, iguana will be on the menu for sure and only partly because that bull iguana scared the crap out of me.

Pier Ecstasy

I changed my underwear after the iguana exchange and drove to my next stop: Dania Beach Pier.

Over my 1,500-plus lifetime fishing trips, I've fished a lot of piers in a lot of places. Dania Beach Pier remains one of the very best I've come across. Yes, it was a pay-to-play pier, but boasts ample nearby parking, competent and kind staff, and angler-friendly amenities such as freshwater taps and a rail with plenty of notches in which to rest fishing poles. Further, it was absolutely lousy with fish, and despite some other anglers, it wasn't packed, so everyone had room to fish comfortably.

I had just a few hours there, but the 33 fishes I caught didn't care. Grunts made up the bulk of the catch, and every time I dropped bait, something bit. When I dropped a truncated sabiki without bait, oily baitfish made up the bulk of the catch.

The myriad of colors each fish I caught there nearly made a rainbow:

> Squirrelfish, *Holocentrus adscensionis* (pink/red).
> Redear Herring, *Harengula humeralis* (red/orange/yellow).
> French Grunt, *Haemulon flavolineatum* (yellow).
> Scaled Sardine, *Harengula jaguana* (green).
> Blue Runner, *Caranx crysos* (blue).
> Sailor's Choice Grunt, *Haemulon parra* (silver).
> Hairy Blenny, *Labrisomus nuchipinnis* (brown).
> Black Margate, *Anisotremus surinamensis* (black).

Had I kept them all, I could've made a beautiful fish rainbow or maybe a literal Rainbow Roll. Then again, most of those fishes weren't sushi quality, so that would've been too culinarily adventurous — even for a guy who would readily try iguana.

Given that I let all of them go (save for a few Scaled Sardines I tried using as live bait), just imagine it. I didn't really have to imagine it because I was there. Also there? Some sort of Pride event with a sea of rainbow flags.

Perhaps in befriending Jay that day and taking his Pride in stride, this rainbow of fishes was my reward? I don't know, but I do know I added six species — one species shy of a full, seven-color rainbow — at Dania Beach, and I was quite happy about that. Some might even say a little gay.

> Species #293 — French Grunt *(Haemulon flavolineatum)*.
> Species #294 — Squirrelfish *(Holocentrus adscensionis)*.
> Species #295 — Redear Herring *(Harengula humeralis)*.
> Species #296 — Sailor's Choice Grunt *(Haemulon parra)*.
> Species #297 — Blue Runner *(Caranx crysos)*.
> Species #298 — Black Margate *(Anisotremus surinamensis)*.

Chapter 18
Tropical Storm Casey

June 28, 2019

Day 14
Origin: Miami, Florida
Destination: Marathon, Florida

"Major Key Alert!"
DJ Khaled || American DJ

    The next morning, I got up early and bid Jay goodbye and good luck. I left a thank-you note with a Starbucks gift card on the counter and went on my way.
    Miami had been pretty great. I'd scored some Cuban food and lived a few days in one of America's most iconic cities. Though I never saw DJ Khaled blazing down the canals in a jet ski and failed to run into any cast members from *Jane the Virgin*, I was still happy to have marked the city off my list and will definitely return someday.
    Then again, I was more excited for the next leg of my journey that would take me to the Florida Keys. So much of what I'd read and seen about the Keys made me believe it was this warm water paradise, with sprawling white sands and crystal-clear water. It more or less lived up to the hype, except that most of the infrastructure was still decidedly "Old Florida" in every way. Very little of what I saw was the white glistening stucco with pastel accents, palm trees, wave pools, and destination resorts I'd imagined. There were a few places like that, but it was mostly just

like any old part of Florida before the influx of ultra modernity and the strip malls, parking lots, and Starbucks that come with that conversion.

My first stop at a bridge somewhere near Marathon gave me the chance to break out the chum bag I'd purchased on my way down. Nothing like manhandling a 25-pound bag of blood and fish carcasses in tropical heat to make you realize you might be just a little off. I was crazy. Crazy excited. I mean, I was in the Florida Keys, for goodness' sake!

Immediately, I could see different fishes come up and nibble at the chum bag the minute it hit the lukewarm water.

My go-to sabiki with shrimp hadn't failed me yet, so I started there. That first stop yielded 51 fishes in a few hours' time, and apart from the parrotfish that wouldn't acknowledge my bait or the Scrawled Filefish, *Aluterus scriptus* I would've landed if I'd just grabbed the bloody thing by hand instead of trying to lift it up onto the rocks, none of the species I saw avoided me.

In short order, I landed 12 species, six of them brand-new.

Species #299 — Yellowtail Snapper *(Ocyurus chrysurus)*.
Species #300 — Bermuda Chub *(Kyphosus sectatrix)*.
Species #301 — Slippery Dick *(Halichoeres bivittatus)*.
Species #302 — Buffalo Trunkfish *(Lactophrys trigonus)*.
Species #303 — Beaugregory *(Stegastes leucostictus)*.
Species #304 — Puddingwife Wrasse *(Halichoeres radiatus)*.

Of course, I'd be remiss not to make a juvenile comment about the Slippery Dick, a wrasse species prized by juvenile anglers looking for the quick joke. Naturally, I have several:

1) Of note is the fact that at the time of writing there was no world record for this species. I guess that just goes to show that size doesn't matter.

2) Despite its name, most wrasse species are hermaphrodites, meaning they change gender during their lifetime to accommodate different phases in their life cycle. So yes, a fish called a Slippery Dick might be at different times in its life both male and female.

3) An online publication from the University of the West Indies - St. Augustine Campus includes this line, which, taken completely out of context, is hilarious given the name of the fish: "due to their reduced motion or sensitivity during the night," so I'll just leave that there.

4) Upon death, the Slippery Dick will experience rigor mortis (death stiffness) like most other vertebrates. He he.

5) If you hook a Slippery Dick and pull it out of the water, it will gyrate wildly, making it a literal swinging dick.

6) Like most species of fish, the Slippery Dick has no external sex organs and simply releases eggs and milt (fish sperm) through an orifice called a cloaca. So the Slippery Dick is actually dickless.

7) The Slippery Dick can reach 13 inches, though that is incredibly rare. No, I'm not just saying that. Most you'll encounter will range from five to eight inches in length. My own Slippery Dicks have averaged about seven inches in length, for what it's worth.

Well, this segment of the story has reached its climax, so let's move on.

Starbucks

This trip wasn't cheap, and I mentioned all of the efforts I made to keep costs down: Couchsurfing, staying with friends, eating food I packed myself, and not flushing to save water.

Apart from eating dinner out most nights, coffee was my vice. Every morning, I'd pay for a solid cup of coffee and every afternoon, I'd get a cold brew if I felt like I needed a little more caffeine than an iced tea could provide for me. Sometimes, iced tea was enough. Sometimes, I found myself looking for coffee later in the day. Given the lack of small-time coffee roasters, something that this Oregon boy finds absolutely alien, Starbucks became the go-to.

I also mentioned how the combination of my IBS and Florida's intense heat makes me benefit from a well-maintained private bathroom, and so Starbucks shined there, as well, just not quite as brightly after I flushed.

It just so happened that as I left my first stop in Islamorada, I noticed a Starbucks logo with a sign below it that read "LAST STARBUCKS FOR 80 MILES." I kid you not, I flipped a U-turn and went back to it, ordered my Nitro Cold Brew with cream and made all sorts of untoward sounds as I enjoyed the blessed A/C, my coffee, and some only mostly melted chocolate chip cookies.

If this was my last shot for 80 miles (a much further distance in the Keys given the perpetual 45 miles per hour speed limits and heavy summer traffic), so be it, but I was sure going to enjoy it.

Starbucks in hand, I further indulged my inner White girl by uploading my day's catches to my Instagram Story, keeping all 37 of my Followers apprised of my trip. Naw, at the time, I was somewhere between 1,500 and 2,000 Followers and an average of 450 tuned in to each and every Insta Story. I probably would've had more if I posted more racy photos, but Starbucks is about as far as I can channel my inner White girl.

Casey

Earlier on my trip, I'd met up with Casey Shanaberger in his native Iowa. Well, it just so happened that as I worked my way south, he messaged me and said he was planning a family vacation down to the Keys. It was a great coincidence, and we decided to meet up once again to fish.

Our first stop was a little inlet near his hotel. I arrived first and quickly added a few more grunts to the catch list, though none were new. As I waited, some guys nearby told me they'd just seen a shark. I put out the chum bag and kept a close eye on the dark waters below. Sure enough, a Nurse Shark quickly showed itself. Sprinting to the car, I grabbed my sturgeon rod. It was short and powerful, like that one hot girl every gym seems to have.

Hooking a live grunt just above the anal fin, I tossed it out and waited. I didn't have to wait long.

The shark grabbed my bait soon after Casey arrived, and he filmed the entire fight. It took about 10 minutes from hookup to picture, as I battled the 35- or 40-pound shark. It wasn't a fast or intense fight, but the fish was strong and pulled consistently, sort of like a big catfish.

Walking down the short seawall, I managed to turn it into a little inlet used for launching canoes and kayaks. Barefoot and shirtless, I wrestled the shark in the warm, shallow waters until it was unhooked.

A few pictures later, and it was on its merry way. Still shaking with excitement and adrenaline, I was thrilled to have caught my largest fish of the trip and certainly the coolest yet.

Species #305 — Nurse Shark *(Ginglymostoma cirratum)*.

Casey didn't have a heavy rod, so I reset the live bait and let him fish while we dinked around. Nothing new came out for me, but he added one or two species.

While I began to pack up all 83 of the rods I'd brought to the water's edge and prepared to make some hyperbolic complaints about packing light to Casey, I noticed some small gobies in the rocks below our feet. Though I misidentified them at first, I knew they were new, and I'd quickly added yet another new species: the Notchtongue Goby.

Species #306 — Notchtongue Goby *(Bathygobius curacao)*.

The day was young, and so were we. We moved down the road a bit and started fishing the channel below another bridge. Weather was moving in, and the winds were picking up steadily, screaming at us and ramping up the flow speed in the bridge channel.

We had been using half-ounce sinkers, but we were forced to switch to one- then two-ounce weights. The fishes didn't seem to mind, and we continued catching fish after fish. Grunts came on every other drop, but we began puzzling together other species.

My next Lifers came on successive casts: Dusky Damselfish and Tomtate Grunt.

Species #307 — Dusky Damselfish *(Stegastes adustus)*.
Species #308 — Tomtate Grunt *(Haemulon aurolineatum)*.

The Tomtate Grunt stands out amongst other grunt species because the inside of its whole mouth — not just part of it — is a vibrant orange-red, sort of like the flesh of a Roma tomato. Though their external patterning can vary a bit as the fish matures, the mouth is a dead giveaway. So to answer the age-old question "What that mouth do?" — helps identify the fish, that's what.

I'd added some new species, but by then, it was raining, and winds were up to 20 or 30 miles per hour. In addition to fishing, Casey loves weather. He is a storm chaser who routinely studies meteorology and weather patterns. We had been fishing at the edge of the bridge but had slowly crept under the shelter it provided, and I figured if I was gonna be trapped in a tropical storm, he was probably about the best companion for it.

I'd yet to have any weather colder than 70 degrees on this trip (save my lone night in Rock Springs, Wyoming). That day in the Florida Keys, I was anticipating nothing but stifling heat, and I was in shorts and flip-flops. The sky grew darker and angrier, and we burrowed further and further below the safe confines of the bridge.

Windspeed hit 40 miles per hour. You couldn't really talk without yelling at this point given the wind tunnel effect.

When I hooked the next sizable grunt, rather than release it, I impaled it on a 5/0 circle hook and threw it out under the bridge to let it soak in the current. I propped the butt of the rod between a seam in the artificial bedrock poured at the foundation of the bridge and left it there, continuing to catch smaller fishes with relish. The more unique and tropically beautiful fishes finally decided to play, and in no time I added Porkfish and Spotted Scorpionfish to my list.

Species #309 — Porkfish *(Anisotremus virginicus)*.
Species #310 — Spotted Scorpionfish *(Scorpaena plumieri)*.

Both fishes were vibrant and broke the plain lines of the grunts and snapper that had dominated our catch that afternoon. Porkfish are colored in brilliant yellows, whites, and blacks but are actually closely related to the Black Margate — a grunt I'd first caught the day before — and not at all related to the angelfish their coloration most closely resembles.

That Spotted Scorpionfish was the third true scorpionfish I've caught, and I knew to handle it with care and avoid the dorsal spines.

Winds hit 50 miles per hour. It was definitionally gale-force at this point. Though inland, wind speeds faster than 50 are rare, they're much more common in the narrow strip of land essentially surrounded by the ocean that we call the Florida Keys.

Shortly after releasing my 10th and 11th new species of the day (the area was living up to its reputation), the storm hit full force. Gale force winds exacerbated by the wind-tunnel effect under the bridge, likely pushing 60 miles per hour, began blowing heavy gear bags over and rolling them uphill. My bag weighed about 15 pounds, and it was rolling uphill like a ball. I sprinted toward it.

My hat whipped off and Casey's followed. He was able to save mine, but I couldn't return the favor, and his hat was lost forever.

Moment of silence, please.

I briefly stepped out from under the bridge and regretted it. I was having to put all of my weight into every step to keep from losing my balance. It wasn't easy.

The monsoon rains began in earnest but given the wind, the bridge proved little help in staying dry. We huddled against the bridge pilings and watched as everything we'd brought was soaked by the horizontal deluge.

It was harrowing and bracing all at once. There was no telling how long the storm would last, but we waited it out, patiently, until Casey said "I think you have a fish."

I'd completely forgotten about the live bait I'd left on my heavy rod, but sure enough, that forgotten fish wasn't forgotten for long. It wasn't a monster, but it was big enough to put a bend in the Ugly Stik Tiger, a rod designed to catch sturgeon and rays from a boat.

Combine my skill in fighting any fish (I've caught a big fish or two throughout the years) with the heavy gear and sloshing seas, and the fish didn't stand a chance. I expected to pull up a small Nurse Shark but was pleasantly surprised — shocked even — when I pulled ashore a small grouper.

Species #311 — Black Grouper *(Mycteroperca bonaci)*.

My first grouper didn't disappoint. It was about seven pounds and pushing 30 inches in length — not a bad fish by any measure. It had inhaled my 10-inch grunt, and we took a few pics and a short video in which Casey shouts, "How does it feel?" while gale-force winds blow me this way and that as I hold the grouper.

I shout back, "Awesome!" before releasing the fish.

We huddled like scared children for another 15 minutes or so before the storm calmed down. Casey was staying nearby, and he offered to let me dry off and change in his family's nearby chalet. They were incredibly kind, and we talked briefly during the exchange.

The Shanabergers had made the trip regularly with their son, Casey, and were looking forward to a chartered fishing trip out on the flats later in the week. Though I desperately wanted to pay for such a trip, I'd vowed to limit expenses on this weeks-long journey and hadn't booked a single charter or guide. Maybe next time I'd chase Bonefish, *Albula vulpes* and Tripletail, *Lobotes surinamensis*, but this time around, I was going to get my money's worth from shore just as I'd been doing each and every day of the trip so far. We parted ways for a while while I went to grab some lunch at a nearby seafood restaurant.

Though the food was good enough, I'm constantly reminded how much better seafood from the Pacific Northwest is than seafood from almost anywhere on earth. Give me Dungeness Crab and Cabezon, *Scorpaenichthys marmoratus* over grouper and Blue Crab any day of the week.

Still, in the storm, sitting and eating was my best option, so I enjoyed the meal. It would be my only hot meal that day.

After the storm, fishing was uneventful. All I caught in the low light were grunts, but the Bluestriped Grunt was new, and it made 13 Lifers on the day — my personal best one-day new species tally at that point.

Species #312 — Bluestriped Grunt (*Haemulon sciurus*).

I slept soundly after that kind of production despite the loud, stereotypically Florida music being played at Looe Key Resort's karaoke night.

Storm
In the middle of the night, I awoke with a start.

I'm a light sleeper, so I sleep with the aid of a white noise app on my phone. My white noise app plays a loop featuring someone from National Public Radio (NPR) listing organic, overpriced products from Whole Foods read by young twentysomethings with names Millennials give their children, like "Mackynzlei" or "Janyssicah".

I kid. It's usually just static.

Regardless, my entire room was illuminated with bright light.

Aliens?

CIA raid?

Cartel abduction?

Dear God. Not Florida Man!

Half a second later, I heard the loudest thunderclap I'd ever heard. The lightning hit something nearby because I heard a loud explosive sound that drowned out my white noise app for two long seconds.

This tropical storm wasn't kind, and the "Boom-Clap" repeated itself with as much frequency as the chorus from the song of the same name by Charlie XCX but markedly more ominous.

For 15 minutes I didn't sleep. Then the power went out. Well, the lights were off, but I knew because suddenly my phone screen flashed on to indicate it had been unplugged. I don't know when the lights came back on, but I was lights-out within minutes, dead to the world while I weathered the storm.

Chapter 19
A Really Bad Day

June 29, 2019

Day 15
Origin: Marathon, Florida
Destination: Looe Key, Florida

"Live every week like it's Shark Week."
Tracy Jordan || From *30 Rock*

    Since I was young, I've been absolutely fascinated by sharks. Great White, Mako, Thresher, Blacktip, Loan, it didn't really matter. Their raw and savage mastery of their world always terrified and impressed me all at once.
    Of course, once I'd caught that first Nurse Shark in the Keys, sharks were all I could think about. Sure, there were dozens of other non-shark species to be had, but I couldn't stop thinking about the sharks.
    The Keys had Bonnethead, Spinner, Blacktip, Bull, and Lemon Sharks for sure — those were just the ones I'd seen pictures of. In the Florida Keys, where sharks are afforded some of the protections they actually deserve, densities are relatively high, and anglers can expect a reasonable shot at a shark almost anywhere. So even as I threw a sabiki and caught smaller fishes to ratchet up the species count from a broken bridge hundreds of feet in the air, I had a large rod at the ready to fish for sharks once I got down closer to the water and actually had a prayer of landing one if the maritime gods smiled down on me.

I started under the bridge where others were fishing, but it had proven nearly fruitless between the ripping current, other anglers, and the guys in the kayak who were spearfishing or something that required frequent dives under the surface. So I stopped messing around and climbed around the bridge to another, more isolated spot and began fishing in earnest.

Once I had an appropriately large Bluestriped Grunt maybe 12-14 inches in length (which quickly became my favorite shark bait), I tossed out the live bait, wedged the pole in between some rocks behind the chest-high seawall I was fishing from and got to work catching small fishes to pass the time.

In short order, I added Smallmouth Grunt, a juvenile Red Grouper, and the strange-looking Sheepshead Porgy (not to be confused with the Sheepshead, also a porgy and also found in Florida, so shoutout to the taxonomists who named them).

Species #313 — Smallmouth Grunt *(Haemulon chrysargyreum)*.
Species #314 — Red Grouper *(Epinephelus morio)*.
Species #315 — Sheepshead Porgy *(Calamus penna)*.

I filled in the blanks with dozens of fish, mostly snappers and grunts, that kept me busy until my first shark came out to play. It was a big Nurse Shark, more than five feet long. The seawall from which I was fishing was three feet above the surface of the water, and the water at its base was much too deep to jump down into, so I was forced to slowly fight the fish down the quarter-mile length of seawall to a rocky beachhead.

As I was pulling, I noticed a Florida Game Warden come down the steep slope on a mission. He passed me at a distance, but I assumed he would make the rounds and eventually come check on me.

Just as I got the large shark up to the pock-marked rocky beach (beach being used very loosely here), the warden started his approach. I was wearing flip-flops, and that made fighting a large, powerful shark on slippery, uneven terrain a logistical nightmare; eventually, I got the shark close enough to me that I could handle it. Reeling the line tight to control the shark's head with the rod in my right hand, I grabbed its tail with the left and moved the fish into the shallow tidepool, ensuring its gills and head were fully submerged while I unhooked it and took measurements.

The warden grew closer, but I was able to take some mediocre pictures of myself with the shark and release it long before he arrived — it would've been wise to just wait for him to arrive to get a better picture. Hindsight is 20/20, though.

Unsure of his intentions, I was cautiously friendly. He responded in kind and asked if I'd seen anyone poaching lobsters. I didn't know what exactly that entailed, but then it dawned on me: the guys in the kayak. I told him about what I'd seen, and he seemed to think those were his guys. Unfortunately, they'd left hours prior, and it didn't look like he was going to have any luck tracking them down.

"What type of shark was that?" he asked before we parted ways.

"Big Nurse Shark," I half-bragged, half-replied.

"Those are really underrated," he said.

"No kidding," I agreed, rubbing my sore shoulders.

We parted ways with a smile, and I encouraged him to check Fishbrain. Numerous game wardens use the app to catch poachers who effectively self-incriminate by posting their illegal catches. In my home state, it is a popular tool with local game wardens, and at my first ICAST the year before, I introduced it to each of the two dozen wildlife management agencies present. It was an instant hit.

He thanked me for the tip, and I got back to fishing.

Grunt. Grunt. Grunt. Grunt. Grunt. Grunt.

Some of the grunts were fish, some of them were noises I made as I climbed back to the car to get something to drink and snack on in the ungodly heat.

After a revival, I threw out another large grunt with an audible grunt of my own and didn't have to wait long. Though I was fairly far from my shark rod when something took the bait, it hit with enough ferocity and speed that it was almost free-spooling line by the time I got to it. The oversized Cabela's Salt Striker spinning reel is cheap but effective, and the 100-pound braid was flying off at an impressive rate. The beast continued its initial run for 10, 20, 30, 40 seconds. Almost a minute passed before it slowed, and I was grateful for the 300 yards or so of line capacity. I battled the monstrous fish, praying all the while I would be able to land it. It just gained ground on me for the first five minutes. I still had plenty of line, but if the battle continued going that direction, I would be spooled in another five minutes.

Carefully, slowly, painstakingly, I began to fight back. I recovered a few hundred feet of line and after 15 minutes of fighting, the fish was back within 100 yards or so of the shore. I could see where the line entered the water despite the weight of the saturated, 100-pound braid. This fish was pulling hard.

I wondered if it was a massive Jack Crevalle or Atlantic Tarpon, perhaps, given that both species were present. Maybe a massive 50-plus-pound Red Drum, *Sciaenops ocellatus* or a Black Drum?

Then it jumped.

It was none of those things. It was a massive Blacktip Shark, *Carcharhinus limbatus* or Spinner Shark, *Carcharhinus brevipinna*. At that distance, the white or black anal fin that distinguishes one from the other was not visible, but boy was it massive.

My Nurse Shark had measured just over five feet. This fish was every bit of seven feet long, maybe eight. I'd hooked sturgeon that big before, so I had some comprehension of the scale. Only this fish wasn't a sturgeon; it was a big ass shark.

I continued to make headway, albeit slight, and slowly crept down the top of the seawall toward my rocky beachhead. This fish would be much tougher to land, but it was possible. I had to believe that.

Almost 20 minutes into the fight, and the fish did feel slightly weaker. Then again, I felt more than slightly weaker. I was tired, but I wasn't letting up.

Without warning, the shark decided to go on another blistering run. It ran, jumped again, and then hit the water at full speed. Though my drag was relatively loose, that next full-speed run made the reel sing for a second before the line went slack.

Heartbroken, I reeled it in, unsure of what had happened. The fish had broken my 60-pound steel leader in half. The hook was gone, and the end of the coated wire leader was frayed as though it had stretched and stretched and then just snapped.

Devastation hit me, and I ran through all seven stages of grief in the ensuing hours. Fortunately, a small Bonnethead Shark took the next grunt and helped me rebound.

Species #316 — Bonnethead Shark *(Sphyrna tiburo)*.

The grunt had been a large, 14-inch specimen over a pound, and this Bonnethead was barely three feet long. It would go just over 10 pounds.

In an unfortunate turn, the little shark had swallowed my bait and somehow managed to puncture its stomach with the circle hook. Large circle hooks are specifically designed to reduce gut-hooking, instead cleanly hooking a fish in the corner of the mouth for the best survival rates, but this one had failed. It would be my only gut-hooked fish on a circle hook of my life, but it saddened me nonetheless.

In between the time I'd hooked the monster Spinner/Blacktip and the time I caught the Bonnethead, four other anglers had shown up and joined me. Now, this was a seawall almost half a mile long, and they all decided to set up next to me. Siiiiiiick. Further, there was a formal fishing area below the nearby bridge, so they had no reason to crowd me, but there we were.

Rather than fight the breach of decorum, I realized it was probably my signal to begin wrapping up, so I vowed to get one more shark before leaving.

The three on my left were Latino teenagers, Lateens if you will, who had absolutely no idea what they were doing, fishing whole shrimp on large hooks too small for big predators like Nurse Sharks or Black Drum but much too large for most of the reef fish. I helped them out and set them up with smaller sabikis, and they instantly started catching fish. They were very kind and grateful.

On my other side was a middle-aged Asian man who set up way too close to me. I only found out he was upwind of me when he started chain smoking. That settled it. One more shark, and I was out.

Upon the realization that the Bonnethead was dead, the older guy asked if he could have it. Unsure of the laws, but not wanting it to waste, I told him he could keep it, but he should check the rules first.

He thanked me, grabbed his rod and bucket in one hand, the shark in the other, and booked it to his car. With a cigarette still in his mouth, this guy sprinted over broken terrain with full hands. It was admittedly quite impressive, but it made me wonder about the legality of what had just occurred. Still, the fish was 100 percent dead, so at least it didn't go to waste. I later checked, and Bonnetheads are a harvestable species in Florida; you're just limited to one shark from the list of harvestable species per day, so at least my pragmatism hadn't made me a criminal.

Still, I'd had enough. An older White dude in an open Hawaiian shirt who looked like the type who'd be a player at his retirement home started down the rocks with a 40 and a fishing rod. He was loud, obnoxious, and clearly hammered, and that was my cue to leave.

The Asian guy had left behind pliers and a few pieces of gear, so I grabbed it all, loaded up my stuff and tried to catch him in the parking lot. I was still wearing flip-flops, and the temperature had climbed to just under 100 degrees, so there was no way I was going to run.

As you might have guessed, I missed him.

The pliers he'd left were nice, so I considered it a small consolation for the shark's sacrifice and moved on to my next spot, still reeling from the loss of that massive shark and wondering if sacrificing the pliers for a shark was worth it to the other guy.

Key Deer

Though the loss of that massive shark weighed heavily upon me, I shook it off, realizing how blessed I was to be in the Florida Keys. For years, I'd dreamed about coming here to tangle with sharks and the dozens of exotic fishes that called these waters home, so I forced myself to be positive and appreciate my good fortune.

I arrived at Big Pine Key, home of the Key Deer, a subspecies of Whitetail Deer about the size of a large dog. In high school, I subscribed to as many as 15 outdoor magazines at a time. There were the big names like *Field and Stream*, *Outdoor Life*, *American Hunter* and *North American Fisherman*, as well as smaller titles like *Fur, Fish, Game* and the out of print *Fishing and Hunting News*. I loved them all and had every intention of becoming a professional hunter, outfitter, or fishing guide someday, but as I discussed earlier, life didn't work out that way for me.

As my life changed, so, too, did my expectations. Who I was changed. This included my interests. Fishing remained an all-consuming passion, but hunting, which I'd once loved almost as much, just sort of went away. I wasn't opposed to it, but a successful big game hunting trip means the season is over. A successful fishing trip, on the other hand, involves catching and releasing fishes all day then coming back and doing it again. It was an easy choice for me.

That said, the knowledge I gained from the decade of reading hundreds of hunting articles didn't leave me, nor did my fascination with wild animals. One of the things I learned was just how much hunters and anglers do for conservation. In fact, the majority of funding for fish and wildlife management in the United States comes from hunters, trappers, and anglers. I once wrote an article for the Recreational Boating and Fishing Foundation (RBFF) with special regards to angler participation in the state of Oregon. It specifically addressed the financial impact of sportsmen and women in the state of Oregon, a fairly representative state in terms of how wildlife funds are derived.

In Oregon, federal funds account for exactly one third of all monies (33.4 percent) but are only received if sufficient matching funds are raised. Where then, does the Oregon Department of Fish and Wildlife make up the difference? Simple: hunters, trappers and anglers.

"You can do a lot of other outdoor activities, but the one thing that's different about fishing is that by actually fishing, you're conserving the great water resources you're playing on," RBFF President Frank Peterson said to me at ICAST a few years before. It got me to look into it further, and when I did, I was taken aback. Fully $130 million annually (using 2019 numbers) comes from hunters, trappers and anglers in the state of Oregon, but the benefits of these funds are realized by anyone who goes outside.

While boaters, kayakers, paddle boarders, canoers, snorkelers, scuba divers, birdwatchers, hikers, bikers, runners, spelunkers, beachcombers, climbers, skiers, snowboarders, sledders, campers, swimmers and other outdoors enthusiasts may individually elect to contribute time or money to the betterment of our wildlands, they are not automatically paying to preserve our natural resources like anglers are. Though some might contribute individually, you don't need a hiking or snowboarding license, so while these activities might not technically be consumptive, they also contribute nothing to wildlife and wildlands management.

Key Deer are a federally protected endangered subspecies of Whitetail Deer, so what does hunting have to do with that? Well, as noted above, hunters have long been leading conservationists in the United States and abroad, second only to anglers in their financial contributions to the outdoors. So when I got the chance to see the Key Deer I'd read so much about over the years, I was stoked.

It didn't take long, either. Almost immediately, I saw a pair of them.

Though about as tall as a German shepherd, Key Deer have the body size of a border collie; it's just elevated on spindly legs. I was able to get shockingly close to the little deer to take some pictures, but of course I didn't touch them or get close enough to frighten them. Apparently, most Key Deer mortality is from automobile collisions each year, so the last thing I wanted was to contribute to the human familiarity that caused these accidents in the first place. Snapping a few more pictures, I moved to the other side of the island and made another stop to fish.

Crappy Behavior

The next stop was disappointing. I caught some Pinfish, Lane Snapper, and Bermuda Chub, but after the latter pooped all over me, I figured that was my sign to move. Bermuda Chub are famous for that, actually. Most of the Bermuda Chubs I've caught sprayed green-brown filth with unfortunate volume and power of stream. Much of this just landed on my hands and arms, but enough got on my pants and sunglasses that I did a lot of rinsing in the brine. I wasn't about to let one crappy experience cramp my style, so I pressed on.

The next stop looked promising, so I felt validated in my choice to move. On the upstream (at least, given the tidal patterns at the time) side of the bridge, there was a small landing area. It offered maybe 20 feet of waterside access, but it was tightly hemmed in by trees to the north and a large concrete bridge to the south. I set up my shark rod, realizing a stingray was probably more likely here given the way the shallow, sandy channel looked.

Then I got to work fishing my sabiki.

Before I landed the third grunt or snapper or other time-filling skunk-stopper, a group of six people came up. Had I not been there, it still would've been uncomfortably cramped for them. Only three or four people could realistically fish here, and that would be shoulder-to-shoulder.

Given that I'd arrived first, I was centered in the small space.

They came to the edge of the platform I was on and started pointing, speaking loudly in Spanish. Now, I don't speak a lot of Spanish, but I speak a little. I spent a few weeks in Spain as part of a teaching fellowship with *National Geographic* magazine one summer (yes, that's a flex), and I get by with survival Spanish. Add in all of the recreational indoor soccer I've played over the years, and I also know a lot of slurs and profanity. Without even turning around, I could hear "susto" (scare) and "gringo" (slur) multiple times. I rolled my eyes and braced myself.

These weren't young men, as I'd expected. It was a group of three couples, two younger (maybe in their 30s) and an older couple that appeared to be their parents in their 50s or 60s.

Despite what I knew I was about to endure, I tried to be friendly, going so far as to offer them some bait. Optimistically, I thought maybe only one or two of them would try to fish and would at least give me some space. Not a chance.

They all butted up against me, immediately snagging the line of my shark/stingray rod and then cursing me for it. Realizing that it was a lost battle, I reeled it up and continued working with my sabiki.

Out came the alcohol.

The women were already quite intoxicated when they arrived, and in such close proximity, I could smell it on all of them.

Because I'm a damn good angler and fishing for small stuff in the Keys is remarkably easy if you know what you're doing, I outfished their entire group 5:1. They didn't like that.

Again, I offered advice and bait, but they refused.

They began making comments and though I was fishing almost straight down, they snagged my last line.

One of them got dizzy from fishing "tan alto," which means something like "from high up" or "so high," I think. Again, there's a reason Spanish isn't listed on my resume. Regardless, she had to go sit down.

In reality, the seawall was 10 or 12 feet above the surface on one end and slanted down to about two feet on the other, but alcohol does lots of harm to the human body in intense heat.

By the third time my line was snagged, only two of them were still fishing, the rest having resigned themselves to drinking on the ground behind us while jeering at the gringo.

A normally chill Luke can be stubborn when push comes to shove. There were other places to go, other places to fish, but I just didn't feel like bowing down to let a bunch of drunk idiots bully me away. So I didn't. For some reason, I was ready for a fight.

When one of the more inebriated women cussed at me in Spanish, I said "You know, there's really not room for all of us here. Since I was here first, you really should just go to the other side. It's flat, the sunset is visible from that side, and you'd have a better time drinking there with more room to sit."

Her husband or boyfriend or whatever stood, and I thought I was about to be attacked, but I figured I could just parry and toss them harmlessly into the ocean behind me if need-be.

Instead, he stood, cussed at me again and then realized I was probably right. I think it was the sunset comment, because the older couple sitting and drinking White Claws or wine coolers or whatever it was pointed to the sunset, shrugged, and they moved.

The particularly venomous woman threw her can on the ground near me (maybe at me?), cussed aloud, and then stomped off. They were still close enough that I could hear them yelling and smashing glass bottles minutes later on the other side of the bridge, but crisis averted, right?

I like Assertive Luke. He doesn't come out often, but he usually does when he needs to. Assertive Luke lucked into a large school of Redear Herring moments later, and, using one as live bait, hooked into a large Jack Crevalle moments after that. I fought it for a few minutes before it broke off the 60-pound steel leader. Two in one day?! Keys fishes are something else.

Minutes later, I hooked a smaller stingray on the sabiki, but the 10-pound mainline wasn't enough to hold it away from the bridge piling when it ran, despite my best, most gentle efforts, and it broke me off. You win some, you lose some, but I was glad I'd taken a stand for that spot even if I hadn't caught anything big or new. I'd still cleaned up on smaller fishes and earned an early dinner.

It wasn't Shark Week, but I lived like it.

Lockout

This night should've ended with me getting a nice dinner and going to sleep. It should've, but it didn't.

I returned to Looe Key Resort. For some reason, my reservation had been two separate reservations, one per night, so I returned with the expectation of checking in at the same time that night. Except this was a Saturday night instead of Friday. That shouldn't have made a difference, but I returned to silence when I'd expected an endless loop of mediocre-at-best Jimmy Buffet renditions. The resort was deserted.

Nobody was in the office, nobody was in the bar, and there was no "Manager" or "Caretaker" office. I knew I had to be in the same room, so I tried to see if I could get in somehow, walking around both sides, trying both doors, and trying to get through the window. No dice.

Not only would I not get in, but I'd almost get arrested. Hedging my bets, I called the police to see if they happened to have an after-hours contact. They did not.

"Cool cool cool cool cool," I said aloud.

"What?" asked the dispatcher.

"Oh, nothing," I replied, failing to realize I'd said something I'd picked up years before from Abed Nadir's character in *Community* aloud.

"Have a good night," I said.

After 20 minutes of fruitlessly exploring my options, I shifted gears and began calling nearby hotels, hoping I'd be able to get a refund after the fact.

I called every hotel, motel, lodge, and resort within an hour. Everyone was booked or closed that wonderful Saturday evening. Finally, I got a place about 40 minutes away. The night manager was just leaving, but she assured me she'd stay until I arrived.

Skipping dinner, I drove straight there and checked in just before midnight. I was exhausted but grateful I'd found a place to sleep. I wasn't quite ready to be a beach bum, so it panned out.

To the credit of the Looe Key Resort, I got a refund for that second night.

Chapter 20
Shark Weak

June 30, 2019

Day 16
Origin: Looe Key, Florida
Destination: Marathon, Florida

"When life gives you Lemons, you unhook them and let them go."
Luke Ovgard || American Shark Aficionado

I was in a different spot than I'd so meticulously planned for, and that hurt the anal-retentive planner in me, but it also fed the whimsical, spur-of-the-moment part of me, and the internal turmoil raged. I overslept and decided to get breakfast (something I hadn't yet done in the Keys), but it was a Sunday morning, and that was a bad life choice. Still, hot food in the morning helped me rebound from the past two evenings' worth of ... eventfulness.

What did I do? I went right back to the place I'd had the confrontation the night before. This time, however, I was completely alone; apparently my inebriated friends were sleeping it off.

Dinking around with the needlefish in hopes one might be an Atlantic Needlefish, *Strongylura marina* (the other needlefish I'd long tried and failed to catch) proved successful, but both fish I caught were Redfin Needlefish, *Strongylura notata*. Being neither large nor hard-fighting, I gave up on the needlefish and turned my attention back to sharks and stingrays.

The bite was much slower that morning, probably a combination of factors, but the bright sun and higher tide couldn't have helped. It took me a while longer to get a White Grunt for bait, but once I did, I didn't have to wait long before a shark took it.

It was a respectable Bonnethead Shark, just a little larger than my first one. Fortunately, this one was not gut-hooked, and I was able to pop the hook and let it go. Then, the bite died.

Not even Pinfish or grunts seemed interested anymore, and I'd learned the hard way — from dating — not to pursue quarry that has no interest in you. Dating sucks, but there are, in fact, plenty of fish in the sea (I use fish here and not fishes because even though women are a different species than men, all women — err, fish — are the same species).

Sketchville, USA

You've probably seen anglers waist-deep in aquamarine waters casting flies for bonefish on the flats in the Florida Keys or read about it in flowery, almost romantic language. If not, Google "Florida Keys Bonefish" to see what I'm talking about.

I'll wait.

No, really.

It's a pleasant image to have in your mind, that tranquil calm of a tropical oceanscape. With that image in mind, I passed a long, low bridge with that same crystalline, aquamarine water. It spanned out in every direction, there was little wind, and I figured maybe I could get a bonefish from the bridge. This almost never happens, but if I let long odds deter me, I wouldn't be a Bengals fan. For those who don't follow football, the Bengals have never won a Super Bowl (they've lost three, one to the Rams and two to the stupid 49ers). At the time I took this trip, they hadn't won a divisional playoff game since the 1988 AFC Championship. Apart from a Wildcard win in 1991, at the time of this trip, my team hadn't won a single playoff game in my lifetime. In recent years, they're finally good again, and made strong runs in the 2021-2022 and 2022-2023 seasons, but they still haven't won a Super Bowl. Yet, I'm still a fan.

I parked and walked back to the bridge.

Like many bridges in the Keys, there was a walkway designed for fishing, strolling, and photography parallel to the highway bridge. Also like many bridges in the Keys, it had been damaged by a recent hurricane, and the powers that be hadn't gotten around to fixing it yet. I was ready to just give up and go back to the car. Well, not ready, but resigned to it. Then I realized there was access for me to fish under the bridge. It likely would've been productive when the tide was up and though I saw some fish, they were skittish.

So I did what any logical person who'd seen the die-hard flyfishermen chasing bonefish do: I waded in. The water was warm and not terribly deep. Deep enough to give a newer, less crass meaning to "balls deep" and deep enough to make me face some logistical issues. Where did I put bait? Where did I put my phone? After all, I was wearing board shorts and flip-flops. I removed my T-shirt to keep that dry, and just sort of waded out until I saw fishes hovering around a piling. They were mostly parrotfish, and I was desperate to catch one. So I tried. Then I tried again. After a few attempts that only resulted in spooking the vibrant creatures with every cast, I tried casting well upstream of the piling and allowing the current to push it down. Still no.

There were probably better options, I convinced myself, as I headed back to the safety of shore.

Walking under the bridge to my car took me past the rusty, chain-link fence that closed off the fishing pier. Hmm.

With a fluid grace you'd have to have seen to believe, I slid under the fence. My serpentine form stayed low to the ground because I figured if I could get under the fence undetected, maybe I could catch some fishes before an overzealous citizen called me in. The signage didn't prohibit fishing; I think it was just a safety issue to keep people off the post-hurricane structure. I'd just waded almost half a mile into the ocean, so I figured I'd just keep the string of questionable decisions going. YOLO.

Below me, I could see dozens of parrotfish, wrasse, and schools of silvery fish I later found to be Bermuda Chubs almost everywhere. I even hooked a parrotfish, but the fish bit through my small hook. Though I managed to land a Buffalo Trunkfish, a species I'd only caught once before (earlier this trip), no parrotfish or wrasse found my bait again.

Chubs kept me busy. I can take a lot of crap. Heck, I took plenty at work over the years from petty people who ruled petty fiefdoms, but at some point, you just can't take anymore. After I had more Bermuda Chub crap on my hands than sweat, I decided it was time to move.

Adios, Sketchville, USA.

Channel 5 Bridge

Anywhere I stopped would be better than Sketchville, USA, I told myself. So I drove to another bridge, one that hadn't been fenced off.

The Florida Keys are latticed with channels. Some are natural, some were put there to allow access for boaters, anglers, and commercial vessels. Since the Keys is a string of islands that is largely uninhabited, something has to connect the islands between the channels.

U.S. Highway 1 does the primary connecting in the Florida Keys, but Tinder is a close second. The highway actually runs up the East Coast all the way to Maine, but in Florida, it is the central artery for the Keys, and as such, it must cross all of those channels. Each crossing requires a bridge, and each bridge requires limited parking. This, my friends, is where shore anglers can focus their efforts.

No bridge in the Keys is more popular with anglers than the Channel 5 Bridge, which has officially produced more than 100 species (and probably has the potential for many more) in its tenure. The very next day, my species count for the trip (not just new ones, mind you, but total species I'd caught on my cross-country road trip) would hit 100. So yeah, it was a special place. As I pulled up, I glanced at Fishbrain and noted the hundreds of catches reported just within the past month. It. Was. Loaded. It almost lived up to the hype for me, too.

Fishbrain's platform is one that relies, like all social media platforms, on crowdsourced data and community building. When you first sign up for Fishbrain (which is free), you can choose to follow Species of Fish, Bodies of Water, Brands, and/or specific Anglers. It operates similarly to Instagram in that you have a feed composed of pictures and videos from whom and what you follow. You can upload a "Catch," which serves much like a post would on other platforms. That's great and all, but I use it most often for its map, where I can scroll through all catches posted within a given area. If the fishing is slow, I can covet these catches, but when the bite is hot, I don't always check.

The bite was hot that day.

After putting out a live bait in a rock pile near the shore, I immediately hooked into a large fish that fought a little differently than the sharks I was used to catching. There was no consistent pulling of line, nor was there a rapid run, jump, or display of raw kinetic force.

Instead, it was just as if I'd hooked a rock that would pull back ever-so-slightly if I let up the pressure. So I refused to let up on the pressure. It took a few minutes, but I was loaded for sharks, and I got the five-foot Green Moray, *Gymnothorax funebris* all the way to the surface. I was up on a small seawall, and as I debated what to do with it, I considered just jerking it up and out of the water. Likely I would've been the first and last person to "boat flip" an eel that size. These famously ill-tempered fishes have put many an angler in the hospital, and I wasn't about to join that list because my out-of-state emergency room copay is ridiculous. I was going to just gently lift it up to my side, avoiding the small crowd that had gathered.

In my moment of indecision, I let up on the pressure. The eel dove over the nearest rock with my 60-pound steel leader hanging out of its mouth, grating the line on the rocks so, as the angle steepened, it snapped the heavy line like twine. That one stung.

Though I saw a few stingrays and sharks in the hours that followed, I caught neither a large fish nor a new one. The Channel 5 Bridge did me dirty.

Channel 2 Bridge

Sort of dejected and listless, I planned to grab an iced coffee somewhere. Normally, I drink two cups of coffee in the morning before leaving home and don't touch it again during the day. Turns out that standing in tropical heat fishing 16 to 18 hours per day takes a toll on the body after weeks and weeks, and I needed the caffeine. Starbucks was only 15 minutes away, as I'd done a bit of backtracking that day to get to Channel 5, so I again embraced my inner White girl. Unsweetened Nitro Cold Brew never tasted so sweet.

The break timed out well, and before I could slip into the depression that had only hit me late at night in the loneliest waking hours thus far, Casey messaged me, asking to meet up that night to do some fishing. It was on.

We both did some research and decided to subtract the three strikes from Channel 5 and head to Channel 2. There had been several sharks caught and logged there on Fishbrain, and he said he'd driven by and thought it looked promising. Promising was more than I could see in my immediate future, so I headed out, arriving there shortly before him.

There was a little isthmus of sand, reef, and rock stretching out past several bridge pilings, an obvious wreck, and a sort of back-eddy where the isthmus met the wreck, and it looked as "sharky" as anything I'd seen this side of the Discovery Channel — save for maybe *Street Sharks*.

Though Redear Herring and snappers kept me busy for 15 minutes or so, once I had some bait in my bucket, I moved to the wreck. I tossed out my live bait and hoped for the best. I kid you not, it was less than two minutes before I got a hit. The fish wasn't massive, but it pulled.

I battled to keep it out of the wreck. The current helped me do this, as did the heavy gear. I corralled the shark around the isthmus (I've now written that word more in this chapter than during the rest of my life combined), between another, smaller wreck, and a sharp rocky outcropping and into a sheltered pool at the foot of the bridge piling. Though I wasn't sure what it was at the time, I suspected Lemon Shark. After keeping its head submerged while I dug around for my pliers to unhook it, Casey arrived (perfect timing) and took a few pictures while I got it unhooked and released.

It was, in fact, a Lemon Shark.

Species #317 — Lemon Shark *(Negaprion brevirostris)*.

Casey had yet to catch a shark, so I offered him my heavy rod. He chose to use his own, and though grossly undermatched for any large sharks we might encounter, it would've handled smaller sharks (like the Lemon I'd just caught) without issue. He did hook into one soon after, but it got off. He hooked one or two more while I continued using my heavy rod, repeatedly offering him its use.

A lighter tackle shark would be incredible, so I didn't begrudge his hope, but it meant he had to let them run and couldn't power them in and around the wreck as easily, and therein stood the problem.

I hooked into a Nurse Shark next, which I fought to shore, photographed and released just as night fell. Casey then agreed to use my rod, but at this point, the tide shifted, and the sharks disappeared.

While I dinked around with the lighter rod, I heard a group of kids behind me hook into something impressive. It wasn't a shark, but it was definitely a respectable game fish. I assumed a small tarpon, jack, or a big snapper. Turns out, it was the latter. They'd hooked into a massive snapper, maybe 10 pounds or so. Just as we got into the excitement of the moment, it stopped fighting. The kid looked flustered as he sat there for a moment and watched his slack line while still feeling weight. Then, in a heartbeat, the line took off, the rod bent over, and there was a sudden slackness again.

He reeled in the front third or so of what had been a 10- or 12-pound Mutton Snapper, *Lutjanus analis* with a single, shockingly large bite just behind the pectoral fins that arched back and removed the better part of the fish.

His eyes went wide, and then ours did, too.

Casey and I shone our lamps into the water and quickly spotted the culprit: A seven- or eight-foot Bull Shark, *Carcharhinus leucas*. Naturally, we tried to get it to bite one of our much smaller baits for as long as we could, but by then the tide had brought in all sorts of thick, soupy muck and surface vegetation that caused us to repeatedly get hung up.

We held out until reality struck, and our last live bait over eight inches died on the hook. Though I would've loved to catch that shark, a part of me is also glad I didn't...

Chapter 21
The Conch Republic

July 1, 2019

Day 17
Origin: Marathon, Florida
Destination: Lauderdale-by-the-Sea, Florida

"Empires do not in fact appear, rise, reign, decline and fall according to some recurrent and predictable life cycle. It is historians who retrospectively portray the process of imperial dissolution as slow-acting. Rather, empires behave like all complex adaptive systems. They function in apparent equilibrium for some unknowable period. And then, quite abruptly, they collapse."
Niall Ferguson || Scottish Historian || From *Los Angeles Times*

July 4, 1776.
February 17, 1815.
July 16, 1861.
April 15, 1865.
December 7, 1941.
June 6, 1944.
October 1962.
September 11, 2001.

Though not comprehensive, this list includes the dates most significant to the independence and sovereignty of the United States. Had events on these days been just slightly different, America as we know it might have ceased to exist. These dates shaped the future of the independent United States perhaps more than any others. Chronologically, these keystone events in American history are listed below:

July 4, 1776 — The United States declared its independence from Great Britain and plunged into war.

February 17, 1815 — The United States finalized peace with Great Britain after the War of 1812 and cemented itself as a capable and independent nation on the world's stage.

July 16, 1861 — The Confederates routed the Union at First Manassas. Gray troops celebrated just 20 miles from a largely undefended Washington, D.C., but failed to press on and capture the city — a move that likely would've split the U.S. in two or at the very least, perpetuated slavery in a likely no longer United States for decades beyond the Civil War.

April 15, 1865 — President Lincoln was assassinated, rocking an already unstable country to its core.

December 7, 1941 — The Empire of Japan attacked Pearl Harbor. Had it not been Sunday, the U.S. Navy would've been devastated, but given ships were relatively empty and many not in the harbor, the U.S. entered the war close to full strength.

June 6, 1944 — Allied Commander Dwight D. Eisenhower prepared for the D-Day assault. He wrote speeches for both victory and defeat, placing the odds of success at Normandy and those of failure and the subsequent Allied defeat in Europe at 50/50.

October 1962 — The Cuban Missile Crisis brought the U.S. closer to nuclear war with the Soviet Union than ever before or since.

September 11, 2001 — Terrorists attacked the World Trade Centers, setting a new precedent for war against ideologies and not overt national interests, thus changing the American way of life.

Add one more date to that list: April 23, 1982.

Setting the Scene

In homage to the podcast I listened to quite a lot on this trip, *American History Tellers*, imagine it's 1982. You're a waitress at a restaurant near the beach in Key West, Florida. It's a slow night, really slow for a Friday night during Spring Break.

"Man. It's dead," says Janet, the 43-year-old mother of two you're on shift with tonight.

Your manager, Dale, already sent home the third waitress, realizing there was no need for her.

"No kidding," you reply.

This place is normally hopping with tourists, college coeds, and a host of retirees escaping south to enjoy the perennially nice weather, but it's been dead over the past few months.

"It's that damn inspection station!" complains Janet.

"I don't care if Cubans are fleeing Castro. Let them come! I'm sure they'd tip better than an empty table."

You laugh uneasily. She's not wrong.

Ever since the United States Border Patrol set up that check station north of town on Highway 1 and started implementing mandatory vehicle inspections, the once-steady flow of tourists has turned into a slow trickle.

President Reagan's new minimum wage of $3.35 went into effect last year, but prices are catching up now, and without all the tips from happy vacationers, you'll have a hard time making rent this month. After the holiday season, you fight through a lean January and February every year and really count on Spring Break, but this has been a disaster.

"I'm gonna take a break," you tell Dale, who just waves you off, clearly engrossed in the Braves game he's watching. Why he cares so much about baseball, you'll never know. Florida doesn't even have a team!

Shaking your head, you pop out to the alley.

One of the cooks, Ernesto, is smoking a cigarette. He smiles and nods at you.

"Hey Ernesto," you say, stealing away below the naked bulb overhanging the door.

You reach into your apron and pull out two crumpled bills and some change. Disgusted, you count out $2.79. For a Friday night, during Spring Break?!

You shake your head, following Ernesto back inside. Part of you wonders what he thinks about the inspection station, being from Cuba himself. You almost ask, but you keep it to yourself. You know he fled Cuba after they passed the Cuban Adjustment Act back when you were a kid. That allowed Cubans who made it to the United States to pursue citizenship legally. He's been here, what, 15 years now? You've met his wife, Sonita, and their daughter Yanet. Yanet is going to college in Tallahassee next summer.

You voted for Reagan, as did almost everyone else you know in Monroe County, but why is his administration doing this? Can't he see how Key West's economy is suffering?

Why does the government want to stop Cubans from coming? You'd be fine with more people like Ernesto and his family around; their money is just as green as anyone else's, and you need people spending money for Key West to survive.

Maybe the mayor is right. Maybe something drastic needs to be done...

Secession

On April 23, 1982, Mayor Dennis Wardlow of Key West declared independence from the United States of America, establishing the Conch Republic.

A roadblock border station was set up on the outskirts of Key West to perform vehicle searches earlier that year. The citizens of Key West relied heavily upon tourism, but this roadblock discouraged tourists from driving there. Further complicating the issue, only one airline flew into Key West commercially, so tourism dollars dried up quickly after that station opened.

Residents of Key West had long been at home with the "end of the world" feeling of living there, but they always had a lifeline of out-of-area dollars keeping their economy afloat. Without tourism, Key West was in trouble. The logic behind the secession was: "If you're going to treat us like a foreign border crossing, we might as well be one."

Mayor Wardlow, who became Prime Minister Wardlow in the new nation, hit someone in an American Naval uniform over the head with a loaf of bread as a mock declaration of war, waited for about a minute, and then formally surrendered with the condition that the United States supply $1 billion in foreign aid. It was more a publicity stunt than anything, but it worked. Soon after the secession, the checkpoint was removed, and Key West's economy rebounded. The move had unintended conch-sequences, though. The faux secession would fuel increased fervor amongst secessionists nationwide, leading to at least half a dozen serious secession attempts in states such as Alaska, California, Florida, and my home state of Oregon in the decades that followed.

Key West

I couldn't leave the Keys without visiting Key West, so I made sure to detour down to the Conch Republic before making my way back north. Key West is a tourist trap, and the "Southernmost Point of the Continental United States" marker had a long line full of people waiting patiently for heat stroke, so I walked by and snapped a picture after making the sacrifice and opting not to have my picture taken with it. I have no photographic proof I stood there, so you'll just have to take my word for it.

The "Conch Republic" theme prevailed everywhere, and I spent a few hours appreciating the kitschness of Key West. It almost felt like a foreign country. Everything was brightly-colored, tourists were Disney-thick in some places, and every business on the main streets seemed to cater to visitors rather than residents.

The unique history and otherworldliness could only entertain me for so long, though, so I began making my way north.

Sure, I'd surrendered a lot of time indulging the nostalgia and unique history of this place, but it could've been worse; I could've been stopped by Border Patrol and had my car searched. Even though I had nothing to hide, the inconvenience of it all was horrifying. My car wasn't searched, but I was almost pulled over.

Cellphones

The date was July 1, 2019, which will hold no significance in American History but will go down as a significant date in Florida's history. Now, Florida gets a bad rap, but it tends not to have as much legal or judicial red tape as other places around the country. That's great for business, for people who want to retire in peace, and for criminals. It's also largely why so many exotic species have been released into the ecosystem here.

One law Florida simply didn't have prior to this date involved cellphone use while driving. Virtually every other state I'd been to (and I'd been to 33 states by the time I finished this trip) had laws prohibiting or at least limiting cellphone use while driving. To be fair, texting and driving was already illegal in Florida, but you could use it for other purposes such as phone calls, emails, or streaming your favorite Netflix series. This ban simply mirrored the bans found in most other states by broadly prohibiting handheld cellphone use while driving.

Obviously, I'd never use my phone with someone else in the car, but when it's just me, and I'm traveling hundreds of miles through desolation, I'll admit I've used my phone. Okay, not only in desolate places. That day, I was using it to find and navigate to a restaurant in Key West before heading back up north, while driving. A cop saw me, but I'm not new at being a petty criminal. As I always do when I come across a cop while using my phone, I simply let it drop from my hand and immediately reach for my water bottle, bringing it up for a long draught and holding it there. This makes it appear as though I was just fiddling with my water bottle, and as always, this cop bought it.

Now, am I proud of being a lawbreaker?

I mean, if I wasn't willing to live life on the edge, I probably wouldn't have been in Florida, right? Besides, only a day before, it hadn't been illegal, so that justifies my bad behavior, right?

To the kids at home: please don't use your phone while driving. It's really not wise.

Do what I say, not what I do.

Retrospect

In retrospect, one of my biggest mistakes on this trip was not spending more time in the Florida Keys.

Okay, apart from that one drunken night at the strip club, it was the biggest mistake. I'm kidding, of course! There was more than one drunken night at the strip club.

After such an incredible time in the best part of Florida, it was hard to leave. During my first three days there, I'd landed 277 fishes representing 33 species. This was without microfishing or fishing from a boat. I also spent fully a third of my fishing time in the Keys targeting sharks, which limited my species haul dramatically.

This final day, as I made my way north from Key West to Lauderdale-by-the-Sea for my next Couchsurfing stay, would reaffirm my hesitance to leave. Fishes are everywhere in the Keys, and even though I'd tried all of my key "spots" marked out and researched ahead of time, I decided to just look for a slightly different habitat. My next stop wasn't planned. It was simply a place I stopped because I wanted to fish, and I'm incredibly glad I did so.

A 30-something guy with a beard and a regrettably dark T-shirt for the punishing heat pulled out a respectable Mangrove Snapper before I'd even set up below the bridge. It was every bit of two pounds, and he tossed it into his cooler with that subtle swagger only an angler who's just caught a decent fish in front of another angler can know.

I smiled, complimented his catch, and then proceeded to flex on him myself. I caught a half-dozen snappers and grunts before he caught his second fish. Mine were all smaller, but he didn't seem to care, telling me he'd "Fished his spot out," before heading back to his car 100 feet away and then driving off into the asphalt mirage.

Without company, I began getting serious, noticing the parrotfish that had eluded me thus far feinting in and out of view below my feet as they nipped particles of something or other off of the seawall. Without a doubt, catching one would make my day, so I spent the next incalculable period of time in the summer heat trying to land a parrot. It was difficult getting past the churning, almost mechanical swarm of fishes that mobbed my bait every time it hit the water, but I learned the pattern and got into a rhythm.

Side note: Even as someone who has written for (at least part of) a living since 2013, some words still trouble me. The two words I can never spell are camaraderie and rhythm Sad for a fairly sociable if untalented drummer, no? As I typed those words above, both attempts spawned the telltale red squiggly lines, proving my point. This chapter isn't about spelling, though, so before I get out of rhythm (misspelled it again), I'll get back to what matters: fishing.

If I could get my bait to the bottom quickly, I had a chance, but the dozens of little sergeants, grunts, and snappers kept my blood pressure almost as high as the humidity. Blessedly, a new species, the Spotted Trunkfish, kept the ulcer away.

Species #318 — Spotted Trunkfish (*Lactophrys bicaudalis*).

Well, that was something, at least.

Three times I hooked parrotfish, and three times the colorful bastards broke my line or hook or spirit with their beak-like teeth. The fourth fish was much larger — well over five pounds — and I knew I had a solid hookset. What I didn't have was line strong enough to avoid being grated on the cement edge when the large parrotfish dove under the concrete lip near the base of the seawall.

Another guy showed up, cooler in hand, and started catching snapper, but I was in another world. I was irritated. Those little fishes were stopping and inspecting every bait I tried to get down to the bottom, and suddenly I sympathized with the Conch Republic and its complaint with the Border Patrol.

Just as I was about to secede from my spot and head north, I hooked parrotfish No. 5, and that Lou Bega song played in my head as I battled the fish. It was a small Rainbow Parrotfish, but that didn't stop me from asking my new neighbor to take a picture for me. After all, it was a fish I'd desperately been targeting with no success, and I'd only posed with sharks and groupers thus far in my trip.

Species #319 — Rainbow Parrotfish (*Scarus guacamaia*).

I put the fish in the freshly dipped bucket of saltwater I carried with me to keep the hapless creature alive and fresh while I walked over to the other fishermen.

"Do I look like a sweaty beast?" I asked, laughing awkwardly as I grabbed my parrotfish from the bucket for a photo.

"Yeah, but who cares?" he replied, taking the photo too quickly for it to have been any good and then getting back to his work.

"Oh," I thought to myself. "So I guess I won't have a memorable parrotfish picture after all."

The photo was about as bad as I'd expected, but I had to let the fish go. Shrugging, I began targeting the indigo and azure parrotfish that ghosted in and out of the living throng below me. They had to be Blue Parrotfish, *Scarus coeruleus* and Midnight Parrotfish, *Scarus coelestinus* and they were much larger than the Rainbow Parrotfish I'd just landed.

When I finally hooked one of the big ones, I was excited. This would not only be a new species, but the Midnight Parrotfish is just about the coolest-looking thing that swims. With a deep blue-black coloration interspersed with all-white scales reminiscent of stars on a night sky, it's truly one-of-a-kind and a mascot nominee for Key West.

Unfortunately, it wasn't a Midnight Parrotfish.

It was a massive Rainbow Parrotfish.

The IGFA world record for this species is 10 pounds 12 ounces. Had I known this when I caught my eight-pounder, I would've likely been a little less excited, but I made sure to get good pictures and measurements before letting that fish go.

World record or not, it was a fish I was very proud of, and I rewarded myself by heading to my car and grabbing an ice-cold coconut water, a cheese stick, and granola bar to go with the slice of humble pie I'd been repeatedly served by parrotfish all week.

With my commitment to the spot renewed, I spent another hour there. I threw out my heavy rod in hopes of catching another Nurse Shark while continuing my surgical removal of every small fish below me. While the Nurse wasn't in, the doctor was. My final new species at that spot was a fairly surprising catch, the Doctorfish Tang.

Species #320 — Doctorfish Tang (*Acanthurus chirurgus*).

Interestingly enough, once they reach adulthood, the Doctorfish Tang is a somewhat solitary fish. As such, it's one type of doctor that spends far less time in schools than its human namesake. Tang, that was a bad joke.

Afterthoughts

Once more I stopped at the Channel 5 Bridge, and once more I was disappointed. A few common fishes weren't enough to keep me there longer than a few hours, and that Green Moray I'd lost at the seawall days before was nowhere to be found.

So, in the waning moments of my trip to the Conch Republic, I returned to my very first stop in Islamorada, hoping for one of the Scrawled Filefish I'd twice hooked and lost there.

Naturally, I also set out a live bait for sharks because sharks are so awesome we give them a week-long holiday. Only a handful of our national heroes get holidays and even then, it's a day. Sharks get a whole week. #SharkWeek.

In fact, Jeff Winger from the TV series *Community* said it best: "You know what makes humans different from other animals?

We're the only species on Earth that observes Shark Week. Sharks don't even observe Shark Week."

Though the trunkfish never materialized, and I failed to catch another new species, the Doctorfish Tang was not my last medically-themed fish of the day. That honor went to a five-foot Nurse Shark that crushed my live bait and left me with an incredibly risky climb down a slick, rocky slope in flip-flops.

I landed it, kept its gills submerged and prepared to take the most epic selfie of my life. I'm used to fishing alone (cue world's smallest violin), so I've become proficient at propping up my phone on a stick, tying it to a tree with a scrunchie, or creating elaborate lakeside cairns that will induce speculation by future generations just to brace my phone and enable me to use my front-facing camera with a timer.

It's how I've captured trophy shots for posterity since I first got my iPhone, and like the latest iPhone's camera, today I'm light years ahead of my origins. Still, propping up your phone, bending over to grab a 60-plus-pound shark, and then posing with it in frame is a selfie not even the most vapid Kardashian wannabe could accomplish. So when I did it, TMZ was there waiting.

That maverick, one-of-a-kind, fearlessness of the Conch Republic must've rubbed off on me because I got an epic picture of me holding a shark just a foot shorter than me at eye level. You can barely even tell that holding it that high was straining my body to the absolute limit.

I finished my time in the Keys with an independent feat that Mayor — nay, Prime Minister — Wardlow would appreciate.

Chapter 22
Snakeheads

July 2, 2019

Day 18
Origin: Lauderdale-by-the-Sea, Florida
Destination: Lauderdale-by-the-Sea, Florida

"No two persons ever read the same book."
Edmund Wilson || American Author

Thus far on my trip, I'd spent a lot of time Couchsurfing, and I'd seen a spectrum of houses and apartments ranging from poor to palatial.

When I arrived at Bob Zanengo's place in Lauderdale-by-the-Sea, I went into the parking garage below tower apartments. After spending about 10 minutes actually getting lost in the massive underground parking structure, I met Bob at my designated parking space, and we quickly hit it off.

Bob was taller than me, which is out of the ordinary. He had silver hair and the summer glow Florida seems to generously bestow on its residents. He was retired from a career in HR technology — a very niche career, to be sure — and he had an eternal youth about him that I found refreshing.

Of all the folks I would Couchsurf with this summer, I got on better with him than anyone. I appreciated Bob's uniqueness. I'm different myself, and so was this conservative gay Catholic Southerner with a penchant for travel and cutting-edge technology. He wasn't the Dos Equis man, but he could certainly enter the contest for the Most Interesting Man on Earth. We talked about life, faith, politics, work, and even shared our tastes in television, which had moderate overlap.

Not only did we get along, but his apartment was incredible. It wasn't massive, but it was clean, sleek, and European, well-appointed and boasted an incredible view from the patio that looked over the shoreline within throwing distance for someone with a better arm than I possess.

I sound like his realtor, but it was truly a great place. Perhaps my favorite part was the ultramodern shower in the guest bathroom that, while not a true rain shower, was an experience in and of itself.

I was Bob's first Couchsurfer, so he didn't know what to expect, but I think he was just as glad to find himself not murdered in the night as I was during my first couple of Couchsurfing stays. His hospitality bespoke his Georgian roots, and he made me an incredible breakfast that included homemade biscuits. He made cookies. He even made me dinner one night. Not all Florida men are Florida Man.

The stay with Bob was so different from any of my other Couchsurfing stays on my trip that it really stood out. We exchanged numbers and even shared television series recommendations in the months that followed, and I watched the unique Irish comedy *Catastrophe* on Amazon at his recommendation. It didn't disappoint.

In fact, the only thing Bob and I didn't seem to bond over was fishing. I invited him to go both days I was there, but he politely declined. No worries, but I was there to fish, so each morning, after a delicious homemade breakfast, we'd part ways, and I would go explore Broward County's fishing opportunities in the stifling heat to earn my fancy shower every night.

Snakehead

The first day was tough fishing, so thankfully I had Audible to keep me company, but there was a time when audiobooks and television weren't my time-fillers. Prior to college, video games and outdoor magazines filled this void. Perhaps one of my mildly popular tweets said it best:

"Things men should outgrow some time in their 20s:
- Video games
- Partying
- Snapchat
- Sweeping generalizations"

Follow me @LukeOvgard on Twitter if my unique brand of funny *and* pitiful is your thing.

I definitely outgrew video games sometime during or just after college. Regardless, video games in my youth were somewhat beneficial, as were the magazines, but like much of what I tend to enjoy, I can easily become obsessed. I mean, I subscribed to 15 outdoor magazines, and I spent hours every day playing video games after work, school, or practice for whichever of the five sports I played in high school was happening at the time. For a cash-strapped high school student, that represented a sizable chunk of my income and time. Still, I played. Still, I read.

Ten to 15 years ago, popular topics in these magazines included wolf management in the Lower 48, restoration and expansion of elk populations south and east, and managing invasive "monster" fishes such as snakehead.

Snakehead were vilified early as they began to expand their territory into South Florida and the Potomac Basin. While Northern Snakehead, *Channa argus* reigned supreme up north, Bullseye Snakehead, *Channa marulius*, specifically the Mae Khlong Bullseye Snakehead, *Channa aurolineata,* reigns in Florida. I was directed to a 2019 paper by Eleanor Adomson and Ralf Britz published in the *Raffles Journal of Zoology* titled "The Mae Khlong Basin as the potential origin of Florida's feral bullseye snakehead fish (Pisces: Channidae)" by my friend Ryan Crutchfield of FishMap.com, which narrowed it down.

These fishes are capable of breathing air and moving — albeit at an excruciatingly slow pace — overland in serpentine arcs. In a place like Florida, where you can stand at one waterway and find another creek, pond, ditch, canal, or glorified puddle a drop-kick away, it's no wonder that snakehead terrified wildlife managers. What terrified them even more was the Northern Snakehead, which is capable of withstanding much colder water temperatures than the species established in Florida.

Fear of the snakehead led to a widespread hysteria resulting in documentaries, countless doomsday articles, and even a 2004 horror movie called *Snakehead Terror.*

In reality, like all invasive species, the snakehead is a problem at first, but the ecology adapts around it, and eventually, the biome reaches a new normal. Florida has far more widespread and problematic invasives such as the Mayan Cichlid and various tilapia species, and the state has been so inundated with aquarium releases that non-native fishes outnumber native fishes in many waterways. That said, many of these invasives are tolerant of salinity and poor water quality and tend to fill ecological niches that are at best unpalatable for native species and at worst unlivable. Somehow, they've reached some sort of balance.

I guess all of those "COEXIST" bumper stickers spelled with various religious icons finally worked. Good job, Subaru and Prius owners. You did it!

I had marked several locations for snakeheads, some from friends and others from USGS and Fishbrain data. So, one at a time, I began my hunt for snakehead. Like dating apps, I had to strike out a few times before I hooked up. JK. Like Kelly Clarkson, "I Do Not Hook Up." Except on fish. Just not that day, apparently.

I found myself fishing a roadside channelized stretch of the New River. Admittedly, it wasn't very appealing, but you should've seen the Old River. Trust me, this is an improvement.

I more or less just walked the bank, casting lures between the bank and weed bed ahead of me. Though I saw just a single snakehead, I managed to catch several Butterfly Peacock Bass and Mayan Cichlids to keep the skunk off. No snakehead, though.

After walking more than a mile in one direction (but not the band), I came across a giant crusty pipe spanning the river. Since I didn't want to walk back, and I'd parked on that side of the water, I scaled it. It was gated off on one end, but I'm spry and kinda dumb sometimes, so I put my rod between my teeth, tied my flip-flops to the drawstring of my board shorts, and climbed up and around it barefoot. It was rusted metal and exposed to the sun, so I danced atop the pipe while I untied my flip-flops to relieve my feet from the hot steel. Catwalking across made me feel pretty badass until I saw a gator. Then I was just nervous.

I made it down from the pipe and then fished the other side of the river on the long walk back. No dice.

Returning to my car was a bit of a relief, and I quaffed an iced tea, ate a cheese stick and an apple, and began questioning whether a single species was worth all of this effort when I was so close to the brine. By brine, of course, I mean the nearby Atlantic Ocean and not the sweaty miasma brewing beneath my board shorts.

I gave myself an ultimatum: go to the boat ramp, ask for snakehead advice, and then move on. The boat ramp was unassuming. I saw a father and his two tween boys fishing there with one bucket full of Mayan Cichlids and smaller Butterfly Peacock and Florida Bass and another bucket full of live shiners — still no snakehead, though.

Though they weren't exactly killing it, they provided me with the bit of intel I needed: they'd seen a curious snakehead several times, but it just wouldn't play. Pocketing that information for later, I walked the shoreline nearby. It was more natural than where I'd been earlier that day, with undercuts and root wads that sheltered numerous Mayans and peacocks more than eager to gobble my worm with all the vigor of a lonely cougar.

Maybe 30 minutes passed, and I decided to head to the pier and chase saltwater fish. After all, it was a single fish I was after, and odds weren't in my favor. I loaded up my car but noticed the dad and his boys were gone. Shrugging, I went up to the water's edge and looked for the coy fish. Not koi fish, mind you, but that coy snakehead. Sure enough, it was lurking in the shadows at the edge of the deeper water.

Huh.

I grabbed my ultralight rigged with a small jig. I impaled two whole red worms on it in an "X" and slowly fished it along the bottom like a football jig while lying flat on my stomach and peering over the edge of the dock. Once the jig came within a few inches of the snakehead, the fish raised its eyebrows. Okay, that was me. Humanizing fishes is difficult, but I swear that fish was intrigued. I was prone on the dock with just my eyes visible. It looked up at where it expected to see a human, and, failing to see the right profile, chomped down on my bait. I set the hook and landed my first snakehead.

Species #321 — Mae Khlong Snakehead *(Channa aurolineata)*.

What happened next is embarrassing. Not quite "used 'adventure' as a verb on Instagram" embarrassing, but close. Subconsciously, I'd bought into the hype about snakehead because instead of lipping it for the picture, I used pliers. I didn't hurt the fish, but still. Disgusted, sidelong eye emoji, right?

Those magazines had indoctrinated me, I guess. I did realize the error of my ways later that afternoon, but it was too late. I had already been *that guy*.

Anglin's Pier

The hard-won snakehead built up some momentum, and I fully expected to go to the renowned Anglin's Pier and add a few more new species. I mean, it's called "Anglin's Pier," so it had to be tailor-made for fishing, right?

Strangely, despite catching 109 fishes there in the few hours before I'd promised to meet Bob back at the house for dinner, I caught nothing new. Grunts, snapper, Pinfish, Bermuda Chub, and Blue Runner dominated the catch. Before the pier was damaged in a storm and the end closed off sometime in the recent past, I'm sure the access to the deeper water and additional structure held more species and warranted the reputation in its day, but that day had passed.

After dinner, I returned to the pier to try night fishing for a shark or ray. Though I did see several barracudas caught in the wan light, and I even netted a massive one for a rando using a dropnet, I never caught my own. I got the four-foot beast up on my first attempt, photographed the toothy torpedo for the guy who caught it, and this helped me feel like a fractional success even though I failed to catch anything special myself.

Eventually, I gave up on catching small fishes with sabikis and just sat on a bigger live bait while I perused Tinder and Bumble and Hinge. Hot women are native to Florida, but there are plenty of non-natives there, too. In combination, I swiped right more times that night in South Florida than any other single day before or since. But just like the sharks and rays, timing was off, and by the time I noticed the dozen or so matches the next day, I was already on to the next area.

Chapter 23
The Pursuit of Happy

July 3, 2019

Day 19
Origin: Lauderdale-by-the-Sea, Florida
Destination: Fort Lauderdale, Florida

"Your gayness does not define you.
Your Mexican-ness is what defines you, to me."
Michael Scott || From *The Office*

My next Couchsurfing stop took me to the home of Sebastian.
He gave me instructions on where to park and said "look for the big flag." I automatically assumed he meant the United States flag, so I drove past the place the first time around. The second time, I noticed the large Pride Flag, realized I shouldn't assume things, and pulled in.
I knocked, and a friendly face greeted me inside.
Sebastian was watching Netflix, but he said I could shower and relax before settling in, so I did. His home was small but pleasant, and though the decor wasn't really my speed, it was well-appointed. I laughed internally as I thought this because this guy was letting a complete stranger stay with him, so what the hell did it matter if I didn't share his taste in interior design?
I was grateful to be there.
On the way to the bathroom, I counted no fewer than three small Pride Flags, and I must admit, I was impressed with just how much pride Sebastian had. At least until I got to the bathroom.

Then I was awed.

I hopped into the shower and almost bumped into a brightly colored floral Speedo that must've been very tight. It had recently been worn and was drip-drying on the towel rack at the end of the shower.

At the other end stood a shower rack filled with no fewer than 20 varieties of shampoos and shower gels, all bearing a different scent. Admittedly, I was a little jealous of this second side of the shower and was tempted to try one of the fruity shampoos, but I limited the urge for herbal and used just one shampoo and one conditioner.

Interestingly enough, most of the people I Couchsurfed with were older gay men. I don't know what that says about me, but since I don't believe my straightness to be one of my defining characteristics, I don't often list it as one. Instead, I'd consider my Christian faith, obsession with fishing, love of food, intelligence, and sense of humor as my defining characteristics, but to each their own. Regardless, I got along just fine with everyone, and I was grateful for a free place to crash — so long as the host didn't try to kill or drug me. Neither of those things happened. Well, not on this trip.

I was only ever drugged once, and that was in high school. Long story short, a friend thought it would be funny to crush up a bunch of sleeping pills, put them in orange juice, and ask a pretty girl to offer the drink to a 15-year-old me. Of course I said yes. This was one of the only occasions a cute girl had ever initiated a conversation with me, after all. I obviously didn't die, but I slept for way too long, woke up with a migraine, and felt awful for a few days.

Moral of the story? I'm not sure. I just sort of got sidetracked when I remembered that. Oh yeah! I didn't get drugged while Couchsurfing. That's what I was saying. In fact, Couchsurfing was a pretty great experience. I got to meet people from circles I ordinarily would've never intersected with, and I was happy for that.

As I got to know Sebastian, I learned he was from Colombia, worked part-time in tourism and was from Medellín, a techtropolis and cultural anomaly in comparison to most of the rest of his country. The show he was watching was a dramatization of the life of Simon Bolivar, the man credited with leading the independence movement for many former Spanish colonies in South America, including Bolivar's native Venezuela and Sebastian's native Colombia.

While we talked, Sebastian's straight (well, he said he had a girlfriend) friend came over to visit. Marco, a Venezuelan import, was equally friendly. I quickly realized how my education had failed me as I learned about the rich and fascinating history of the respective independence movements of their homelands.

Though both men had different upbringings, Sebastian's included a relatively easy and willing journey to the United States. His biggest complaint was the limiting effects of a Colombian passport when traveling, and he told me he wished Colombia had remained a Spanish colony — apparently not an uncommon sentiment where he was from.

Marco, on the other hand, was forced out of Venezuela. His father had committed egregious crimes in the eyes of the powers that be: he was an educator who spoke out against the government. Marco's family was forced to flee the country or risk imprisonment or execution. Everyone but his ailing grandmother was able to escape, and he lamented the fact that he could not return to say goodbye to her. Just as my eyes were thoroughly opened to their realities, it became clear it was also time to close them. Sebastian's boyfriend knocked on the door, picked him up for a date, and Marco took off, leaving me alone to crash hard on the couch.

I drifted off to sleep that night with a nagging feeling telling me that despite being fairly unbiased toward new perspectives, I still had a ways to go to fully understand those around me.

Happy

Pride flags adorned the walls, and as I rubbed my blurry eyes, I couldn't make out anything but color.

Imagine my surprise when I awoke gay.

While the dictionary defines "gay" as happy and carefree only in the second-most-common, dated use of the word, it is nonetheless valid. I awoke that morning feeling gay in the happy sense of the word. Today was all about the pursuit of happiness, well, at least the pursuit of Happy, and I was up for the task. I headed out before Sebastian woke up.

My plans that day included chasing Happy, specifically the Eastern Happy Cichlid, *Astatotilapia calliptera*, in a small shopping center pond, more snakehead in the margins of the Everglades, and then looking for whatever new saltwater species I could find at Hillsboro Inlet Park.

Despite circling the entire pond and obviously making several employees nervous with my presence, I failed to catch my first target. Happy eluded me again. I did catch a ton of Bluegill, Mayan Cichlids, Florida Bass, and even a relatively massive Mozambique Tilapia, but the Happy eluded me. Apropos, really.

Depression is a dirty opponent. It doesn't play fair. Some days it sneaks up and attacks your psyche; others it's there from the moment you wake.

Though I'd woken happy and in pursuit of Happy, failing to find it dampened my spirits a little. This book was originally titled *Fishing for Happiness* (which I split into its own book partway through), and if I'd caught an Eastern Happy, I might be able to end it here, but that didn't Happ-en. So the search for Happy presses on.

Back to the Everglades

The Everglades is a massive area, spanning more than 7,800 square miles, and it's mostly uninhabited; however, it butts up against civilization at its margins.

This makes for a strange dichotomy in which the Everglades is entirely detached from humanity yet right on its doorstep. Its proximity to Miami and Fort Lauderdale makes a quick jaunt over to the untamed wilds fairly easy.

After failing to find Happy, I figured I'd move on. Maybe another snakehead would at least make me content? I made my way to a spot in the Everglades where they'd been sampled before, and I began scouting the bank. Almost immediately, I found one.

It was a monster fish, probably close to 40 inches long and reminiscent of my lower half. Not for the reason you frat boys are giggling about; the snakehead was about as thick as my calves.

Now, I hadn't been to the gym in almost seven years at the time (I began working out regularly shortly after returning from this trip and continue to do so now), but at the time, I was far from buff. Fit, sure, but not buff. That is, everything except my calves. For some reason, my calves stayed large and well-muscled. I mean, some girls are into that, I assume, so I guess it's a positive, right?

Well unfortunately, my body is weird. Despite skipping leg day (and arm day, to be fair) for the better part of a decade, my legs were still fairly large and strong even if my butt didn't measure up. When shopping for pants, this means I typically have to buy much larger pants and get the waist tailored down to size. In fact, most of my pants are tailored. For a few dollars, I can get a perfect fit that requires no belt, and since the pressure of a belt on my abdomen causes issues with my digestive tract, I avoid belts like the plague. On the rare occasion my tailored pants still don't fit perfectly, I'll take two small binder clips and clip the waistband of the pants to the waistband of my underwear. #LifeHack. The elastic holds taut and keeps me from committing public indecency.

Enough about the quirks of my body; this isn't that type of book.

It's a book about fishing, in part, and that snakehead was a fascinating fish. With it were dozens of juveniles, all about the size and shape of hot dogs. The juveniles would swarm in place at the entrance to the little nook in the rocks the adult had established. Once I got within sight, though, they vanished like smoke, and the large, menacing head of the adult would reappear. This production repeated half a dozen times as I'd leave, wait, hide, return, and fail to elicit a strike. Even a live sunfish proved ineffective. Cutting my losses, I decided to make like a snakehead in a rockpile and head out.

Hillsboro Inlet
Redoubling my efforts and still hoping to catch a new species, I headed east to the coast. I arrived at Hillsboro Inlet Park and was immediately impressed. The park is chiefly an inlet from the Atlantic Ocean to the network of saltwater arteries running through South Florida that provides the region's lifeblood.

The inlet itself runs under a drawbridge where anglers congregate in moderate numbers to catch all sorts of fishes. There is also a wooden overlook pier plus the bridge and a fishing pier that juts out into a sort of back bay off the inlet, a rocky point, and a sandy basin. Virtually all major habitat types are covered save for flooded mangroves. It is a veritable buffet of potential, and I caught a lot of fish, but I failed to catch anything new, save for a handful of Night Sergeants.

Species #322 — Night Sergeant *(Abudefduf taurus)*.

They look a lot like Sergeant Majors, but instead of black-and-yellow coloration, it's more of an indigo-and-black color scheme. They're pretty fish, prettier than their more common cousins, but still annoying after you've caught a few. In fact, "relentless" is a great way to describe the damselfish, snappers, and grunts that mob your partial sabiki on every drop. Knowing full-well there were other species to be had, I was hesitant to leave, but when darkness blanketed the park, the bite died, so it forced my hand.

The morning had been gay, but that night was uneventful, perhaps because the Night Sergeants set it straight.

Chapter 24
The 324th of July

July 4, 2019

Day 20
Origin: Fort Lauderdale, Florida
Destination: Fort Lauderdale, Florida

"The Constitution only guarantees you the right to
pursue happiness. You have to catch it yourself."
Attributed to Benjamin Franklin || American "Renaissance Man"

At this point, I'd been on the road for three weeks, essentially on my own for most of that time. It was a fitting realization given what the day was: Independence Day.
In my 28 years, it would be just the second Independence Day I wouldn't be spending with my family. The first was superseded by Officer Training School (OTS), and given my diarrhea-laden experience with OTS, that Independence Day was miserable. This holiday couldn't be much worse than that one had been, but I hoped for better than just "not terrible" as I grabbed a coffee and embraced the dawn's early light.
Spending a day fishing the salt in South Florida was about as American as anything I could imagine, and as the parades and fanfare announced the holiday, the traffic responded in kind. South Florida already has traffic on a normal day, but it turns out patriotism increases traffic flow even more.
I was in for a battle today.

In the twilight hours the night before, Hillsboro Inlet showed a gleam of promise, and I knew that's where I wanted to start my day. I spent hours there that morning, and it wasn't long before my opponents showed themselves: parrotfish.

Some were red, some were blue. None were white, or it would've been particularly patriotic, but Dr. Seuss still would've been proud.

They were Stoplight Parrotfish, *Sparisoma viride* and Blue Parrotfish, the elusive and cunning fish known for being extremely difficult to catch yet impossible to resist trying for. Stoplight Parrotfish have such a uniquely spangled pattern that consists of patches and stripes in various hues of red, gray, and white.

There were also some yellowish parrotfish I couldn't identify, and they seemed to be the most numerous. I hooked one or two but failed to land even one due to the perilous nature of each fight — I was dodging a railing, bridge pilings, the wooden fishing pier, and all sorts of floating debris. I was fishing behind a handrail, and the parrotfish were just big enough that I couldn't boat flip them without breaking my line yet small enough that they were tough to grip. Of course lipping a fish capable of biting barnacles off of rocks was out of the question, and my net was helpfully in the car, so I lost the first few parrots.

Repeatedly, I lost the fight. Unphased, I enjoyed watching the endless chain of luxury boats zipping in and out of the channel, music blaring and attractive women baring. I didn't have a particular sweetheart in mind, but Florida's women kept me in the fight. Why would I leave my post when it came with a view?

I made some progress thinning out my real enemies: non-target species. An onslaught of grunts and accompanying sergeants were the most numerous, but some sailors even got into the fray — Sailor's Choice Grunts, that is. The odds weren't in my favor, and I realized I would lose this war if I didn't change tactics. Just as I prepared to throw in the white flag and move on to another spot, I noticed something out of the ordinary: one of the little yellow parrotfish gallantly streamed up from the bottom to bite a floating piece of vegetation. This process repeated.

That was it! If I couldn't defeat these bastards the old-fashioned way, maybe I should use the age-old tactic of playing on the indulgences they afforded themselves. When the next floating weed cluster drifted by, I scooped it up. Ripping off several small pieces of the spongy yellow-green plant, I tied a piece to each hook of my sabiki using stretchy string, a thread-like material used primarily to tie soft bait fishes to large hooks.

The tactic was certainly new, and I was skeptical as I dropped my vegetarian bomb down to the bottom. Seconds after it impacted the seabed, it impacted my day. I got a hit! Then another. Then another. On the first three drops, my bait was stripped, but on the fourth, I hooked up. It was a parrotfish.

Pulsating energy ripped through my arms, and I was impressed with the vigor of the compact fish. Unfortunately, I failed to land it. Fireworks erupted around me, and in the shaded water below the bridge, I could see those rockets' red glare reflecting wanly on the surface. Refusing to quit, I quickly dropped down again. My enemy was gone. It had disappeared after coming so close to defeat, when I was hot on its heels, ready and willing and (almost) able to bring my might to bear.

Rethinking my tactics, I removed the weight and just floated the weightless sabiki in the current, hoping that would help eliminate any lingering doubts. It worked, and once again we battled. This time, I bested my opponent, bringing the vivid red, yellow and pink fish to hand. Its beak-like teeth were menacing, to be sure, but as a captive, it was harmless. I quickly photographed the fish — a trophy and testament to my victory over it. In accordance with the Geneva Convention, I treated my captive well.

Species #323 — Yellowtail Parrotfish *(Sparisoma rubripinne)*.

Despite releasing the fish, the rush of victory it gave me reinvigorated my resolve, and I pressed onward, hoping to find its Stoplight or Blue counterpart. Another maiden-laden boat passed, and I was feeling myself enough to nod at the bronzed woman who looked at me. She smiled, and I smiled back.

Flirtily, she waved. On the back of that boat, an American flag waved, too. I waved back.

At this point, I was beaming to beat the band and when I threw shrimp on one hook, the slow drumroll played me up to another new species, the Bandtail Puffer.

Species #324 — Bandtail Puffer *(Sphoeroides spengleri)*.

I was so incredibly free after finally catching that parrotfish, that I decided once again to brave the traffic and head to another spot nearby. This one promised slightly different conditions, and I hoped it would mean different fish.

I wasn't wrong; I immediately hooked what was now my fourth Scrawled Filefish of the trip, but I was fishing a platform about six feet up from the water, and when I tried to lift it up, it snapped my line. Though I doubled back to the car to grab my EGO E3 Slider Net, a net capable of reaching down that far, the filefish never showed itself, and I filed yet another failure into my "Unpleasant Memories" folder.

Grunts and sergeants once again proved to be my cannon fodder, getting in the way of my more valuable targets. Just as I'd cleared them out, the French Grunts came out to play. Had it been Bastille Day, maybe they would've been distracted, but it was Independence Day, and the French Grunts were relentless.

I caught 67 fishes at that spot, but nothing was new. After seeing a little girl walk up and catch a Caribbean Sharpnose Puffer, *Canthigaster rostrata* (a species I'd never caught) on her first cast, I'm sure I got a sour look on my face despite being excited to see it. She was very excited to have caught a fish, and I told her how cool that was. She puffed up her chest and beamed like the fish in her hands, asking me to help her unhook it. She was so proud to show her dad when he walked over, and she wanted to take a picture, but her dad called it a "trash fish" and she deflated faster than the puffer. It broke my heart.

Next time she caught a fish, this time just a little grunt, I made a big deal about it and told her I couldn't beat her, so I had to call it a night. She smiled with her whole person in a way only little kids can manage so easily, and I smiled, too.

Traffic was lighter in the darkness, and I returned to Hillsboro Inlet to fish a few more hours. The fireworks reflected on the black water, and the warm night air filled with smoke, some from the pyrotechnics, some from impromptu barbeques. All manner of music played in the night, from Cuban to reggae to country, and I basked in the Americana as the bite died down. Grunts and sergeants were fighting to the last man, but the snapper and parrotfish had evaporated with the sunlight.

A guy next to me caught, mishandled, and released a respectable barracuda on a live bait. I caught my umpteenth sergeant and the smell of barbeque kickstarted my metabolism which started screaming for me to leave. Reluctantly, I became a slave to my stomach even as I watched the freedom celebration all around me.

I couldn't find a melting pot for dinner, so I opted for Hot Pot instead. As I sat at the table doing some rough math, I came to the realization that I'd caught more than 1,000 fishes on my trip so far — 1,061 to be exact. I really wish I could come up with some creative parallel to draw to the number 1,061, but apart from being a subsection of the Internal Revenue Service Tax Code, 1061 is not particularly significant to anyone but a July 4, 2019, Luke Ovgard. And the beauty of America is that that is completely okay.

Chapter 25
Housekeeping and Sweepers

July 5, 2019

Day 21
Origin: Fort Lauderdale, Florida
Destination: Fort Lauderdale, Florida

"The more decisions that you are forced to make alone, the more you are aware of your freedom to choose."
Thornton Wilder || American Playwright

After sleeping off my victory, I again woke up early. My host was asleep, so I left the thank you and Starbucks cards on the kitchen table, made like a ball and bounced.

Light was still creeping over the skyline as I drove to a nearby coffee shop. The warm gray urbanity took on a soft glow as the Florida sun began to heat up the day, a day already pushing 80 degrees and promising to be much, much warmer, but that didn't stop me from pulling up to the coffee shop with every intention of having a cup of piping hot coffee.

My last pre-written column was slated to run that day. I calculated the difference between Eastern (Florida), Mountain (Idaho), and Pacific Time (Oregon) and realized it was already on doorsteps back home in Oregon and Idaho and probably had been for a few hours now. Though I had another week before my next column would run, I wanted to get ahead of it, so I grabbed the laptop my cousin, Ben Taucher, had mailed me weeks before and set to work, hoping I could send my columns to the editors and/or other contacts of the papers I was writing for at the time. This included Holly Owens (editor at the *Herald & News* of Klamath Falls, Oregon), Andrew Cutler and Renee Struthers (editor and community records editor at the *East Oregonian* of Pendleton, Oregon), and Elisa Magagna (editor at the *AM Morning News* of Blackfoot, Idaho). Author's Note: The post-COVID newspaper industry is in a very sad state. Huge downsizing in the industry has led to sweeping layoffs and forced many folks to choose new lines of work, including three of the four editors I mentioned above.

For years I'd written only for the *Herald & News,* my local paper, but after a conversation with my friend, Holly Dillemuth, she convinced me to try syndicating. A syndicated column or cartoon is just one that runs in at least two papers at the same time. Whether weekly, monthly, quarterly, whatever. At the time, I was syndicated in three papers every week and a handful of others on a monthly or quarterly basis. I owe that to Holly. Once she told me about it, I bought a book on syndication written before the rise of the Internet. It took hundreds of phone calls and rejections before I made progress, but I finally did, and the rest was history.

Given how much time I planned to be on the road during my trip, I asked if anyone would be willing to sell me a cheap old laptop I could use to write on my trip, preconceiving how awful writing every column from my phone would be. My cousin, Ben, had replied on my desperate Facebook post that he had his old laptop from college he was willing to share.

Ben was always brilliant and funny (it runs in the family, obvs), so I wasn't surprised when the box arrived with a return address under the name "Cam Pewter" that drew out a chuckle.

I had a lot of housekeeping to accomplish that day, but I hoped it wouldn't stop me from fishing a little, too. If I had to enjoy a few delicious pastries along the way, so be it.

I hauled out the old laptop and walked into the coffee shop. Opening the door, I immediately appreciated the aesthetic of Switchbox Coffee Roasters. It was at once clean and industrial, the brushed steel and wood parlayed with modern decor spoke to the coffee culture I was so accustomed to in the Pacific Northwest. I had high hopes when I ordered a coffee, but I also noticed the pastry case sitting next to the cash register, and my unbreakfasted stomach overcame my writer's voice. Before I knew it, I found myself ordering two savory empanadas and a scone. Though it was a carb-heavy meal, it was delicious enough to keep me distracted from my writing until I was completely finished, satiated and smiling like a fat kid at a free sample stand. The empanadas were legit; the scone was buttery and its texture perfect. Paired with some excellent coffee, my mood soared. I ordered a refill and powered on the laptop. It was fairly old, and once I refilled the diesel tank and turned the crank, it started loading slowly.

Ten minutes or so passed, and I was surprised to see a fiery sunset covered in white words typed in what was obviously a font from the *Legend of Zelda* series. Ben's thoughtfulness never ceases to surprise me. He's that one cousin who messages every single member of the extended family on his or her birthday, actually pays attention to what you post on Facebook, and can speak to what is going on in your life even months or years removed from last seeing you or communicating with you directly. He's the cousin I wish I could be sometimes.

Yet again, his thoughtfulness shone through, and I read the message on the desktop, truly touched:

"No, this isn't a motivational Pinterest quote, despite the sunset pic behind it. Just wanted to say I'm happy you can use this! This was my high school graduation gift from my folks and carried me through college. As for sentimental value, it makes me happier that someone in my family can actually use it, or it would be collecting dust under my twin bed. Hope it works for you. It should, but it may be a little slow. I kept a few disc-burning programs on here, a basic antivirus, some fonts I'd collected (enjoying the *Zelda* font here?) and a folder of Def Leppard music. I kept it that way to make it easy for you to use, but if you'd rather start from scratch, there's an option in the Control Panel to restore it to its brand-new factory default state.

"The battery is also pretty terrible, but if you absolutely need to use it without plugging it in, I'm sure you can find a replacement online.

"Let me know if you have any questions. Have fun on your trip, dude! Maybe you and Jed [Ben's brother, and another cousin I'm close with] and I can go fishing sometime this summer.

"Proud of you, man.

Ben"

I was floored. The girl behind the counter was cute, so I tried not to show too much emotion, but I was nonetheless choked up by his thoughtful and earnest display. It wasn't just a handwritten note; he took the time to type that out and then set it as the background. It really meant a lot.

It took me a moment to recenter on the task at hand. My column that week would be about Florida's water, comparing and contrasting it to the Pacific Northwest. I already had some semblance of an idea about how to tell the story, but I often go in with just an idea and write whatever flows into my head. A story about water should flow, after all, and this one felt ready to spring forth. Desperately, I tried to open the Internet, but couldn't.

For some reason, the laptop just wouldn't sync to Wi-Fi. I tried again and again, but after 30 minutes, it was clear it wasn't happening, so I just wrote the story, begrudgingly, on my phone and submitted it via email. That process of typing anything larger than a text or Instagram caption on a phone is a bit convoluted, and it requires a bit of practice — especially for those of us not a part of Generation Z (the Screeners), but I managed.

I'd try to sync the laptop to Wi-Fi several more times on the trip in motels, coffee shops, even the houses of my Couchsurfing hosts, but I couldn't get it to work. Ben warned me it was old, but it was completely free and an incredibly nice gesture, so I wasn't bothered. Sure, I can type 80- to 100-words-per-minute on a keyboard and at best half of that on my phone, but it forced me to extend myself, practice a new skill, and keep my fingers limber.

It also kept me cursing at autocorrect every time my phone changed something without my concert. Ugh, there it goes again. Consent. Without my consent.

The only real downside of using my phone is that when I returned from my trip in August and tried to start writing this book on my desktop, it felt insanely foreign to me, and the adjustment period of an hour or so really made me feel out of place.

Sneakerheads

Column completed, I headed next door to the post office and mailed myself some of the shoes and clothes I'd purchased on this trip. Despite vowing to spend money only on purchases directly related to my trip, I faltered early. I picked up several pairs of shoes in Orlando while shopping with my family and friends, and while I was adding three or four pairs to my embarrassment of riches back home, I didn't have a lot of space in my car, so it prompted me to do something to reduce the number of shoe boxes and maximize the space I had available: I loaded those shoes — and several pairs of workout shoes I'd brought along with me in the very unlikely event that I felt like working out on my trip — into a pair of flat rate boxes and sent them home.

Economically, buying clothes in a state with sales tax (Oregon has no sales tax) and then paying to ship them home probably wasn't the most fiscally-responsible move, but then again, neither was buying my collection of 50-plus pairs of shoes in the first place. Admitting you have a problem is the first step, I'm told, but I feel like talking about steps when discussing shoe addiction is a bit trite, so we'll stop there rather than foot stomping the issue. Everyone has their addictions and bad habits, so just remember that if the shoe were on the other foot...

Green Light

For the third time in as many days, I returned to Hillsboro Inlet Park. I paid for parking, grabbed up my gear, and made my way back under the bridge. Inexplicably, at around 11 a.m. that Friday, it was absolutely crawling with people. Not wanting to do battle with anything or anyone but my target fish, Stoplight Parrotfish, I climbed up onto the drawbridge and began walking across.

Naturally, a large vessel decided to pass at that exact moment, and though I tried racing to beat the buzzer, I was too late, and a horn sounded to accompany the red light. I stewed in quiet contempt as the bridge raised and lowered at an excruciating pace. It spanned just seven or eight minutes, but it felt like an eternity in the sweltering heat of the already-imposing mid-morning sun. The man operating the bridge lift kept giving me dirty looks, as though I wasn't supposed to be crossing along the pedestrian path. That, or he assumed I was going to try and bum-rush it completely loaded down with rods, gear, and my bucket like an action hero in a high-budget movie. Oh, sweetie.

Eventually, the bridge fell and my spirits lifted. The light turned green, and I moved to the other side, climbed down, and immediately set to work looking for the mustard-colored weeds (which I'd since learned were sargassum) that floated in and out of the channel. As I peered into the dark water, I noticed a large, dark form maybe four or five feet long. Recognizing it as a massive barracuda, I instantly regretted having carted only light rods across the drawbridge. Profanity.

Apart from sharks, the lone grouper, and one big parrotfish, I hadn't caught anything large, so I couldn't pass it up. Looking both ways, I assured myself no one else was fishing on the same side as I was. On the ocean side of the bridge, there was a serious fence, laced with barbed wire, just a few feet from the concrete footings. On the other side was a private marina, also fenced and connected to a nicer hotel. Confident I wouldn't be robbed blind, I left my gear behind and sprinted back across the drawbridge, the "Thwack!" "Thwack!" "Thwack!" of my flip-flops making me more of a spectacle than my introverted self appreciated. I made it to the car and grabbed my heavy rod. It was already loaded for sharks, and though it may have been a little heavy for a potentially 30- or 40-pound barracuda, I accepted my lot and began sprinting back across the bridge, already soaked with enough sweat that I didn't care if I added more.

Though I'd made the trip to my car without issue, once again, I was stopped by the drawbridge on my trip back. I swear the bastard in the control tower looked at me with a mirthy grin and waited longer than necessary to lower it back down. This time I lost almost 10 minutes.

Miraculously, the barracuda was still there, tucked into shadow and quietly swaying with the current.

I quickly caught a small grunt, threw it on my heavy rod, and positioned the fish just a few feet in front of the toothy monster. It took all of five seconds before the barracuda engulfed my bait. I set the hook, but the ropy, 100-pound braid was heavy enough and the current strong enough that when I went to set the hook, I failed to maintain enough line tension. The fish was on briefly, but the circle hook failed to find flesh in its bony mouth.

Losing a big fish is particularly painful, but I pressed on, knowing there were still plenty of options on this side of the bridge, and the rocky habitat and faster current helped optimism prevail. Sure enough, I could see blue and red parrotfish here and there, and they called out to me.

With wooden resolve, I mowed down grunts, put some damselfish in distress, and kept hoping for just one colorful parrotfish to oblige me before my wan patience collapsed.

"Well," I complained to no one in particular. "I guess my miracle bait only works *sometimes.*"

I was referring, of course, to the sargassum I'd used successfully the day before to catch Yellowtail Parrotfish. The edge in my voice was sarcastic — sargasstic, maybe? — and I felt more than a little petty as I prayed aloud. God answered my whiny prayer shortly thereafter. Apparently, He gave the fish the green light, and it finally decided to nibble on that dirty mustard vegetation.

It wasn't blue; it was red. That meant one thing: Stoplight Parrotfish.

Species #325 — Stoplight Parrotfish *(Sparisoma viride).*

I landed the fish quickly and put it into my freshly dipped bucket of water while I fiddled with my camera. The brickwork underfoot was not only uneven and difficult to walk on in flip-flops; it was also featureless. There were no ledges or benches or posts. This meant I had to walk all the way to the angled masonry ramp leading to the origin of the bridge. Thinking quickly, I used my gear bag and sunglasses to position my phone for a quick picture. I took a few shots of the beautiful fish, which I'd later learn was in its "Initial Phase" of life, complete with brown-and-white randomly checkered scales, red fins, and a red underbelly. It was certainly striking, and had I been within view of the road, it just might have stopped traffic. Then again, many of the women you'll see in Florida have this superpower, too.

In fact, as I walked back to my car, a pair of flawless, sunbathing Latinas caused me to walk straight into a curb. I stubbed my toe, and their subsequent giggles guaranteed I'd remain single at least a little bit longer.

Trophy

While my return to Silver Palm Park that afternoon proved fruitless, I was undeterred. I had caught plenty of fish, but I'd hit a species plateau, where new fishes were few and far between. Just days removed from the Keys, sharks were still ever-present on my mind, so I scanned Fishbrain for areas nearby with numerous logged shark catches as I ate dinner.

It didn't take long. I arrived at a park with a long inlet dumping into the ocean next to an expansive beach that, from a distance, looked to be red. After walking all the way out there, I realized it was thickly piled with mats of floating vegetation that were just as dense in the water as on the beach.

I sighed and said something charming to the attractive cocoa-complected woman relaxing nearby. She smiled but didn't reply, so I notched two losses in my belt and moved to the rocky, fingerlike jetty that was lined with anglers.

Dusky Damselfish dominated the catch here, but rocks came in at a close second. Disheartened, I walked back toward the parking lot to see what different habitats — if any — might present themselves along the way. Sure enough, a much shallower, dog-legged corner of the inlet screamed for me to stop. Not only was it protected by a floating breakwater, but the large rocks jutting up from the surface created deep pockets right up against the seawall that intrigued me.

Daylight was fading faster than a drunk frat boy on a hot day, so I gave myself an ultimatum: "New species be damned; I'll just try to catch 100 damselfish before dark."

I was making headway on my promise when another guy showed up and asked to fish next to me. He had little to no idea what he was doing, but his small, unbaited half-sabiki quickly earned him a fish. He was more surprised than I was as I glanced at what I expected to be a Sergeant Major or Night Sergeant (what I'd been catching on 9-of-10 drops there) but was shocked to see an oddly-shaped purple fish with a body about the size and shape of a bent soup spoon attached with only one third of the handle.

I had no idea what it was. Its oversized eye and unique shape made me think it was something from the deep sea following in the wake of an equally lost Nemo. He tossed it back and proceeded to catch a second one. At that point, I'd landed 31 Sergeant Majors and nine Night Sergeants from my perch, but I eschewed my goal of 100 to get one of those little fish he caught.

He caught a third one before I had my Lifer, but by the time darkness fell minutes later, I had caught two. Never in my life had I seen a fish that looked like this, and it would take hours for me to get an ID, but when I learned I'd caught the fairly rare Glassy Sweeper, I was pretty stoked.

Species #326 — Glassy Sweeper *(Pempheris schomburgkii)*.

As it turned out, most of the high species count guys I'd idolized in the Species Hunting community didn't even have this species. I'm not really that competitive, but the exclusivity of my accomplishment put me back into my 2016 Halloween costume: the emoji girl in the raspberry-colored sweater with one palm outstretched at the ear as if holding it out for a trophy. Two new species, 102 total fishes, and some bragging rights? Yeah, I could live with that.

Chapter 26
Real Unicorns

July 6, 2019

Day 22
Origin: Fort Lauderdale, Florida
Destination: Royal Palm Beach, Florida

"All the beasts obeyed Noah when he admitted them into the ark. All, that is, but the Unicorn. Confident of his own abilities, the Unicorn boasted: 'I shall swim.'"
Ukrainian Folktale

My first stop involved a long walk to a small, rocky point where a channel met a sandy beach. It looked promising, and with both sandy beaches and rocky channels close at hand, I figured there was something new waiting there for me in the varied habitat.

The nearest parking was at a city park almost a mile from my intended base camp. It was pouring rain, so I waited it out under a pavilion for a few minutes before deciding to power through as some inconsiderate twats smoked in our shared refuge. Eventually, I was smoked out and decided to just get wet.

I did immediately catch fish, at least, validating my long walk through the pouring rain. The channel was loaded with fish, mostly Spottail Pinfish, *Diplodus holbrookii* and Hairy Blenny, and in retrospect, I wonder if I caught one of the confusingly similar blenny species or a Silver Porgy, *Diplodus argenteus* in the fray. Given how many of each I caught, there was likely one mixed in, but since I didn't even know those other species existed at the time, I'm left to live with my uncertainty and regret.

Speaking of regret, a mile is a long way to walk on loose sand in the rain while wearing flip flops. It's even worse when you arrive at your destination to find someone already there. Fortunately, the guy was willing to share his space. I quickly caught a grunt, hooked it as a live bait, and threw it out to the surf break near the little structure at the corner of the beach and the seawall lining the channel we'd set up on. In one of those rare moments where everything works out, I quickly felt a bite and set the hook on something capable of eating an eight-inch grunt. Though not the shark, ray, drum, or snook I'd been hoping for, the two-foot Great Barracuda was certainly cooler than a blenny or pinfish. The guy fishing there agreed and asked if he could have it. Since smaller barracuda are, in fact, edible, I made his day.

As the rain cleared and the day warmed the sand, swimmers and snorkelers ruined my pristine corner of the world, and after tiring of catching small grunts on every cast with no sign of anything changing, I started the long walk back.

On my way, from a distance, I noticed the little troupe of men dressed in all black. They had set up an American flag, Confederate flag, and a few other flags I couldn't recognize from where I stood. What I could recognize were the large, military-style guns each man carried or had slung over his shoulder. My first thought was "Neo Nazis," but given that only half of the eight men were White, I ruled that out.

The men appeared to be "shark fishing" while exercising their right to open carry about a quarter mile from the busy beach. At the gated-off, dead-end road nearest them, several cops stood at the ready. The demonstrators were smack-dab in the middle of the only path from the beachside condos to the main street, so I had to walk through them. They seemed at once confident and hostile, so I nodded cordially and walked through, hoping I didn't smell too liberal.

Now, I grew up hunting. I own guns. I even worked a weekend job at a target range for five years. I have nothing against guns and consider myself a moderate supporter of the Second Amendment, but this display was completely unnecessary. Not only did it serve to put everyone on edge, but the fear-mongering tactics they were using likely swayed some folks indifferent to private gun ownership to support tighter controls on guns or even wholeheartedly oppose gun ownership. I felt it was crass and completely extraneous. Own your guns and use them for hunting and self-defense and target shooting if you choose, but don't bring them to a public beach with hundreds of people around. Yes, guns are just tools, but so, in my opinion, were those guys.

As I passed the cops, I said: "God bless. Thanks for putting up with this sort of thing every day."

One of the cops shook his head sadly, but the other replied, "Thank you. I don't hear that a lot."

I made the long walk back to the car, grabbed a coffee, made a lunch of tuna, a peanut butter sandwich, some salad, and an iced tea and then proceeded to my next stop.

Unicorn

Cops were swarming the parking lot at my next stop, too, dealing with something Florida, I'm sure. I was worried they wouldn't let me through, as there was a barricade, flares, and a small fleet of police cruisers. It didn't appear to be an accident, and they didn't stop me as I slowly drove by and into the parking lot. Ask forgiveness, not permission, right?

I parked and began walking around the marina on the far side of the commotion. The water here was as pretty as any I'd yet seen in Florida, its lapis lazuli hue and rippling surface broken only by the schools of Jack Crevalle that cruised this way and that.

I couldn't get my bait out fast enough. That's not an expression. I couldn't get my bait out fast enough to catch one. By the time I'd caught a live grunt, hooked it, and thrown it out on the heavy rod I had to run back to the car for, the two or three minutes I'd lost doing so meant the fish had moved. Frowning slightly, I proceeded to catch small fishes on bait as I messed around with lures in hopes of getting a jack that never obliged me.

The park was large, and I fished sandy flats in the marina, rocks near the access bridge, and finally settled on an elevated fishing platform. I walked to the end of the platform and dropped straight down to the edge of the paired pilings at the end of the structure. Immediately, I caught a fish. Then another. Then another. I caught more than 20 fishes there, most unremarkable reruns of what I'd already caught in abundance. But one fish stood out. I knew immediately it was something different when it pulled line and ran like a gamefish. I assumed it was an Atlantic Croaker, *Micropogonias undulatus*, but to my surprise, I pulled out a small khaki-colored triggerfish with what appeared to be a horn.

Species #327 — Planehead Filefish *(Stephanolepis hispidus)*.

The fish was as alien as any I've ever caught; its roughly diamond-shaped body pinched at each end near its tail and tiny mouth with humanoid teeth. Its horn was collapsible and moved up and down. I was intrigued and slightly horrified by this unique fish. As a Species Hunter, I'm always after the "unicorn" while fishing, that rare, unique, or different fish that stands out, but I didn't expect one to actually resemble a unicorn. The ocean is a strange place, my friends, but it can be intriguing.

Pier Misery

It *can* be intriguing. "Can" being the operative word. My next stop was so devoid of intrigue, I'll just leave it at that. Few fishes and nothing new. I had arrived at a place called Juno. It had nothing to do with the 2007 film about the pregnant teen nor the Roman goddess. Rather, it holds the unique claim to fame as being the most unremarkable and disappointing paid pier you'll find in Florida.

I always joke that when it comes to dating, I've come to expect nothing, and I still get disappointed. Well, that phrase should be the motto of this pier: "Juno Beach Pier: Expect nothing, but you'll still be disappointed."

My first problem was the cost. It was $7 to access the pier. As expensive as any other walk-in only pier I've fished, but I hoped it would live up to its price tag. After all, I'd seen several Lookdown — a flat, almost two-dimensional silvery fish with large eyes, a downwardly compressed face, and a fivehead that make it look like it was plucked straight from a '90s video game and composed only of poorly rendered fractals. These fish are relatively uncommon, so I hoped the pier might be a sort of preserve for these and other uncommon species. It also had a gently sloping beach with breakers and seemed to be the perfect spot to try for species such as Florida Pompano, *Trachinotus carolinus* and other fishes that stay up shallow in the surf, and I'd already caught a unicorn that day, so I figured it was my lucky day.

Oh how wrong I was. Though I caught 17 fishes in my hour there, they were all Blue Runners and Spottail Pinfish.

Nothing else.

Nada.

Further compounding my frustration was the fact that the first third of the pier was closed to fishing to allow beachgoers a chance to try and catch meningitis in the surf. So pompano were out. Add in the fact that the pier closed at 10 p.m. instead of at dark or being an all-night pier like most of its peer piers, and I was livid. This place had been a raging disappointment, but it didn't stop there. It also had rules about using heavy gear that could be capable of catching a shark, so no live baits for me. Signs banned overhead casting, allowed just a single rod (Florida law allows as many rods as you want while shore fishing), and made you store any extra gear in special zones. It's like the pier was designed by the same people who created the U.S. Tax Code but offered no refund.

My idea that it might be a preserve wasn't far off, but it was reserved for special people, not special fish. It would take a truly unique person to fish there twice.

Jupiter Beach

Following a theme of coastal Florida cities named for Roman deities, I finished my day at Jupiter Beach Park. Though it was a goldmine for Black Margate (I caught more than a dozen there), a relatively uncommon species, it was otherwise unremarkable. Still, I don't need to catch new species of fishes to enjoy fishing, so I just fished. My species count was already much higher than I'd ever anticipated, and I had caught some 75 new species on the trip thus far. That's fairly significant given that in 2016, an entire year, I tried to catch 75 species total in my home state and failed miserably. I had already caught 112 on this trip, and 75 were new, so I had no room to complain. So I didn't.

I just caught fish after fish and counted myself lucky with each one. When I caught something new, a damselfish that looked just a little different than those I'd caught up to that point in the trip, I snapped a few pictures. Since I'd been standing all day, and my back was beginning to ache, I sat down and took a moment to identify it. It was a new species, I knew, but it took me a moment to identify it as a Cocoa Damselfish.

Species #328 — Cocoa Damselfish (*Stegastes variabilis*).

Slowly, I stuck out my tongue and tasted it. Surprisingly, it tasted more like vanilla than chocolate. I've never made it past first base with a fish, and then only a quick peck to channel my inner Jimmy Houston.

With my last hour of daylight, I caught more of the usual, and I didn't think anything of the three Hairy Blennies I caught. Save the last one. I'm honestly not sure why I took a picture of it, but I did.

Almost six months later, a friend would post a picture and explanation of an eerily familiar-looking fish. Turns out, I'd caught a Mock Blenny, a species that looks so similar to the Hairy Blenny that it can masquerade as such. Moral of the story? Take pictures of anything you have even the slightest inkling to take a picture of — save your naked body. You will get hacked, and those photos will leak. Trust me, it's not pretty.

Species #329 — Mock Blenny (*Labrisomus cricota*).

I didn't know I'd added the last species yet, but I was still satisfied with my 122-fish day and several new species, so I got in touch with my Couchsurfing host and started driving northward.

Wrap Up

After leaving the water that night, I drove to Royal Palm Beach to stay with George, my next host. He lived in a nice gated community and had a beautiful home. The retired airline pilot greeted me at the door. After exchanging small talk with him and his visiting best friend, I grabbed a shower.

Refreshed and renewed, they invited me to join them for some Key Lime Pie. Ordinarily, I'm not much for cream pies, but this was an exception to the rule. It was really good pie that made for the perfect ending to my evening, and I crashed hard.

Chapter 27
B-A-N-A-N-S

July 7, 2019

Day 23
Origin: Royal Palm Beach, Florida
Destination: Melbourne, Florida

"There's always money in the Banana Stand."
George Bluth Sr. || From *Arrested Development*

    I awoke the next morning and offered to take my hosts out to breakfast as a thank you. I'm not entirely sure why. I'm normally not the most social guy, and though George and his friend (whose name I can't remember) were both easy to get along with, I rarely put people before fishing.
    Yet, there I was, sitting at breakfast with two older gentlemen listening to stories about singles cruises and the thriving gay community in South Florida that I'd already become more familiar with by Couchsurfing than I ever imagined — but not in the way you might be picturing. I suppose it's healthy to see the world through a lens different from your own, and I certainly had.
    Part of me wondered why so many (primarily older) gay men had accepted my Couchsurfing requests, but George's friend told me I have a bit of a "rugged Otter vibe" which might have earned me so many free stays. Otters, for those unfamiliar with the term, is used to describe tall, lean, somewhat masculine hairy gay men. I asked George's friend if this meant he thought I was gay, and he replied, "No, I've never met a gay guy *that* into fishing," adding with a

chuckle "but I suppose if any gay man were to be into fishing, though, it would be an Otter."

My appreciation for the wordplay didn't offset the slight uneasiness arising from what he'd intended as a compliment. Still, it was no more forward than the older women who always hit on me, albeit far less likely to work. Who I am kidding? It would never work for the women, and I'm not even a little bi-curious, so what's less likely than never? Stumbling into the age-appropriate woman of my dreams on a pier, I suppose.

When I went to grab the check, George stole it away.

"It's my pleasure," he said in his Carolina drawl.

I thanked him profusely and wished both men well as I headed out to fish. Well, more accurately, I headed to Starbucks, grabbed a coffee and went to the bathroom. Since I'd eaten out twice in a row and hadn't had any fruit other than apples for several days, I grabbed a banana off the counter and added it to my coffee order. This would prove prophetic.

Bananas

I scarfed down the banana, thinking to myself "Good thing I'm not on a boat." Despite the name of the popular sunscreen brand, bananas are not meant to go on boats — at least, according to legend. Many fishermen consider them unlucky.

Now, I'm not much of a believer in luck, but I tend to at least respect the views of others and keep my bananas ashore. This is normally not difficult because bananas are one of my least favorite fruits. I mean, I'll eat them, but not happily. That said, bananas contain high quantities of prebiotics, which help my oft-troubled stomach. Plenty of foods have this, but bananas are easier to snack on than onions, garlic, leeks, and chicory root, so bananas it is.

What happened next was bananas, B-A-N-A-N-A-S!

My destination that day was one I'd long been preparing for.

After seeing Zain Khalid (whom you may remember from my visit to Florida near the beginning of this book), post several fairly rare species, including: Bigmouth Sleeper, *Gobiomorus dormitor*, Mountain Mullet, *Dajaus monticola* and River Goby, *Awaous banana*. He'd caught them on Florida's east coast, and I was very intrigued. These are all native fishes that range in freshwater and brackish water but can be difficult to locate. In terms of difficulty, all three fishes are tough to locate, but Bigmouth Sleepers are fairly easy to catch; River Goby are insanely rare and supposedly very difficult to catch; Mountain Mullet are fairly common but one of the near-impossibles to entice to bite. I fully expected to find Bigmouth

Sleeper and Mountain Mullet. I fully expected to catch a Bigmouth Sleeper, not catch a Mountain Mullet, and not even see a River Goby.

As it happened, Zain caught them over a span of trips after his friend, Magnus Billings, had discovered them. One of the Species Hunting community's accepted principles is that when one person shares a location and asks you to keep it quiet, you do so. Zain's spot was really Magnus' so when I asked for the coordinates, Zain said I should ask Magnus. So I did. Magnus was kind enough to share the spot, so I drove out into relative isolation, parked under the only tree for miles, and began the long walk in, carrying all manner of gear.

Not only were those three rare natives present, but so were a host of other fresh and saltwater species, including Atlantic Tarpon, Florida Bass, snook, and various cichlids. Situations where there are any number of possibilities and each possibility requires different gear make for frustrating conditions. Do you throw out live bait? Cast lures? Fish small baits? Jigs? Micro gear? With so many choices, it can be overwhelming.

Initially, I threw minnowbaits (small lures that look like fish) for tarpon or snook. Though I'd caught both species before, they're incredible fish, and I figured it was worth a few minutes. It might have been, but I failed to catch any, so I went to the other end of the spectrum and started using micro gear for the tiny fishes near the shoreline that proved to be mostly tilapia and Mayan Cichlids.

Clouds rolled in, visibility declined, and I decided I should change gears.

The area I was fishing sits below a small dam, maybe 15 feet high. At the base of the dam, limited flow charges through a densely packed field of melon-sized rocks into a large catch pool of several acres. This, in turn, narrows into a small creek that flows all the way to the ocean — thus the tarpon, snook, and myriad other saltwater and brackish species.

I began hopping around on the rocks below the dam, dipping a small baited jig into every nook and cranny I thought might be holding a Bigmouth Sleeper. After almost two hours of this with nothing to show but a few Bluegill and Mayan Cichlids, my frustration forced me to change gears once again.

Returning to the shoreline, I decided to go fish the creek at its formation where the pool narrowed. It looked promising. As I returned to the shoreline, however, the sky thickened, a soiled cottony mass threatened to smother me, and I knew a storm was minutes away. By some strange quirk of weather, a gap in the clouds enabled a ray of light to shine down and illuminate a patch of water near the sandy shoreline maybe six inches deep.

I noticed a fish that was hugging the bottom, moving slowly this way and that and behaving completely unlike the cichlids that dominated the area. The illumination from the sky extended into my mind, and in a moment of clarity I knew it was an elusive River Goby!

The most common microfishing setup involves putting a tiny (most microfishermen agree Size 20 or smaller constitutes microfishing) hook between one and eight inches below a tiny split shot. You bait the hook and typically sightfish for whatever tiny critter you're after. Normally, it's quite effective.

For almost five minutes I bounced my bait in its face, leaving the peppercorn-sized piece of worm within that bloody River Goby's grasp. For almost five minutes it refused all of my presentations, either ignoring the worm or moving away from its (apparently) unnatural presence.

I sat there, stumped, for what felt like much longer than the five minutes it probably was.

Then, I remembered how I'd captured the most finicky sculpins while micro-sightfishing at night back home in Oregon. Sometimes, sculpins will hit the split shot (especially when your headlamp reflects off of it at night). Other times, the split shot scares the fish. I was getting exactly zero strikes, so I figured it wasn't after the split shot. I removed that and just let my unweighted rig sit a few inches from the fish.

In comical fashion, it would lift its head from the sandy bottom and look up, side-to-side, then move an inch forward and wait a few seconds before moving again. It would do this painstakingly, inch-by-inch. It took over a minute for it to close the foot between itself and my bait as the sky continued to sour. Then, it engulfed my bait, and I did a micro hookset and pulled out my River Goby, shocked that this was the new species I caught here first. Hell, I was surprised I'd caught it at all.

I hadn't even seen a Bigmouth Sleeper. I hadn't seen a Mountain Mullet. Now I'd both seen and caught a River Goby. Remember how bananas are supposed to be unlucky? Remember how I said River Goby was the longshot of longshots? Well, a little-known fact about River Gobies is that their scientific name is *Awaous banana*. Yes, banana.

Species #330 — River Goby (*Awaous banana*).

Call it luck, or cosmic irony, or God having a sense of humor, but it was certainly something memorable. The banana had been money, and I smiled wryly as I thought of the running joke in my favorite series, *Arrested Development,* in which family patriarch George Bluth Sr. repeatedly tells his family "There's always money in the Banana Stand." I proved that day that bananas aren't unlucky for fishermen; they're money.

The River Goby was lucky, but in the same vein, I experienced some bad luck. I never saw a sleeper. I never saw a mullet. In my subsequent self-pity, I probably said something cliché-like "Could it get any worse?" because the sky opened up, and a downpour started.

Florida is semi-tropical, so thunderstorms are as common as retirees. Unfortunately, I'd parked my car far away below the only tree for miles, so I had nowhere to hide from the thunder, lightning, and pouring rain. There was a metal footbridge that seemed to be my best option, so I sprinted — in flip-flops — to take shelter beneath it. More unfortunately, it was a bridge with wooden slats containing more pores than a strawberry, and it only kept some of the rain off.

So I sat there, soaking under the bridge and choosing the constant dripping of rainwater over the deluge just off to either side. It wasn't great. The rain poured for a while, but after 30 minutes, it went from downpour to drizzle, and I decided to make my move. I ran back to the end of the pool below the dam and drifted a worm-tipped jig in the current repeatedly. I caught several Bluegill and Mayan Cichlids before catching something else. No, not a cold, thankfully. Though it was a bit chilly. It was a small snook, and I immediately knew it wasn't a Common Snook. After some research, I identified it as a Smallscale Fat Snook.

Species #331 — Smallscale Fat Snook (*Centropomus parallelus*).

It, too, was a surprise species, and I was soaked — sorry, *stoked* — to add it to my list. I was not stoked to be soaked, so after catching a second little snook, I began the long soggy slog back to the car.

O'Reilly & Taylor

I returned to the stretch of creek I'd discovered with Zain that spring, and I parked right next to the O'Reilly Auto Parts store nearby and walked to the water. Unfortunately, it was blown-out with the recent rains, and the bigger snook I'd hoped to entice out from under the bridge wouldn't play. In fact, nothing would, so I detoured to a restaurant, grabbed dinner in my sopping-wet clothes, and proceeded to my next Couchsurfing stop.

My host, Eve Taylor, was one of only two single women who hosted me, and she was one of my favorite hosts. We sat and talked at her counter after I showered off, and the 60-something divorcée reminded me of several of my aunts. I inherently liked her. She sipped wine while I sipped iced tea, and we had fancy cheeses, crackers, and chocolate. It was not at all what I was expecting, but the humanity of it all was pleasant. I don't know how long we talked exactly, but it was several hours before we called it a night.

Chapter 28
Worms

July 8, 2019

Day 24
Origin: Melbourne, Florida
Destination: Titusville, Florida

"Every single living thing is food to at least one living thing."
Mokokoma Mokhonoana || South African Author
From *The Confessions of a Misfit*

    I awoke the next morning, but before I took off, Eve left me with a present. Men may be, but not all worms are created equal. Since Adam called them one by one, mankind has classified and compared animals. For most of us in the North and West, worms mean nightcrawlers. It was for this reason that my first few experiences fishing with worms in the American South — particularly Florida in the summer — weren't the best.
    "Canadian" nightcrawlers are not limited to Canada. In fact, they're not even *from* Canada, instead originating in Europe, but they certainly range into Canada now and prefer the cooler temperatures offered in northern latitudes to the hot swampiness of the American South. Nightcrawlers don't like heat. I can't blame them, though. After all, temps above about 70 degrees Fahrenheit will kill them. Temps above 70 won't kill me, but they burn me and make me sweatier than an (insert colloquialism here). This, in turn, can kill a fishing trip if you'd planned to use worms and suddenly find your bait has turned to stanky goo.

Fortunately, there is a solution.

Now, I've long used coolers to store bait, but shrimp and squid smell. Worms don't present that problem, but worms packed in dirt tend to come in paper containers. Even when contained within a plastic bag, water finds its way in and (1) drowns the worms and/or (2) the resulting mud finds its way into the water in your cooler, painting a thin film of dirt onto can mouths, fruit, your love life and anything else you decided to put on ice while fishing. Not to mention carrying a cooler over the river and through the woods is not something grandma will enjoy.

Logic notwithstanding, I just accepted worm limitations and carried a few in a paper towel in my pocket and would return to the cooler when I needed a refill. Then, friend and fellow angler Gerry Hansell told me to just buy a cooler lunch box. It changed the game. Suddenly, I could use fresh bait all over the South, and that dynastic shift in my routine had far-reaching ripple effects.

The toughest fishes to catch are those that won't touch store-bought bait, and it just so happened that I decided to target one of these (apparently) pickier fish again the next day. I'd failed to get my Bigmouth Sleeper, so I figured maybe I should change it up and use different bait despite never even seeing a sleeper to know it was rejecting my bait instead of simply not being present to see it.

One of Eve's hobbies is gardening, and to produce the kind of rich soil that her tomatoes and eggplants and other vegetables prefer, she farms worms in bathtubs in her backyard. She encouraged me to take some for bait in hopes that the local fauna might more readily hit a local worm. Her intuition was spot-on, and the second day I used worms from Eve's garden to catch not one but four Bigmouth Sleepers in a nearby river.

Species #332 — Bigmouth Sleeper (*Gobiomorus dormitor*).

I also hooked and lost two Spinycheek Sleepers — a much rarer species — and my hopes inflated and deflated in an instant. Then again, I know where these fish are, and I'll be back to catch those and the Mountain Mullet I did finally see just long enough to watch them dart out of my field of view and out of my life forever.

So as I continue to classify and record the fishes I catch, I'll think no more of Adam, a garden, and a serpent, but Eve, a garden, and a worm.

Lowlander

In the springtime, I'd struck out trying for Pearlscale or Lowland Cichlid. The pond had been right on the way, so the stop was quick, easy, and disappointing. I'll let you come up with your own sexual metaphor.

That said, I'd had to beg for this spot, and unlike the Highlander, this wannabe Lowlander was not immortal. I only had so much time.

In my finite mortality, summer was upon me before I knew it, and I was back in Florida.

Once again, the chance to become a Lowlander presented itself. The pond was right on the way, so I stopped for a second attempt at what is arguably the most beautiful cichlid in the Sunshine State. Just as before, I caught bass and Bluegill but didn't immediately see the cichlids. Suddenly, I found a rockpile and let my worm-tipped jig sink to the bottom. Out popped the black head of something neither bass nor sunfish. I leaned forward. It didn't take much work to get it to inhale the jig, and I quickly landed my first Pearlscale Cichlid.

Species #333 — Pearlscale Cichlid (*Herichthys carpintis*).

I was incredibly pleased to have become a Lowlander, and I notched a win for mere mortals and celebrated by breaking my own rule about not eating hot food during the day with a few slices of pizza nearby.

Parrish the Thought
I finished my evening fishing at Parrish Park right in Titusville. I'd stopped here once before but never spent much time actually fishing, and there were several catches logged on Fishbrain that intrigued me — Black Drum and Atlantic Stingray chief among them.

Dual-wielding rods, one light and one heavy, I made my way to the water. A group of people stood spread out across most of the causeway, and I nestled into the nearest corner. They told me it had been a slow day, and I smiled a little to myself when I caught a fish on my very first drop. American Silver Perch. The small croakers are widespread, but a fish I hadn't caught many of since the beginning of my trip. That changed quickly, and I caught fish after fish, hooking one live and throwing it out on my other rod while I continued slaying with the light rod. Before I called it a night with the light rod, I'd caught 28 of them. Add in Hardhead and Gaftopsail Catfish, *Bagre marinus*, Pinfish, and the lone Southern Kingcroaker (a new species), and I had caught 41 fishes on the light rod in under an hour.

Species #334 — Southern Kingcroaker (*Menticirrhus americanus*).

Even the heavy rod got some action, and something hit the live bait with a vengeance and ran for about three seconds before the line went flaccid. I reeled in my disappointment as I reeled in my rod. Only half of my bait remained. It could've been any number of fish, but it screamed small shark. I soaked live baits until darkness fell and even awhile after that, but to no avail.

When I arrived at my skeevy motel that night, I slept like a baby.

Chapter 29
Twenty-Five

July 9, 2019

Day 25
Origin: Titusville, Florida
Destination: Orlando, Florida

Spongebob: "Hey Patrick."
Patrick: "What?"
Spongebob: "I thought of something funnier than 24."
Patrick: "Let me hear it."
Spongebob: "Twenty-five!"
Spongebob Squarepants and Patrick Star
From *Spongebob Squarepants*

When I first fished for tarpon in 2018, it was one of the best experiences of my life. I'm admittedly romanticizing it in my mind because while it was one of the best, it was also one of the worst. On the first trip, I'd walked a mosquito-infested mile in 100-degree-plus heat in between thunderstorms as gators soaked in the water on both sides of the narrow grassy path. Biting ants kept climbing onto my flip-flops, and I began to wonder if I'd mistakenly entered the wrong coordinates. My only consolation was being able to breathe in the saturated, stewing air whenever I got thirsty — which was constantly.

The 16 Ladyfish, *Elops saurus* I landed kept me occupied as I hooked and lost tarpon after tarpon. It was infuriating. Of the 15 tarpon I hooked, I landed just one, but it was enough to hook me on tarpon.

It had been almost a year, but here I was again, walking through the crispy grass and clouds of mosquitoes to my destination. Minutes after my arrival, a flyfisherman appeared out of nowhere and scared the fight out of me when he walked up behind me and asked how I was doing. Before his sneak attack, I'd just hooked and lost a tarpon at the net.

"I've had better days," I replied with a chuckle that only slightly masked the bitterness I felt.

We chatted for a few minutes, and I reached to give him my card, but didn't have one on me. Neither did he have his. You may recall my whole trip had been built around Austin and Darian's wedding and ICAST, the fishing conference. As it happened, he was also in Central Florida for ICAST, which was now just two days away.

"Well," he started, "If I go out and do any more fishing, I'll give you a call."

"Thanks!" I replied. "Good luck today!"

I really doubted I'd hear from him anyway. He dove further into the mangroves, in the direction of the wild pigs grazing in the flooded grasses, and I proceeded to hook and lose more tarpon. In total, I hooked five, but eventually, I did land one. It was tiny, barely 20 inches long, but it still put up a commendable fight. Along with my single tarpon, I'd landed 25 Ladyfish and a Common Snook. Though not nearly as exciting as tarpon, Ladyfish passed the time, and each one brought a smile to my face.

Since I'd spent just a few hours this time around, and I'd already caught one, I decided to move to the next stop. I relished the 20-minute walk out. It was miserably hot, but hear me out: it was also riddled with mosquitoes.

Cops

My next stop was a few miles away. I pulled up to find someone fishing the spot from a boat, and I wondered why he'd decided to set up at the primary shore access point when he could take his boat miles in either direction, but I didn't feel like pressing it.

In the water at my feet, there were numerous small fish, including needlefish. You remember needlefish, my collective nemesis? In dozens of attempts, I had failed and failed and failed to catch one. I'd finally caught several Redfin Needlefish earlier in the trip, but the more common Atlantic Needlefish continued to elude my grasp. You know why they call them needlefish, right? Cuz those little pricks really needle your self-esteem.

After a few more failed minutes trying to get the needlefish to bite as they swam around on the surface in my immediate vicinity, I gave up and began soaking shrimp again for the little Mangrove Snapper and Pinfish flitting around the shadow line at the edge of the shallows. It was very rocky, and I snagged and broke off shortly thereafter. I hadn't brought gear from my car, so I walked back to get out another rig and cool off for a bit.

Just as I made it to my car, a game warden pulled up in a truck. During the weeks I'd been in Florida, I'd never run across a game warden. In fact, outside of a handful of Oregon and California warden interactions, I'd never really come across wardens in more than 1,000 fishing trips. I struggled to find my paper license, but fortunately I had service on my phone and was able to pull it up satisfactorily. He was friendly, and we talked a bit about microfishing — which he was absolutely fascinated by — before he moved on.

I told myself I'd spend no more than 15 minutes trying the spot before heading in to get some dinner. Light was fading fast, I was tired, and I was beginning to suspect I wouldn't get a new species today. I'd been on my trip for 25 days thus far, and I'd fished 23 of those days. I'd caught at least one new species every day I fished but for two. It looked like I was going to have a third without any new species.

Then, in the eleventh hour, I reeled in a puffer. I'd caught puffers, but I knew most of the species I'd caught were out of range, and when I looked at the little guy, it was immediately obvious I'd caught something new!

Species #335 — Southern Puffer (*Sphoeroides nephelus*).

At once excited to have caught one and incredibly entertained by puffers, generally, I felt briefly invigorated. Perhaps growing up watching and appreciating *Spongebob Squarepants* and the titular character's infuriating behavior around his boating school teacher, Mrs. Puff, influenced me. In fact, I know it did because every time I've handled a puffer that inflates itself, I see Mrs. Puff sitting in the passenger seat of a wrecked boat, inflating, and saying in a suddenly deep voice: "Oh Spongebob. Why?!"

I'm smirking to myself just thinking about it. *Spongebob* is truly a timeless classic. My mood lifted slightly by the memory, I decided I'd try to catch the needlefish again. I know, I know. It was likely an exercise in futility, but I was willing to experience probable disappointment in the off chance that I might get what I was looking for. That was my exact line of reasoning when it comes to dating, so it wasn't a philosophy new to my life, just new to the moment.

Just as I'd done successfully for Redfin Needlefish, I opted to use a micro sabiki without weight. I baited each hook and dragged it slowly along the surface near the cluster of needlefish. Getting bites is never the problem with these fish, but getting a solid hookset and then landing the fish is. These were small, so I had no risk of breaking off, and this emboldened me. When I finally had a serious take, I set the hook and to my barely contained shock, landed one.

A quick check confirmed the fins weren't red, but I failed to unhook it before checking, and it went into a gator-like death roll, tangling up my rig and connecting itself to my now equally hooked hand. Sadly, I couldn't get the whole mess sorted in time, and the fish died.

Species #336 — Atlantic Needlefish (*Strongylura marina*).

Rarely do I kill fish, but it happens. If possible, I'll eat the aquatic casualty or use it as bait, but sometimes I have to leave a dead fish. It won't go to waste, and this one didn't. Minutes after it sank to the bottom, small crabs were already picking it clean.

Circle of life, I suppose.

As easy as it is for some fishermen to get holier-than-thou about killing fish, and I'll admit I'm like that sometimes, but at the end of the day, angling is hooking a fish in the face for sport. Sure, I try to respect each fish and treat it with as much care as possible, but we can't pretend as anglers that we're not inflicting some level of pain — or at the very least, discomfort — upon our quarry. Proper handling will severely limit mortality, but it does still happen.

Still, I know I'll never again try to catch needlefish now that I've caught the irritating little beasts, so that lone needlefish served as a final sacrifice on behalf of its kin. That's probably overblown and earned an eye roll from you, dear reader, but that's okay. Like many of my questionable statements, I say it partly tongue-in-cheek.

Orlando

That night, I returned to Orlando. Before I checked in to my Airbnb, I rang up Zain to see if he was free to fish for an evening. Time was short, and the weather was in that ominous pre-thunderstorm stage that accounts for about 20 percent of all summer weather in Florida.

Zain, always up for fishing, told me he'd be down to run to a pond near his house and help me try to get a Golden Silverside, the small metallic baitfish apparently quite common in Florida for anyone not actually looking for them.

I arrived at his house, and picked up the CaughtOvgard-branded hats and T-shirts I'd had my mom mail to him earlier that summer in hopes of handing them out at ICAST. My intent was to have them ready before I left, but time is rarely an ally of man, and this instance was no different.

Instead, when they were finished, I had my mom pick them up and ship them to Zain's house, knowing full-well I'd meet up with him once I made it to Orlando. In the end, it worked out.

After losing my tenkara rod the day I did my best Humpty Dumpty impression and fell off the seawall in Miami, I'd immediately ordered another on Amazon and had it shipped to Zain's house as well, knowing we'd be meeting up in a week or so.

Two packages were waiting for me at his house, and I thanked Zain with his choice of hats, said hello to his family, and thanked them for serving as my post office box-away-from-home.

Zain and I grabbed some gear, and we hopped on bikes. Where we were fishing, there wasn't much in the way of parking, and it was a short ride from his house. It was a bold play in the impending weather, but YOLO.

Zain and his crew take a special interest in using ultralight gear for larger fishes such as Florida and Largemouth Bass, Bowfin, and a host of saltwater species most people would never throw ultralight, finesse presentations for. It usually pays dividends, and as I failed to locate any silversides, he struck gold time and again with his little jig. He caught several bass before the weather forced me to give up any hope of finding the silversides, and we rode like madmen back to his house to flee the deluge.

We agreed to fish again when I finished the conference, and I headed to my Airbnb.

Fishbrain, my sponsor, would pay for my lodging again this year in exchange for helping out and representing them at ICAST. Though I'd gotten into the Pro Staff or Ambassador Program when Bojan Lazic ran it, Hanna Grevelius had since taken over, and I'd gotten to know her well through email, phone calls, and a few conference calls and video chats. She invited me to return to ICAST, and that, along with Austin and Darian's wedding, had precipitated my entire cross-country trip, so I made sure to get a full night's sleep to be ready for the next day.

The only problem was that, upon arriving at my Airbnb, I learned it was a third-floor walkup. Ordinarily, this would be fine, but given that I had to completely unload months' worth of supplies, fishing gear, coolers, clothing, and food one load at a time, it was an inconvenience. But the apartment itself was nice, and it let me sleep soundly while I imagined Spongebob and Patrick counting the Ladyfish I'd caught that day, on my 25th day of my trip, all the way to 25, laughing uproariously when they hit that magically comical number.

Chapter 30
ICAST

July 10, 2019

Day 26
Origin: Orlando, Florida
Destination: Orlando, Florida

"A bad day fishing is better than a good day at the office —
unless you work in the fishing industry."
Unknown || Twitter

The kid-in-the-candy-store Luke who had attended ICAST the year before faded into the background this year. Yes, I was still enamored with the massive scale of the conference and the presence of all my favorite brands, but having experienced it once before, this time I felt I could be less of a tourist and more of a participant.

I was the firs to arrive that morning, and I waited in the lobby outside the entrance, musing quietly to myself as dozens of fishing personalities of widely varying levels of success as YouTubers, bloggers, podcasters, writers, television hosts, and tournament anglers filmed themselves in front of the conference center. Most of them were small-time, even more so than I, and let's be real: did anyone actually care that they were there, in some jersey covered with logos? Heck, I had almost 100,000 people reading my column every week at that point, and I can assure you my readers didn't care. But hey, I was a wonderstruck tourist my first time, too, so I let it slide.

When I first sighted the black-and-white Fishbrain hats, I made my way over to the group and introduced myself — most of the crew that was in attendance this time was new to me. I finally met Hanna, and her smile and personality were just as big and infectious as I expected. Accompanying her were a group of others that I would get to know in short order. This included Fishbrain's CEO, Johan Attby, whom I'd met at ICAST the year before, and Niklas Eklund, a prominent Swedish investor and Fishbrain's Chairman of the Board. Alphabetically, the Fishbrain team also included Jens Beckemeier, Austin Buck, Johan Klintbo, Robert Kornfeld, Petter Norberg, and Martin Roos.

Before long, Hanna introduced me to Ross Cocheo, a kayak bass specialist who lived in New Jersey but talked with the British accent that bespoke his upbringing in the United Kingdom. He seemed like a genuinely nice guy, and we hit it off.

The previous year, Fishbrain had held a booth and members of its staff hosted a press conference every few hours. The Ambassadors such as myself were asked to attend, answer questions, and look pretty. Though our roles were fairly limited, that was our only requirement. I felt privileged to be in that group of Ambassadors, and though I was wide-eyed from the scope of the conference, I lived up to my limited role and actually expanded upon it, spending time speaking with each and every wildlife management agency present at the conference about the potential data tracking and enforcement potential of Fishbrain. It had scored me some brownie points, and given that the other Ambassadors that year hadn't really put in the same level of effort, I'd been the only one asked back. I genuinely liked the others who'd attended, but they were more about furthering their own careers, sponsorships, and (one in particular) about smoking his dab pen at every opportunity. Simply by not being high and actually showing up when I was supposed to, I think I would've locked in a return invite, but I did a little extra work. After all, Fishbrain had brought me, so I felt a fair amount of loyalty and obligation to work *for them* first.

It paid off, and I was back. This time, Ross and I were the only Ambassadors present.

Essentially, our job this year was to speak with as many brands as we could about putting their respective product catalogs on the newest piece of the platform, the Fishbrain Store. Envision Amazon but with a specialized set of gear for anglers, complete with reviews and products attached to specific catches, showcasing its effectiveness and taking reviews to the next level. It's a great idea but with a much smaller commission than similar affiliate referral platforms, so it wasn't that difficult to sell.

Our secondary goal was to speak with individual anglers and get them to sign up for Fishbrain. Preferably, Fishbrain Pro (about $60 per year), but the free version if nothing else. Fishbrain Pro is a necessity for the serious angler. You should sign up now if you're interested. Click one of the Fishbrain ads at the bottom of my blog (www.caughtovgard.com) if you feel like giving me credit for that signup, but sign up regardless. After all, in the world of tech, Average Daily Users (ADU) is a very important metric, so driving traffic to the app would certainly be beneficial if we accomplished nothing else. We had some giveaway items, hats and backpacks, and we made a strong effort that day, covering almost a third of the show floor.

In the process, we did a little self-promotion to those brands that aligned with our own respective values and goals as anglers. Obviously, my platform, CaughtOvgard, included the blog and written word in newspapers and magazines with a special focus on wild trophy trout and multispecies angling. Ross, by contrast, was a YouTube presence. His entertaining YouTube channel, theenglishchannel, serves as a sort of everyman's channel focused primarily on bass and pickerel angling from a kayak.

Between us, we covered a lot of bases, and we were able to carry on with most brands. Of course, getting traction with smaller brands was easy; many of the owners were staffing the booths. It was the larger brands that took more work, and we often had to set appointments or go through half a dozen people before we got to decision makers.

We made a solid team, and we managed to get some personally beneficial contacts in the process that we would follow up with later in the conference. We broke for lunch, resumed our duties, and the day wound to a close.

Despite having walked miles on the mostly carpeted concrete, we agreed we'd like to fish if given the opportunity. Just outside the parking lot, there were ponds. Well, it was Orlando, so there were ponds within a half mile of any given point. Weather was ominous as we drove about 100 yards from the parking lot, pulled into a muddy field, and made our way down to the water. It was windy and cold, and the bass didn't seem to love it. I'd brought just a fraction of my bass gear, so we had limited options. Topwaters weren't productive, and the winds drove us to try another spot.

Hopping to a nearby pond we'd found just by alternately scanning our Maps app and Fishbrain (Pro pays for itself time and again), we found ourselves at some shopping center pond. By now, it was pouring rain. We waited in the car for a few minutes, hoping the deluge would lessen, but it didn't let up, so we said "Screw it!"

and fished anyway. Neither of us hooked up, despite covering the pond thoroughly, and we were forced to call it a day after a while. I dropped Ross off and went to grab dinner.

On the menu that night: Ethiopian food.

In the perennial road work and thick traffic of Central Florida, it took me 40 minutes or so to get to the restaurant a few miles away. I scarfed down the food, overeating as I usually do at East African restaurants, and walked out to my car slightly bloated.

As I walked into the apartment where I was staying, I realized something: this was the only day I'd gone fishing and gotten skunked on this trip. Fortunately, time would allow it to be the last such occurrence on my entire road trip.

If I'd known that then, I might have felt better about it, but despite the productive day on the conference floor, I was a little dejected by my failure. After all, tomorrow was packed with more of the same, as well as some scheduled meetings and a group dinner that evening, so I likely wouldn't even get to fish the next day. But hey, if I can't be fishing because of work, it might as well be fishing-related work, right?

Chapter 31
Meet Your Heroes

July 11, 2019

Day 27
Origin: Orlando, Florida
Destination: Orlando, Florida

"He's a great American fisherman, he'll fish anywhere.
Anywhere there's water, Lord knows he'll be there.
He's just like a gypsy: mighty hard to hold.
Great American fisherman got fishin' in his soul."
Fishing with Roland Martin|| Theme Song Chorus

    The second day of ICAST began with a special breakfast, just as it had the year before. Once again, Fishbrain had pulled together its lesser Ambassadors (like yours truly) with some of its greater Ambassadors (some of the biggest names in fishing) and a number of Fishbrain staffers for a hosted breakfast.
    The previous year, it had been held at a Denny's. Okay, technically it's called "The Diner," but it's the look, feel, and menu of a Denny's with a facelift. The Diner sits right across the street from the Orange County Convention Center, and is markedly more popular than a regular Denny's — particularly with foreign guests who don't know any better — but it's still just a glorified Denny's. Apparently, it used to be called "Danny's" but now it's like a Denny's Plus.
    You might be wondering why I'm going on about Denny's/Danny's/The Diner so much. Well, it just so happens to be

where I met one of my heroes in 2018. Flashback with me, if you will.

ICAST 2018

What differentiates a dream from reality?

As our Lyft pulled up to the restaurant for a group breakfast sponsored by Fishbrain, we saw arguably the greatest bass fisherman to ever live talking on a cellphone outside. Was I dreaming?

"That was Roland Martin," I said to my companion in the car, Stacy Barawed, calmly and without the slightest hint of giddy squealing.

Trying to remember everything I learned in that one yoga class I thought about taking once, I began deep breathing exercises to calm myself down. After all, I was about to meet one of my heroes, and the last thing I wanted to do was fangirl and fawn all over a living legend.

We walked in and waited for our assigned table, but it wasn't ready. My nervous bladder sent me to the bathroom, and I made sure I looked my best. You snicker, but put yourself in my shoes and see if you aren't nervous.

The party began arriving, and we went into our private dining room. I was seated next to Shyanne Orvis, who is descended from the original Orvis family but has made a name for herself as a flyfishing guide in Colorado. We swapped trout stories until the celebrities began arriving.

In walked not only the king of bass, Roland Martin, but his son Scott Martin, and the Canadian princess of trout and salmon, April Vokey.

Bruh.

The quickening of my heart rate must have been audible because Shyanne whispered, "They're just regular people. You're good." It calmed me just enough for me to not make a fool of myself as Scott Martin and Johan Attby, the Fishbrain CEO and founder, sat down at my end of the table.

Conversation proved Shyanne right; they were regular people.

We swapped fishing stories, shared information and our food arrived. The building's facade and decor weren't the only souped-up elements of this Denny's; the food was actually edible. Go figure! Then again, I could've eaten anything that morning — not just Moons Over My Hammy — and still been over the moon.

Though I met Scott early, it wasn't until after breakfast that I had a chance to meet Roland and April.

Roland, then in his late 70s, could've passed for 60, a testament to what a lifetime of fishing can do for a person. He was swarmed by my fellow Fishbrain ambassadors, so I took a moment to talk with April — I'd get a chance to catch up with him later, anyway. She was warm, friendly and we quickly exchanged information. Then she followed me on Fishbrain.

April Vokey followed me on Fishbrain.

So that happened. No big deal.

These folks were all celebrities in the fishing world, and there I was, standing and talking with them, taking pictures with them. Admittedly, I felt a little out of my league. Sure, I consider myself a capable fisherman, and I have world records and a few "firsts" and "onlys" to back that up, but I was among some of the best ever. I guess if it's anything like real estate, being the least house in the best neighborhood is promising for the future, right?

I know I'd had this dream, but since we were at Danny's — Denny's — I knew that strange little detail was too ordinary for my unconscious mind to conjure up because as a fisherman and a writer, I have a very active imagination. Fortunately, as in fishing, the proof is in the pictures.

ICAST 2019

Round Two was different, though. The breakfast was to be held at another location. Already, that was a positive change. Unfortunately, April wouldn't be there, but Roland and Scott would be back.

"So let me get this straight," Ross said, "We get to meet Scott Martin, Roland Martin, and get a good meal?"

Ross, an aspiring YouTube presence, had nothing but respect for Scott Martin, the angler who has been far and away the most successful on YouTube, routinely reaching the milestone of one million viewers on his videos and boasting almost half a million subscribers.

A year prior, I'd been seated next to Scott Martin and listened to him speak about his growing business, and he'd done quite well for himself. Sure, name recognition helped, but he knew what he was doing, and that slingshotted him from famous-adjacent to actually famous.

Scott was great, but Roland was the icon I was most taken with. After all, I grew up watching his television show, and he was one of my first heroes I wasn't related to. So color me no less pleased than Ross.

The breakfast was great. Like legitimately great. It was buffet-style but with an omelet bar and a host of other luxuries that accented and improved upon an already great experience. It compounded the experience, and I was sure to relish the moment. Ross and I were given a special thanks from Fishbrain for all of our efforts at the conference, and that was a nice nod. Humbled to not only be in the presence of greatness but also to be acknowledged in front of them was incredible.

We finished breakfast, and Ross and I spent a few moments chatting with Chasten Whitfield, a 20-something who spends her time tournament fishing and taking disadvantaged kids fishing. She is another Fishbrain Ambassador who had just attended the breakfast, having had other obligations during the conference itself.

Fully stuffed, it was time to make our way to the convention center. It was kind of cool to see a place so packed with people not interested in sports or music but *fishing*. We thought about how many of these people had actually made a career of fishing in one way or another, either as professional anglers, guides, brand managers, product designers, or via a host of other avenues. I mean, in part, my career was fishing. Though it didn't come close to paying all of my bills as a fishing writer, it paid some of them, and that was more than most of the attendees at the conference could say. Same with Ross, who also hand-paints lures with custom logos as a side business. Counting ourselves blessed for those opportunities we'd been given and seized, as well as the opportunity to attend ICAST provided by Fishbrain, we walked tall to the show floor.

On this second day, we were in a rhythm. We spoke with Hanna and her team about the opportunities and expectations of the day. She told us to redirect interested brands to her, Petter, or Austin. Petter worked heavily with the Fishbrain Store, while Austin was the newly hired Stateside Fishbrain representative based right there in Florida. For part of our rounds on the second day, Petter accompanied us.

The three of us got on well, and we enjoyed ourselves as we cruised the stalls, schmoozing and making contacts. If the opportunity presented itself, Ross and I pitched ourselves for potential sponsorship, but primarily we were focused on making Fishbrain's investment in us worthwhile. Throughout the course of the conference, we spoke with almost every single one of the 100-plus vendors and got more than 20 referrals to Fishbrain's staff for potential inclusion in the Fishbrain Store — not to mention the dozens of people we convinced to sign up for Fishbrain, many of them as Pro members. I think we earned our free lodging.

It wasn't seamless, though. Almost immediately, we brushed by a competitor of Fishbrain. At the time, Fishbrain had more than six million users, while this particular competitor had yet to break a million. Okay, they had yet to break half a million. So, the rivalry wasn't strong in our minds, but the folks at that other app certainly thought so.

One of the attractive female employees of our rival stopped Ross and me. Hey, we're just men, so we had a quick chat. Ross' British accent drips charm, and he had that girl wrapped around his finger. I watched, bemused, as the guy behind the table sort of encouraged it. This particular app had taken to hiring scantily clad female anglers to pose in their gear, so the strategy of having an employee flirt with someone wouldn't be entirely new. Regardless, while Ross chatted up the attractive young lady, the guy tried to make inroads with me.

He tried to ask questions about strategy, user metrics, and glean anything he could. I played it cool and acted like I didn't know much, asserting I was just a pretty face hired to walk around and make introductions. I'm not sure if he bought it, but he tried to recruit me right then and there.

"I don't know what they're paying you," he said with all the nonchalance of David Rose's sweatshirt in television's *Schitt's Creek* (another all-time great series), "but we treat our Pro Staff very well."

I thanked him for the offer, but mentioned that I was happy with Fishbrain for now. He was undeterred. He continued trying to butter me up, but the five minutes or so we'd spent there were already long enough, so I sort of cued Ross to land the plane. His new female friend invited us to a hosted event at their booth later that night, and I just smiled wryly. We wished them well and moved on down the aisle.

The next few hours flew by. We spoke with some of my favorite brands, including St. Croix (rods) and FeelFree (kayaks), as well as some of Ross' like Googan Baits (lures) and 13 Fishing (rods and reels). It was a productive day. Not only did we sign up dozens of Fishbrainers, we also got numerous contacts and interested parties to pass up the food chain. We grabbed lunch and split up for a bit before reconvening in the afternoon. Time ran out, and we found ourselves at several afterparties that afternoon and early evening.

Our only scheduled stop was at Mustad's booth. Mustad, a Norwegian company, was the first major brand to sign on with the (Swedish) Fishbrain Store. Nordic solidarity, I suppose. With a name like Ovgard and my large-for-an-American size, I was even mistaken for a Nord several times, which, at one-quarter Norwegian, I technically am.

Mustad gave out free beers in nice metal cups. Now, I don't drink, but I liked the cups. Ross agreed to give me his cup if I let him drink my beer. It was a good deal for both of us, so I stood there holding but not drinking a beer. It reminded me of the one time I tried to fit in at a party in college, but this time, it seemed to be working.

The Fishbrainers present stacked up for a group photo, and we all held the Mustad cups high, smiling our best Scandinavian smiles.

After that, we sort of dissolved into the evening. Ross and I got an invite to join Fishbrain for dinner at a touristy restaurant located inside Disney Springs — a shopping center near Disney World that serves like a free, but equally packed, Disney World outside of Disney World, albeit without rides. It's a worthwhile visit, despite the parking nightmare.

We enjoyed a great meal that was fresh and delicious. Part of the appeal was that they made the guacamole fresh at your table. I ordered fajitas, and they were in the Southwest or Tex-Mex style more than actual Mexican, but great and markedly lighter fare than I'd expected.

Exchanged stories highlighted the evening, and shortly after we finished eating, Jens and a handful of the more lively gents split off to go to the "Costa Party." In my two years attending ICAST, it was *the party* everyone talked about but was invite-only and typically packed. I passed last year, and this time, I repeated my decision. The next morning, that would prove to be the right choice, given it was too full, and our teammates couldn't even get in. I dropped Ross off and called it an early night, failing to wet a line that day for just the second time on my trip.

Chapter 32
Telling Time

July 12, 2019

Day 28
Origin: Orlando, Florida
Destination: Orlando, Florida

"People who love nature find a common basis for understanding people of other countries, since the love of nature is universal among men of all nations."
Dag Hammarskjöld || Secretary General of the United Nations

 Up until this point, being on the Fishbrain Pro Staff had given me bragging rights, a chance to attend ICAST twice, some free meals, a chance to meet one of my heroes, a free subscription to Fishbrain Pro, some shirts and hats, and a few "Featured Posts" which enabled me to get thousands of likes on Fishbrain. Flex.
 I'd never received a check, and apart from my hotel room at the conferences, not a single perk I'd received had a tangible monetary value of more than $50 or so.
 Until the last day of ICAST, that is.
 Fishbrain entered into a partnership with CASIO to include special features for Fishbrain Pro users on the CASIO ProTrek Smartwatch. To solidify the partnership, Fishbrain and Casio invited a group of outdoor writers to a half-day event that included a breakfast, guided fishing trip, and product field test. It also featured a sort of show-and-tell session, wherein CASIO staff showed us how the product worked.

Everyone present (including me and Ross) got a watch to try out as a free gift. Considering it was worth $400, it remains the single most valuable "payment" I've ever received in my capacity as a Pro Staffer, given that it's difficult to assign monetary value to guided fishing trips and access to private water.

I fiddled around with the watch as we drove out to the Lake Toho Marina for a sponsored bass fishing trip. I was hoping to fish with a Florida bass pro, but we just fished live shiners all morning. Given that our veritable United Nations of anglers that morning included American, British, Canadian, Japanese, and Swedish nationals with varying levels of fishing experience, it was probably the right call.

Fishing was fairly slow.

Though I got a few strikes on the shiners, it wasn't really my speed. I swapped out to a finesse jig, thankful I'd brought a small tackle bag along, and caught one of the smallest Florida Bass I've ever seen.

Only about half a dozen of the 20 or so anglers caught fish, so I felt slightly validated. We were encouraged to post our catches to Fishbrain, and even though the tiny bass Hanna photographed for me that I posted on Fishbrain became the "Featured Post" of the day and got as many laughs as likes, I took it in stride and made fun of myself a little, too.

Still, it was good exposure. A significant part of my brand is, after all, making people laugh at my expense.

Debbie Hanson, a guide, writer, and radio host who'd been invited along in the media group, caught two fish to lead our boat. Nobody caught a bass over two pounds in any of the boats, though one guy did hook a monster Bowfin that he lost at the gunwale.

We'd only spared two hours to fish, and we returned to the hotel where we'd had breakfast that morning for final questions and press packages to be disseminated to the media present.

Spoiler alert: This would be my only guided or charter fishing trip of the year, and I had neither paid for it nor caught a new species.

As we piled back into the vans, I got a phone call. The flyfisherman I'd met a few days before while chasing tarpon in the middle of nowhere had actually called me back. He was going fishing and invited me along. Unfortunately, I still had obligations at the conference, so I had to decline, but I thanked him for remembering and a small piece of my lingering animosity towards flyfishing purists went away. Only time will tell if that animosity goes away entirely some day.

Closing Time

The iconic Semisonic song played in my head as the conference wound to a close. Fishbrain had us continue the rounds for an hour or so after our Casio event, but after that, they hopped on return flights to Sweden, and we were free to roam about the cabin. Ross and I decided to try our best to make one final push, following up with loose ends and trying to pick up a sponsor or two ourselves.

A brand called Rheos, which makes floating sunglasses, was our first hit. Nervously, I worked my way into getting a free pair of shades for each of us. Ross would later bring on Rheos as a sponsor, doing some video work for them. I loved the concept, but the pair of glasses I'd hastily chosen were too large for me, so my own hopes for working with the floating sunglasses brand sunk for the time-being. Fortunately, they later replaced them with a better-fitting pair, and I was hooked forever on Rheos.

We spoke with other booths and rounded out the evening with lots of free stuff but few other sponsorship leads until we found ourselves at Reef Safe Sun, an environmentally-friendly sunscreen brand.

We spoke with the owner, Dan Knorr, and hit it off.

In the end, he gave us a smattering of his products on the spot that I would come to love and appreciate throughout the course of my trip. I put a pin in Reef Safe, making a note in my phone to contact him as soon as I got back from my trip. It was by far the most promising potential sponsor I'd brushed shoulders with at ICAST, and though Dan said they didn't currently have a Pro Staff program, he said he was interested in speaking with me further to get one started a few weeks down the road, once his trade show schedule slowed down a little.

As booths packed up, Ross and I went back to the car. He had a few hours to kill before his flight left, and I'd promised to drop him off at the airport, so we figured we could kill a little time. My Lifeproof phone case had been put through the ringer on this trip, so I swung by a cellphone store to buy a new one. Though they're not terribly durable, Lifeproof cases enable me to take underwater photos and wash my phone after I get it covered in rancid bait juice, fish slime, or anything else that would ruin a perfectly functional iPhone. I dropped the $80 for a new case, we grabbed some coffee, then headed to the airport and parted ways.

Orlandope

It wasn't dark yet, so I hit up Zain.

The previous year, on my first visit to Central Florida, I'd made friends with a handful of locals who lived in and around Orlando.

Three guys in particular, Zain Khalid, Jessel Sanchez, and Pierce Sanders, taught me a lot. I was able to fish with Jessel once and Zain on several occasions during the summer of 2019 and while at my conference in the spring of 2018, but I never did meet Pierce in person. Still, all three had become my friends through frequent interactions on social media — primarily on Instagram in a group chat I named "Orlandope."

These guys are incredible anglers — specifically microfishermen — who have caught more "near impossible" species than almost anyone else in the Species Hunting community, including: Everglades Pygmy Sunfish, *Elassoma evergladei*, Least Killifish, *Heterandria formosa*, Okefenokee Pygmy Sunfish, *Elassoma okefenokee*, Rainwater Killifish, *Lucania parva*, and Sailfin Molly, *Poecilia latipinna*, as well as being some of the only people to regularly catch chubsuckers, a notoriously frustrating fish found along the Eastern Seaboard.

Zain was free that evening, so I returned to his house to take another crack at the Golden Silverside. With a tenkara rod that could reach 12 feet, it was pretty easy, and I had one in almost no time.

Species #337 — Golden Silverside (*Labidesthes vanhyningi*).

It broke a two-day streak without a new species, and I was sure to get clear pictures of the fish slightly submerged, given most silversides are distinguished by the anal and dorsal fin origins and the relationship between the two — a feature only visible when the fish is in water.

By the time I landed that fish, it was almost dark, and I was a solid 40 minutes from my Airbnb, so I parted ways with Zain and agreed to meet up with him the next day for a trip to the coast to chase tarpon and anything else we wanted to look for.

Chapter 33
Faith in the Unseen

July 13, 2019

Day 29
Origin: Orlando, Florida
Destination: Titusville, Florida

"But fishermen, I have noticed, they don't care whether I'm Brown or White, rich or poor, wearing robes or waders. All they care about is the fish, the river and the game we play. For fishermen, the only virtues are patience, tolerance, and humility. I like this."
Sheikh Muhammed || From *Salmon Fishing the Yemen*

I picked up Zain early, and tired though I was, we made our way to the coast east of Orlando. Our destination: Titusville.

Sadly, from the very beginning, luck was not on our side. For some odd reason, I wasn't using my GPS, and I missed the turnoff to Titusville. This cost us almost 40 minutes in detours since the next exit was nearly 15 miles away on the divided highway.

To his credit, Zain was much kinder about it than I would've been. With the extra time, we talked quite extensively. One of the topics we stayed on for awhile was the disparity between faith and science in the modern angling world. Zain was still in college and studying genetics and biology. He's quite brilliant. He's also a practicing Muslim.

Most anglers and members of the Species Hunting and aquatic scientific communities alike are staunchly atheistic, or at the very least, coolly agnostic. For those individuals who have faith in God or practice any sort of traditional religion, the scientific community can often be dismissive and even alienating about such beliefs as Creationism or the acknowledgement of any higher power.

As a Christian, my beliefs are obviously different from Zain's, but a Christian and a Muslim share much more in common than an atheist would share with either of us. It was a deep discussion for a fishing trip, but I appreciated the discourse, especially since my rural town in Southern Oregon isn't exactly a haven for Islamic practice.

Once again, learning to find common ground and being able to have a civil discussion with a person whose values and driving beliefs are fundamentally different from your own proved its value. It was refreshing to have two people sit side-by-side and engage in a discourse of commonality and disparity with respect and humility.

I know my own Christian faith, if it were simplified to a single word, would be love, and I think a lot of Christians forget that. Christ didn't marginalize and defame and preach hatred. He certainly didn't shy away from rebuke or compromise His beliefs, but His message was one of loving God and loving your neighbor first and foremost. That's important to remember.

Also important to remember? Your exit.

I had half a dozen potential freshwater spots set out for this day, but we opted instead to try our hand fishing saltwater. It's the ocean, after all, and there were still a dozen species recorded on Fishbrain right in Titusville I'd never caught: Atlantic Stingray, *Dasyatis sabina,* Black Drum, Sand Seatrout, *Cynoscion arenarius,* Striped Mojarra, *Eugerres plumieri,* Summer Flounder, *Paralichthys dentatus,* and Oyster Toadfish, *Opsanus tau* chief among them.

We finally arrived at Parrish Park, where just a few days before, I'd absolutely slayed American Silver Perch, sea catfish, and kingcroaker. Most of those species would be new for Zain, who primarily fishes freshwater near his Orlando home.

It was more of the same, and I quickly realized there would be no lifers for me there that day, but Zain added a few, so that certainly improved the hand we were dealt. I played 52 Pick Up without cards by catching 52 fishes there. In a scenario rarely seen in the World Series of Poker, I was holding out for a jack and was disappointed by the pair of kings I picked up while fishing there — Southern Kingcroaker, that is.

Haulover Canal

We went from there to a place called the Haulover Canal, which had initially been dug as a shorter water route from the Atlantic

Coast of Florida to the northernmost end of the Indian River. It ended up being less economically useful than expected, but today, it is popular with anglers. It is also where I'd caught my first Southern Puffer and finally (oh thank God, finally!) caught my first Atlantic Needlefish a few days prior.

I snagged more sabikis in a few hours there than I had on my whole trip up to that point, losing six or seven of them. Others nearby were fishing for inshore predators, Red and Black Drum and Spotted Seatrout topping the list. This intrigued Zain and me, and we both set out heavy rods. Mine was ignored like a poorly dressed woman at a gay bar, but Zain had found and caught a small crab that he cut in half and used as bait.

I'm not sure how long it took for his epic bite because a friendly but inebriated couple kept chatting us up. They were nice enough to give us some popping corks to try out, and I experimented with them for a bit. Unfortunately, the tide was up, and I couldn't get out past the submerged root wads at the mouth of the canal without wading out. Every time I waded out, my bare feet and lower legs were mobbed by hungry sand fleas.

I caught some Pinfish, some more Pinfish, a Sheepshead, and some Mangrove Snapper, but that was it.

When Zain's rod bent sharply, we knew it was a big fish. Either a big Red or Black Drum, but either way, I was pulling for him as that fish pulled against him. He fought it fairly well, though he was a little undergunned and probably would've been able to tire it out a lot faster with a bigger setup. After 15 minutes or so, without warning, he lost the fish. It was a devastating blow to us both, and we just sort of sat there, stunned, unsure of what had happened.

He fished the other half of the crab for a while as I fished shrimp, but nothing else tried our seafood buffet that afternoon, so we moved to the final spot.

Tarpon
The tarpon were still present, and I caught two. Well, I hooked two, but they were hard-won, and I ultimately lost both. We couldn't see them, but we believed they were there. The larger of the pair would've been my largest tarpon to-date (probably about 13-15 pounds), but it came off about 18 inches from the scoop of my net and soaked me with a swipe of its tail. Mmmm, losing a nice fish and getting a mouthful of brackish water blackened with tannin all at once? Unfair.

Zain, meanwhile, patterned the small snook and caught half a dozen of them on his ultralight rod with a small jig. I was impressed and stupefied at once by the uniqueness of his presentation and subsequent catches, but the results didn't lie. Weirdly, the Ladyfish were nowhere to be found that evening, and I ended up with a goose egg at our final spot.

Light evacuated the sky, and we evacuated the gator-infested sawgrass, each thanking our God for such an enjoyable day on the water.

Chapter 34
The Florida Panhandle

July 14, 2019

Day 30
Origin: Orlando, Florida
Destination: Montgomery, Alabama

"One U.S. soldier wrote: 'If the devil owned both Hell and Florida, he'd rent out Florida and live in Hell.'"
Quoted in *American History Tellers*

I've already expressed some frustration with the tendency of certain public lands to exclude the very hunters and anglers who actually fund their maintenance and operation. Florida is home to dozens of such places, particularly in and around the springs in the northern part of the state.

Many of these areas have long allowed swimming and diving and rafting in these fragile ecosystems while remaining closed to fishing, arguing it would have too much environmental impact and could create issues for swimmers if gear was snagged and lost and wound up in people. The argument that someone standing on shore and catching a fish is somehow more damaging than a swimmer doing his or her best Godzilla impersonation across the streambed is, of course, absurd. Yet, that's exactly how most of these spring parks are operated.

It would make sense to either close all access or allow all reasonable use. Piecemeal exclusion is indefensible.

Though it has since closed to all water access and entry — even for swimmers and divers — a spot called Gilchrist Blue Springs was high on my list for the diversity it was rumored to support. When I pulled up to the state park that Sunday, I found a line of cars, waiting with their air conditioning running full blast. I got out of the car and looked ahead to see a "PARK FULL" sign displayed nearby. As one car would leave, another would be let in.

It was insanity.

I gave it 15 minutes and two of the 20 or so cars ahead of me got in, so I cut my losses and moved on to my next destination. The next park allowed fishing, mercifully, but was not nearly as conducive to the prospect. I soaked a worm on the bottom in hopes of catching a Spotted Sucker, *Minytrema melanops* or the like while I microfished. I spent a fair amount of time chasing small fishes I could neither identify nor catch. There were at least three types of micros there, but after a fruitless hour, I gave up.

I moved on to another spot, this one a hotspot for rafting. After paying another day use fee, I loaded up my gear and started walking down to the river to fish. Just before I arrived at the water, a park employee stopped me and gave me a lecture about how fishing wasn't allowed. I pressed the point, noting how that was not spelled out in the fishing regulations. I was polite, but I asked on what authority it was banned, given that her agency was not a regulatory body for fisheries management.

Naturally, she couldn't answer the question and just told me "We don't want our rafts getting popped by hooks," and my face certainly showed disgust at the gross commercialization of this precious natural resource.

Not wanting to argue, I told her I'd just leave.

"Wait here," she said in an impossibly catty tone, "I'm gonna have you chat with the rangers and see if you're so confident then."

"Thanks anyway," I said back with an equal helping of smugness.

She cussed at me, and I smiled and turned to walk away.

She lost her composure and started screaming something about "You're gonna get a ticket."

"For what?" I replied. "Intent to fish? I never wet a line."

Some lady in line next to me taking in the spectacle said "That's a good point," and the crowd, at first against me, seemed to be rallying to my side in light of the woman's rude behavior. This was pointless.

Realizing I had absolutely nothing to gain, I threw in the towel.

"Have a nice day," I said, turning and walking back to my car. I casually stowed my rods and drove away.

Off the Beaten Path

At this point, I was ready to just skip the Florida Panhandle entirely and head straight to Alabama, but I had three spots left on my radar, and one of them had a lot of promise. I was half-hearted when I tried to find the park, and a wrong turn sent me into some remote reach of the park with a small storage shed and a number of small cabins — a scout camp.

Camp didn't seem to be in session, so I parked my car and walked down the steep trail into a canyon. It looked more like the gorges I fished for trout and salmon and steelhead back home in the PNW than a Florida river, save for the dark, tea-colored water steeped in tannins. The current was relatively fast, despite the river's lazy surface flow, and it took me a minute to find a pocket that would allow my small slip sinker to rest easily on the bottom.

Once it stopped drifting, I got a bite. The small bullhead I pulled up wasn't the Gulf Sturgeon, *Acipenser oxyrinchus* I was hoping to luck into, and I assumed the speckled creature was just a Florida Brown Bullhead. In reality, it was a Spotted Bullhead.

Species #338 — Spotted Bullhead (*Ameiurus serracanthus*).

The next fish was also a bullhead, this time a White Catfish, *Ameiurus catus*. It wasn't a new species, but I hadn't caught one in years, so it was a nice surprise. Despite the surprise new species, my perch on the edge of the canyon wall wasn't exactly comfortable, so I packed up and climbed out of the canyon with enough grace to avoid tumbling backward into the shadowy depths.

Sturgeon

Eventually, I found the main entrance to the park. It was a bit of a walk from the parking area to the boat ramp, the single best access point to the river, and even though the canyon wasn't as steep here as the spot behind the scout camp, it was still all but impossible to access the water given the high banks and loose soil — save for the boat ramp.

I began throwing out small baits and jigs in hopes of catching a Flier, *Centrarchus macropterus* or larger Suwannee Bass, *Micropterus notius*. Neither fish obliged, so I threw out a large bait for the Gulf Sturgeon I could see jumping every few minutes. They weren't nearly as large as the White Sturgeon back home in Oregon, but to catch a fish three or four or five feet long would still have been something to behold and given that few people catch Gulf Sturgeon, it would've given me some serious bragging rights.

So, for several hours, I tried in vain to catch one. It was infuriating, honestly. They wouldn't take shrimp, worms, or cut bait, and I felt impotent. As a result, I wedged the sturgeon rod between the butt of a tree and began microfishing, catching fishes but nothing new.

Just as I began to contemplate leaving, I saw a small darter. Considering I only had a handful of darter species, it stole my focus. I worked for a few minutes before catching a Blackbanded Darter, *Percina nigrofasciata* that turned out to not be a Blackbanded Darter anymore. Author's Note: As I was preparing this book for publication, one of my editors, Zach Alley, pointed out this species has been split into two, and what I caught is now actually a Westfall's Darter, *Percina westfalli*. I'd actually caught Westfall's before, and I would eventually catch what are now called Blackbandeds, but not that day. I've since caught dozens of *actual* Blackbandeds in Alabama and Mississippi, though.

Then, I noticed the other darters. Though they were likely more of the same, I was unphased. I caught four of them, but they were all the same species. Oh well. Darters weren't the only micros present. A school of shiners kept zipping in and out of the shadow line. In a blackwater river, visibility is already limited, but the river was a deeply carved canyon with a sandy bottom, and about two feet from shore, it began diving steeply. These shiners, particularly skittish, would zip out of sight every time I got too close to their shadowy forms. This cat-and-mouse game continued for some time, but eventually I prevailed, adding Weed Shiner to my list before leaving the shoreline and returning to my car.

Species #339 — Weed Shiner (*Notropis texanus*).

Panhandling

The drive from Orlando to Montgomery is about eight hours. Even during the long July days, this meant my fishing was limited by how far I had to travel. Sadly, I couldn't stop nearly as often as I wanted to, so I cut out several stops from the itinerary. Though I probably should've just called it a day after striking out so many times, I had one more stop in mind. I was hoping to catch an Apalachicola Redhorse, *Moxostoma sp.*, a vacant world record, and a fish few people have caught. Plus, there was an outside chance of getting a Shoal Bass, *Micropterus cataractae* there, and those two factors in combination were enough to have me drive into the middle of the inspiration for *Deliverance.*

The more populated regions of Florida have some issues, sure, but the Florida Panhandle is something else. It is as redneck as it is beautiful. Some places are downright spooky, and as I made my way to the boat ramp I could feel the local talent staring daggers through me.

Beer bottles littered the boat ramp, and I could hear the faint sound of country music playing in the distance. There was a sign about how to identify Shoal Bass near the launch, and this briefly gave me hope. Oh how foolish I was to get hopeful.

The fishing was terrible; the boat ramp was constructed in a way that there was nowhere to actually fish. Despite a small overhanging rock outcropping covered in slick mud that I kept slipping and falling off of, there was nowhere to stand. A steady stream of boats put in and out to my left, and to the right, a shocking number of snags reigned supreme. Sure, I caught some sunfish, or "brim" as the locals kept excitedly calling them, but nothing I was after.

That reminds me! One particular boatload hopped out, clearly drunk, and asked me what I was trying to catch. I explained I was after a kind of redhorse, and they proceeded on a two-minute rant about "trash fish" and something racist about the skin color of people who typically targeted those species. Excellent.

I was outnumbered 5:1, but that didn't stop me from kicking five racist asses that night and quoting Nelson Mandela while I burned their Confederate flag. Not really.

One of them was holding a shotgun for some reason, so I had to just bite my tongue and wait for them to leave. I was honestly ready to leave myself. I glanced up to see the drunken Floridians crowded around their oversized truck with the dually tires, a Confederate flag, and an "If you're gonna ride my ass, at least pull my hair" bumper sticker. Classy.

Not for the first time, I wished I'd actually printed the bumper stickers I'd long wanted to order that read "No, it's AVERAGE!" so I could slap one on that truck. I sighed, exasperated.

They finished their last round, threw the bottles into the woods, the sound of glass shattering to a chorus of laughter, and drove off. I figured I'd give them five minutes before I bounced. So naturally when I was ready to leave, something made me stay. At that point, the last and final boat of the day came to the ramp.

On that boat were two of the most attractive women I've ever seen in my life, and this coming from a guy who'd just spent an entire month in Florida which, for all its struggles, is the Mecca of attractive women East of the Mississippi.

The blonde and the Latina could've each won a beauty contest individually, but together? Well, let's just say I'm glad I hadn't left yet. And I know what you're thinking, but it wasn't the "Cheerleader Effect" in action. For one, you need at least three women for the

Cheerleader Effect to come into play. Secondly, these women were each insanely beautiful; not just seemingly beautiful in a group as with the Cheerleader Effect.

Tragically, there were two dudes with them, but this boat bucked the trend of what I'd seen in the panhandle thus far; they were all friendly, completely sober, and showed neither racist language nor symbology in our brief interaction.

We talked fishing for a minute, and given the $40,000 bass boat they pulled up in, I assumed they were out bass fishing. But alas, when I caught my final Redbreast Sunfish, *Lepomis auritus* of the day and tossed it back, they decried my action, saying "That was a nice-sized brim!" Out came their stringer of "brim" as they trailered the boat, and despite how friendly they all were and how smokin' hot the girls were, I couldn't help but think "What a waste of a boat."

Then again, I was chasing "trash fish" as a string of hicks had told me all evening, so who was I to judge? I packed up, wished the group well, and respectfully drank in the beauty of the two women one final time.

It was too late to detour for food, and I was on a paved-yet-forgotten stretch of road far from the nearest freeway late at night. I wasn't going to be eating a typical hot meal that evening, so I pulled out one of the self-heating meals I'd been given at ICAST by the brand OMEALS and enjoyed probably the best freeze-dried food of my life. At this point, any time I wasn't eating peanut butter sandwiches and tuna packets, I was happy. Low bar or not, the meal was delicious, and it gave me the energy I needed to get out of the backwoods to the famously more civilized wilds of Southern Alabama.

Chapter 35
Sweet Home Alabama

July 15, 2019

Day 31
Origin: Montgomery, Alabama
Destination: Madison, Alabama

"No one is born hating another person because of the color of his skin, or his background or his religion. People learn to hate, and if they can learn to hate, they can be taught to love, for love comes more naturally to the human heart than its opposite."
Nelson Mandela || 1st President of South Africa

In 2016, I raised my hand and joined the United States Air Force. The following summer, I drove down to Maxwell Air Force Base in Montgomery, Alabama, for Officer Training School.

All told, it was a pretty terrible experience. A few days before I left, my dad was diagnosed with early onset dementia, a disease that had crippled my paternal grandmother later in life. We would later learn it was a misdiagnosis, but not until long after I returned, so I spent my time down there thinking my dad was dying. It devastated me.

In the high-stress environment, my IBS manifested for the first time. I had chronic diarrhea every single day for six weeks. I used an entire bottle of Imodium and countless bottles of Pepto Bismol. I hardly slept, and I got as depressed as I'd ever been up to that point.

We ran a competitive 5K every week, took graduate-level courses, ate poorly, and slept little, but since it is fairly competitive,

I refused to take "sick call" and fought through it in some misguided machismo. In retrospect, that was stupid, but hindsight is 20/20, right?

Officer Training School in any branch of service is intended to stress test you and prepare you for a leadership role in an austere combat environment, and I really have nothing to complain about compared to those brave men and women who have deployed and endured Hell on Earth, but the version of OTS I was attending called Commissioned Officer Training (COT) was nonetheless awful for me and my semi-charmed life. Seriously, I remember thinking to myself: "What have I done?"

I lost almost 20 pounds I didn't have to lose and felt absolutely terrible for long enough that it stayed with me for weeks after my return home.

Fortunately, my military experience improved by leaps and bounds from there, and terrible as COT was for me, personally, there were a few positive outcomes: (1) I got to take my first cross-country road trip, (2) I met a girl whom I dated for several great weeks, and (3) I ate the best breakfast sandwich of my life at a small, family-run restaurant called Cahawba House with the other members of Juliet Flight in one of the rare moments we were allowed to leave base.

Without the occurrence of (1), I wouldn't have made a subsequent trip for Tech School in San Antonio the following summer (which I loved as much as I hated COT) or gone on the trip that inspired this book.

Without the occurrence of (2), at the end of a pleasant evening we were allowed to leave base, I never would've kissed a girl of another race in the heart of the most historically racist city in America, a fact she pointed out sometime later that made me realize how much life had changed in less than a lifetime. It would've been a crime 60 years before.

Without the occurrence of (3), I wouldn't have found myself eating at Cahawba House again two years later next to a table of COT instructors and overheard them discussing their cohort. I never would've had them tell me it was the last COT cohort ever, as the Air Force moved to more streamlined training courses moving forward. I never would've had closure on that small part of my life.

Maybe the made-from-scratch biscuit topped with homemade jam, eggs, and toppings was so delectable, so mouthwatering, and the fact that I ordered three separate sandwiches in succession had something to do with it, but in that moment, I was able to look back more favorably on COT.

Get in Line

Alabama has its share of problems. I mean, if you want to complain about Alabama, get in line. Problems there include pervasive, systemic racism, poverty, and a lack of education, but it's not all bad. It also has a lot going for it. Not only are there more species of freshwater fishes and other aquatic life found in Alabama than anywhere else in North America, but its landscape is rich, vibrant, and beautiful. There is no shortage of greenery, and the landscape is lush and covered with water. As a result, the intrepid angler can stop almost anywhere and catch a fish or two. That's exactly what this intrepid angler did.

After leaving breakfast at Cahawba House, my only other non-fishing stop would be in Birmingham at Bullet Coffee, a drive-through coffee shop the likes of which is completely unique in the South. When I told the owner it reminded me of Dutch Bros., the fastest-growing drive-through coffee chain in the country and founded in Southern Oregon not far from my hometown, I was shocked and yet not shocked when he told me that's how he got the idea.

The only glaring difference? Bullet Coffee only had one line, and you ordered at one window and drove through to the second. From a process management perspective (my undergraduate degrees are in Operations Management and Marketing), we know a single queuing system is more effective than multiple queuing as long as you have multiple Point of Sale (POS) sites. Reason being that it operates as a pull system in which waiting patrons are pulled wherever there is an opening instead of multiple queue systems that allow one line to be empty while another has multiple patrons. Single queuing with multiple POS sites balances the flow of operations evenly, improves throughput, and increases overall efficiency. But again, that only works with multiple POS sites. One line with one POS will still be less efficient than two lines with two POS sites, so I'm not sure Bullet was improving on the Dutch Bros. model, but the owner seemed to think he'd found the magic bullet. Tehe. Still, it was interesting to see a business idea borne out of another some 3,000 miles away.

Sweet Home Alabama

That day I stopped at so many places and caught so many fish, it's sort of a blur. My first stop rewarded me with two Lifers: Alabama Shiner and Blackspotted Topminnow.

Species #340 — Alabama Shiner (*Cyprinella callistia*).
Species #341 — Blackspotted Topminnow (*Fundulus olivaceus*).

The topminnows were especially fun for me because it's like scaled-down topwater fishing. By skimming an unweighted bait along the surface, you can sometimes see the topminnows chase it down and hit, which is absolutely awesome.

Another stop yielded a bunch of colorful sunfish and shiners, but nothing new.

A tiny creek just a few feet wide was loaded with Mobile Logperch and Largescale Stonerollers, adding two more species to the mix.

Species #342 — Mobile Logperch (*Percina kathae*).
Species #343 — Largescale Stoneroller (*Campostoma oligolepis*).

It wasn't until I had some coffee in me and took a nightmarishly inconvenient walk down to a stretch of river in Birmingham that my luck changed. In a part of the city where three separate bridges span the Cahaba River, I parked on the wrong one. I had to climb down a bridge to the water's edge and then strafe along until I could get to a clearing under the second, cross over it, and then walk down on the third.

It was largely my fault for not being precise about where I placed my pin when preparing for the trip, but live and learn. Fortunately, I did pretty well there, adding two species of bass I'd never caught and some Largescale Stonerollers.

Species #344 — Alabama Bass (*Micropterus henshalli*).
Species #345 — Cahaba Bass (*Micropterus cahabae*).

When I finished, moving on to my next venue, I left my tenkara rod sitting on the ground. This was now the third or fourth time I'd done this in the past year, and I'd already lost two tenkara rods to gross negligence since my trip had begun. I wasn't about to make it three. I drove almost an hour before realizing I'd lost it, and all of the backtracking and wasted time cost me two or three species that day, but when I returned to my original spot, I found my rod sitting there, completely undisturbed.

I was en route to Madison, Alabama, to visit my friend Marcus Moss. I got to know Marcus (whose name you might recognize from the Foreword), years before. He lived down the street from my parents, and we connected over bass fishing, football, and the stock market. He got me invested in the stock market by telling me to buy a gold ETF, $NUGT, just before Brexit. I made thousands of dollars on his advice, and I was sold on the idea.

After a few years, he got a gig as an auditor with the Redstone Arsenal in Northern Alabama, and he relocated there. I had so few close fishing buddies that it was painful to lose one, but I made sure to visit when I had the chance.

I made one more stop on the way north to Marcus' house that netted me a few more species.

Species #346 — Silverstripe Shiner (*Notropis stilbius*).
Species #347 — Bullhead Minnow (*Pimephales vigilax*).

I'd added nearly 10 species in just a few hours of fishing without even touching saltwater — a testament to Alabama's insane diversity.

I arrived in Madison late, and Marcus' wife, DeAnna, had already put the kids to bed, so Marcus and I went to a local brewpub to catch up. It had been almost two years since I'd seen him, so there was plenty to talk about. We talked about work, family, and, of course, fishing. His boys, Dean (then 9) and Mason (then 5), were looking forward to doing some fishing with us, and I was excited to fish with kids for the first time in ages. I mentioned I would be writing a book about the events of the summer, and he started joking that he'd write the Foreword. Marcus is pretty damn funny, and I always get a few good laughs with him.

"Yeah," he began, "Luke isn't the best fisherman. He doesn't catch the most or the biggest fish..." I was laughing pretty hard. Partially because it was introspectively funny, partially because I was exhausted. I remembered the conversation, but I wasn't sure how serious he was. When he sent me the Foreword by email a few months later, it made me laugh just as hard, and I agreed to include it. That's how you began this journey with me.

We retired for the evening, with plans to sleep in and then head to a place I'd long wanted to visit: Shelton's Clothing.

Chapter 36
Shelton's Clothing

July 16, 2019

Day 32
Origin: Madison, Alabama
Destination: Madison, Alabama

"My biggest worry is that my wife (when I'm dead) will sell my fishing gear for what I said I paid for it."
Koos Brandt || Namibian Entrepreneur

    When you envision the big players in the sporting goods retail industry, you think of the national giants like Cabela's or Bass Pro Shops, right? Maybe the regional players like Academy, Sportsman's Warehouse, or Fisherman's Marine? You probably don't think of an unassuming business in the middle of nowhere.
    Neither did I. And I didn't know what I was missing.
    Moulton, Alabama, is small even by small-town standards. About 3,000 people call this little town home. It's mostly churches, fast food restaurants, and motels, but it does have a Walmart Supercenter, given its proximity to other, smaller towns like Mt. Hope, Grayson, and Oakville.
    The unassuming off-white building with green trim is sided entirely in sheet metal. A metal, sliding garage door, a covered patio area, soda machine, and a small white sign with serif green lettering that reads "SHELTON'S CLOTHING Inc." are the only features distinguishing it from a rural storage unit. It looks absolutely nothing like the angler's paradise it is.

Inside, it still looks like a big storage unit. It's dingy, somewhat unorganized, and much of the inventory sits in piles or the original bulk packaging. Most products don't have signage, prices, or anything indicating they're even for sale. The walls are unpainted in places, the floor is dirty, and you can see people rooting in bins, boxes, and piles all over the clothing, hunting, and fishing sections of the store. It's fairly large inside, but without much in the way of shelving, layouts, or displays, it's more densely packed than any retail store you've been in before.

The business teacher inside me was mortified. How can a business operate like this? The answer is simple: volume.

According to its owner, Shelton's sells more fishing rods each year than anyone else (yes, that includes Cabela's, Bass Pro Shops, etc.), cycling some 10,000 units on a monthly basis. That's just rods. Given its sheer volume and market share, Shelton's doesn't put in much effort advertising. They have a website, but most of their products aren't even listed. Why would they be? They often sell out in a manner of days. Since it's Alabama, the fishing section of this multifaceted outdoors store caters primarily to bass fishing, and I'm not a diehard bass fisherman like Marcus is. This fact probably saved my 403(b).

Even still, when I found brand-new G. Loomis rods for $150 apiece and a pair of flawless Shimano Stradic reels for less than $200 apiece, well, let's just say I lost all self-control. I loaded up with gear, and dropped a cool grand on the most elaborate and costly impulse buy of my life. So should you decide to make the journey to Shelton's — okay, *when* — Godspeed. I hope you're stronger than I am.

Greenway

After grabbing lunch at Big Bob Gibson's BBQ in Decatur, Alabama, and trying the famous white sauce on a hearty plate of BBQ and chicken, we ran some errands. I picked up some pool noodles, sliced open one side of them to protect my new rods and carefully wrapped the reels in clothing and packed them in one of the 47 or so clear plastic storage tubs slowly overtaking my car. We grabbed dinner and then headed to the local creek to do some fishing. I rigged up some micro sabikis, and Marcus joined me for his first-ever microfishing experience.

On my first trip to Madison years before, we'd taken out his bass boat and sightfished for Spotted Gar using homemade lures made from frayed rope. It was some work, but I finally got two on my weird concoctions. I'd also earned two strikes from a would-be world record Longnose Gar pushing five feet in length that rhythmically circled and struck my Whopper Plopper twice one sunny morning on the Tennessee River. I cried the appropriate amount.

So microfishing the Indian Creek Greenway near his house wasn't really that much of a stretch, I guess. I laughed a little as we caught shiners, sunfish, Redeye Bass and Logperch on the micro gear and continued fishing for unconventional fishes in unconventional ways.

Species #348 — Logperch (*Percina caprodes*).
Species #349 — Redeye Bass (*Micropterus coosae*).

Logperch are in the same family as Yellow and European Perch, *Perca fluviatilis,* and Logperch look shockingly similar to their larger cousins. They were markedly more aggressive than most darter species I've chased, and on several occasions we doubled or even tripled up on Logperch, with fish each attacking a separate hook on our small string of baited treachery.

The stop proved productive: I landed 27 fish, and Marcus something like that in short order. We could've stopped there and sought shelter as the clouds unleashed a downpour, but we decided to work our way upriver, instead. We walked maybe a mile in the pouring rain, dipping in and out of the canopy to take shelter and try to fish in parts of the creek less accessible to Joe Public. Marcus caught some respectable Redeye Bass on the micro rig, including one over two pounds (bigger than any fish I've ever landed on micro gear), but the lone Redeye I caught during the downpour was small.

Eventually, the lightning forced us back in a stop-and-go scurry to the car, punctuated by an absolute downpour when we finally made it back to the parking lot and tried to load the rods. That night, I had a bit of buyer's remorse, but as I always do, I justified my purchases with a multi-pronged argument culminating in "Well, I really needed a ninth and tenth multi-purpose spinning combo," that shut up my inner critic.

I'm gonna crush it at marriage someday, guys.

Chapter 37
Babysitting Done Right

July 17, 2019

Day 33
Origin: Madison, Alabama
Destination: Madison, Alabama

"Spend your money giving your kids experiences, not toys; they'll treasure them much longer. We should do the same for ourselves as adults. And fishing experiences are like no others."
David Parker || American Species Hunter

Ring. Riiiiiiing. Riiiiiiiiiiiinnng.
In the fog of semi-consciousness, I remember my alarm going off, but then I remember warmth and calm and blacknessssss.
I was supposed to be up around 8:00 that morning. At 10:19, I rolled out of Dean's bed, where I'd been crashing while staying with the Moss family. Ugh. I was tired.
I've never been hungover because I don't drink, but I imagine that is how it feels. I used to get severe migraine headaches, and the day after, I'd have this thickness of thought and muted reactivity and sloshing nausea that I've heard compared to a hangover by those who've experienced both. I was awake, but I wasn't really awake. I stumbled to the shower, and slowly woke up.
I hadn't slept past 8:00 a.m. in almost two months. I went straight from the "five days off per month" reality I lived during

most of the school year to an intense, "fish til I die" and "I'Ll SleeP wHEn I'm DeAD" (yes, from that 2019 *Spongebob* meme) mentality that made my trip so successful. Without realizing it, my sleep debt was so great that it bankrupted half a day. That morning, I was a Millennial stereotype, and I wasn't proud of that fact.

Coffee and breakfast helped clear away the shame, and we made a game plan for the day that included pond hopping, lunch, and then some evening fishing with the boys. DeAnna was at work, and Marcus had taken a few days off for my visit, so the kids went to daycare with the promise of fishing that evening.

We flitted around to several ponds, and Marcus caught bass while I looked like a novice. That was kind of the normal pattern. He's an expert finesse fisherman, and he's caught more bass on dropshots and shakey heads than I've caught bass.

I did the bass thing for a bit before he decided I should make the most of my #SpeciesQuest while I was there. We went from the ponds he frequented to a small lake nearby. He said it held all sorts of fishes — several species of shad being the big draw for me — so I messed around with sabikis and curlytail grubs for a while with nothing to show for it.

We moved around the lake and picked up two new species in short order, sightfishing them with my latest tenkara rod that had survived being forgotten more times than a small market professional sports team with no championship titles. The Blackstripe Topminnow was relatively easy, but the Brook Silverside took a little more work, since the water was milky, and the fish sit just below the surface, nearly invisible even in the best of conditions.

Species #350 — Blackstripe Topminnow (*Fundulus notatus*).
Species #351 — Brook Silverside (*Labidesthes sicculus*).

The origin of the first dorsal fin (where the fin enters the body, on the side closer to the head) lined up with the anal fin origin, so that confirmed the identity of what was my sixth New World silverside species. This is precisely the type of flex almost no one cares about that Marcus had joked about putting into the Foreword. He came through, and you can see why.

As I messed around with the micros, I noticed a handful of Grass Carp feeding nearby. Since I'm not one to thumb my nose at double-digit fish of any kind, I shifted gears. I didn't have a ton of viable bait, but I had the bread I'd been using for my peanut butter sandwiches, and I began lightly chumming. Once one breadcrust got sipped, I threw out my own breadball on a hook. The only wait measured in time and not ounces of lead. I missed two strikes before hooking up on a 12- or 13-pound Grassie, and Marcus netted and photographed it for me before I released it.

Since the Gulf Sturgeon never panned out, and I didn't target big catfish or gar in the Bayou as I'd briefly thought about doing, that Grass Carp was the biggest freshwater fish I caught on my whole cross-country road trip. Again, a flex almost nobody cares about.

We tried one more pond before getting the kids.

Dean and Mason, then 9 and 5, respectively, had a blast. Mason was a bit speculative about touching the fish, but we eventually convinced him they weren't going to bite. He and Dean got the hang of fishing the micro sabikis with surprising speed, and I'm pleased to say neither of them broke off one of the precious, ultralight Japanese imports.

They each caught Bluegill, Green Sunfish, Logperch, Longear Sunfish, *Lepomis megalotis,* and Striped Shiners, adding at least two or three new species apiece — not that they really cared about that fact; they just lit up to catch fishes of any kind.

It was raining slightly, but they remained stalwart, fishing until it was dark enough that the bite died. I'd given them CaughtOvgard hats, and we were all wearing them that night. Mason was still small enough that it barely fit even clamped all the way down, and the crooked orange hat and his tentative look made the pictures all the better.

Dean, of course, was an old pro, smiling like he'd been catching fishes his whole life, and given who his dad was, he sort of had been. It was a blast, and I was reminded how much more fun catching an ordinary fish is when seen through the eyes of a child.

We called it a night and returned home, unwound, and talked as the kids excitedly recounted the day to DeAnna while Marcus and I got a kick out of it.

Chapter 38
Staying Mobile

July 18, 2019

Day 34
Origin: Madison, Alabama
Destination: Mobile, Alabama

"Every species is a thought of God."
Lulu Miller || American Author || Quoted in *Why Fish Don't Exist*

    I parted ways with Marcus and his family and started heading south. My next destination was the Mobile Bay, where I planned to do some intense saltwater fishing after making numerous stops along my route south. It was a solid plan, given that the lower reaches of the Mobile Basin have more freshwater biodiversity than anywhere else in North America and account for the lion's share of Alabama's 450-plus species of unique freshwater fishes. Pretty impressive for a state that ranks 30-of-50 in total land area, right?

    Given the chance to do this trip over, I would've spent more time working through Alabama because I felt like I missed out on a lot of opportunities between Madison and Mobile. The 16 new freshwater species I caught during my brief time in Alabama were a drop in the bucket, less than 5 percent of what was possible.

    Think about that for a moment. My goodness.

    I was already tight on time, but I compounded the problem by striking out on my first stop. There was an area supposed to have spring habitat, but after driving through the middle of a quaint little town with an old white church and a lot of old White people, I found myself stopped at a heavily forested gravel road closed off with a thick steel cable. Naturally, I tried to walk in and found the "springs" were just a flooded, marshy field so overgrown with grass that I never could find water in which to drop a line. That detour took two hours of my life that I'll never get back, and I can't even think of anything conciliatory to say about it.

My next stop came at the Warrior River. It wasn't a spot I had marked, but this stretch was wide and clear with fairly shallow water and a variety of habitats visible from the elevated bridge I safely stopped upon to survey the gently flowing waters below. I pulled off on the shoulder, loaded up some gear, and began walking down the steep incline through the thick vegetation.

Undoubtedly, there was poison oak or poison ivy or poison sumac or some cocktail of the three, but I was committed. I figured if I was going to maim myself, I might as well make the most of it. So I stumbled down the slick rock slide, through the kudzu and chest-high grass, over the river and through the woods but failed to find grandma's house, so I went down to the river instead.

I could see micros, shiners and darters. I could see a school of sunfish. I could see a few decent-sized bass. The opportunities were endless, but each fish required a different approach. I started with the bass because I thought they were Warrior Bass, *Micropterus warriorensis* (a species that not only has an awesome name but a black bass species I find to be one of the prettiest).

Alas, they were just some overeager Alabama Bass.

I did the micro thing next, searching the riffles and runs and current breaks for darters and shiners. I found both but failed to catch anything new.

At this point, I noticed a River Carpsucker holding in the current just upstream of the shaded pilings. Might as well call them River Timesuckers because I spent a fruitless hour trying every presentation to get a strike with nothing to show for it.

Spirit crushed and still worried that despite a thorough scrubbing in the river I was an urushiol-based time bomb, I decided to walk across the broad river and try some new habitat. I saw one drum before I saw the entire school. The school was wary, but the flowing water would rinse off the urushiol if there was any, even if fish in this school proved skittish. I landed one before the small Channel Catfish crashed the party in force.

At this point, I'd yet to catch anything new, and the drum wasn't *that big*, so I stumbled across the slick river rock, flailed through the streamside vegetation up the hill and back to my now very warm car. Without the window shade, I doubtless could've cooked an egg on the dashboard, but with the shade, I could only reheat my lunch:

the unrefrigerated boiled eggs I'd left on the seat next to the mayonnaise dipping sauce and potato salad. Kidding, of course. Eggs stink up the car too much to be an acceptable road trip food — even when refrigerated, and I never knowingly eat mayonnaise unless it has been thoroughly mixed with something else and fashionably rebranded as "aioli" or something equally appealing.

Warrior Bass
Two stops down, no new fish. How can I manage that in Alabama, at the heart of North American biodiversity, you ask? Well, truth be told, it's just like the title of Michael Scott's book, *Somehow I Manage* from *The Office*. Fortunately, the simple fact of probability finally built up enough inertia that I caught some new fishes. First came the Alabama Hogsucker, *Hypentelium etowanum*, a 'nemefish' I'd hooked and lost half a dozen times before, on previous trips as well as this one. I sightfished the handsome little sucker (not a slang term, in this instance) and snapped a quick picture.

Species #352 — Alabama Hogsucker (*Hypentelium etowanum*).

How hogsuckers got their name will forever remain a mystery I don't really want to solve, but they're cool little fishes — especially in the diamond-bright waters of a headwater spring. That particular spring was rich with life, and I caught half a dozen species of fish ranging from the ubiquitous Bluegill to the less common Blackspotted Topminnow.

Then, as I reeled in a small Alabama Bass, I noticed a larger, obviously different bass dart out from under a logjam to investigate. The fins edged in white and orange and the clean, green-brown slimming lines meant one thing: it was unmistakably a Warrior Bass. I had to fight off more Alabama Bass, Bluegill, and Longear Sunfish, but I finally got it. It was every bit as beautiful as I'd hoped, too.

Species #353 — Warrior Bass (*Micropterus warriorensis*).

If you've never seen one, stop what you're doing (hopefully reading this chapter, fully engrossed) and Google "Warrior Bass Fish" add in the word "fish," or you'll get a bunch of guitar-related results. My friend Marcus is a guitar aficionado, and he could tell you as much about the Warrior Bass as I could the Warrior Bass, but let's focus on the one that drifts instead of the one that riffs.

My first Warrior was pretty, but they get a lot prettier. I took my baseline species photo with the bass resting, half-submerged in the gin-clear water. Alas, my tranquil spring was disrupted shortly when a group of college kids showed up drunk and started swinging from the tire swing upstream. I figured it was time to make like a ball and bounce, so I did. I was after bass, and I didn't want any treble, so I went to another part of the same system, this one provided to me by Tim Aldridge, where I managed to get a more representative Warrior Bass but failed to get anything else.

Mobile

By this time, I was a little dejected with my performance, so I did what every self-respecting and serious angler does: I stopped at the French bakery advertised from the road and grabbed some pistachio macarons and an iced coffee.

Consoled ever so slightly, I checked my phone in the parking lot now that I had service. My Couchsurfing hosts in Mobile — Matthew and Rachel Lollar, a wholesome salt-of-the-earth Christian family with two cute little kiddos — had asked that I arrive fairly early, before the kids were asleep. At first, I was irritated, but then I realized I had no right to begrudge them for letting me crash at their house for free. Still hours from Mobile, I hopped back into the Fishmobile (a nickname I'd like to try out for my car, so we'll see if it sticks as much as my legs stick to the worn leather seats in hot weather). I spent the rest of my evening driving to their place, stopping only for a slice of pizza that evening.

When I arrived, I met the family and immediately liked them. Matthew, another Fishbrain user, and I talked fishing, and he gave me a few places to stop before telling me about the Dauphin Island Deep Sea Fishing Rodeo. The 86th annual iteration was scheduled that weekend, and had I known, I would've absolutely signed up. Sadly, it was too late. This would mean Dauphin Island (my planned stop the next day) would be swarming with anglers, which threw another wrench in my plans, and I discussed other options for the next day with Matthew. He threw a few ideas my way before calling it a night.

As I drifted off to sleep, my thoughts reached a finale. I got two new species in the Lifelisting Mecca. I just hoped I wouldn't have an encore performance the following day, instead of wanting ever more.

Chapter 39
Pier Commercialism

July 19, 2019

Day 35
Origin: Mobile, Alabama
Destination: Gulf Shores, Alabama

"White lightnin' bound to drive you wild ... In a flash he was gone, it happened so soon ... Black Velvet if you please."
Alannah Miles || Canadian Musician
From the Song "Black Velvet"

    Not only did my trip to Mobile happen to coincide with the big Dauphin Island Deep Sea Fishing Rodeo, but it also coincided with Alabama's Bicentennial, celebrated as "Bicentennial Day" by offering free admission to all Alabama State Parks.
    I honestly couldn't remember what the anniversary was, but thankfully my editor could. I wrote "it was some sort of anniversary," and she looked it up for me. Like I said, I'm gonna crush it at marriage someday.
    Knowing that, I decided to hop around and try a few different parks to maximize my haul.
    My first Alabama State Park was Meaher State Park, and it was pretty disappointing. More like Meager State Park. Due to the most recent hurricane, the pier was mostly out of the water. Needless to say, I didn't catch many fish. Okay, I didn't catch *any* fish. So I moved to Gulf State Park, where my faith in public parks was forever shaken.

I'm a firm believer in the free market and allowing private industry to flourish, but I also believe there is a place for the government to set the pace — including on lands it owns and maintains for public use.

As a staunch, "little i" independent, I have no affiliation with a political party and strongly believe the two-party political system in the United States has led to the deterioration of American unity, camaraderie, and healthy nationalism. Republicans and Democrats alike have denounced one another en masse to the point where political gridlock, infighting, and open hatred dominate the news cycle and the political landscape. It's a tragic state of affairs. Now, despite what some partisans might think, both parties have played parts in the death spiral of the American political machine, and many Americans have been caught up in it because of the lumping and grouping that having only two options provides.

I'm a hardline social conservative on some issues but a staunch liberal on others. Add in moderate fiscal policy views, and my Political Compass Score is smack-dab in the middle — a true centrist.

Yet, I don't fit into either major political party, which often leaves me feeling disenfranchised. I still vote — unlike a majority of American adults — but I often feel like I'm picking the lesser of two evils. Though I vote in every election, I didn't vote for either President Obama or President Trump, the latter being in office when I took this trip.

When I read about the Trump administration's proposal to further commercialize national parks, it shook me to my core. Certain state parks across the country have already gone down this road, and it's tragic.

Gulf State Park in Alabama is one such cautionary tale. Apart from a full-scale luxury hotel that dominates the beach, it offers cabins, cottages, and nearly 500 campsites with RV hook-ups and even special "glamping" sites. The pier, beach, lake and trails are so choked with people, at times you can't even reach out your arms.

When I fished it, I was at once impressed with the top-of-the-line facilities that reeked of the money that had obviously been poured into the park and horrified by the sheer volume of people there.

Sure, it's profitable and draws huge crowds. Sure, it was still an enjoyable experience.

Is it natural? Does it follow the intent of state and national parks? No. It's more theme park than state park. Further, the area around this park is ecologically damaged due to the high traffic, and that impact will not shrink over time; it will grow and grow in a toxic ripple effect. Still, it is the nicest state park you'll ever visit.

You may not agree with me, and that's okay, but until you see Gulf State Park or similarly overdeveloped, pseudo-natural theme parks in person, I would argue you can't really make an informed decision on the issue.

The debate on whether state and national parks should be developed and if so, how much, is not a new one. It dates back more than 100 years to the Yosemite Valley in California.

John Muir, the man instrumental in preserving Yosemite and helping make it a national park, was not a radical leftist as many in the modern conservative conservation movement paint him to be. Nor was Teddy Roosevelt, his friend with widely different views on environmental policy, a radical right-wing nut job. Both men had a vision of the future, and both men listened to and influenced one another over years of healthy debate.

Muir firmly believed that at least a portion of the natural world should be left in an entirely natural state or as close to it as possible. His ideological successors ultimately conceded that roads were acceptable, but buildings, power lines, cell towers, hotels, outdoor recreation facilities, and the like should be limited to those essential for basic maintenance and safety within a park.

I tend to agree with Muir on that.

Like Muir found his era's commercialization horrifying, I shudder at the thought of today's version.

The whole intent of state and national parks is to give visitors an opportunity to glimpse some of the most beautiful parts of the natural world in accessible yet still largely natural settings. Parks let visitors escape the concrete realities of humanity and trade them for something wild and untamed. This proposal would simply tame the wild, domesticating something meant to run free. Granted, national parks are already somewhat domesticated. Though they vary widely in terms of development and infrastructure, all of them have road systems in place to access the park, trails for those more adventurous, and bathroom facilities to limit human impact on the environment.

During this epic adventure in the summer of 2019, I added Great Basin National Park (Nevada), Biscayne National Park (Florida), and Zion National Park (Utah) to my list of parks visited, bringing my total to 14 national parks in 11 states.

Our national parks are as different as our great United States.

From the ethereal summer mists of Shenandoah National Park in Virginia to the absolute desiccation and desolation of Great Basin

National Park in Nevada, each unique stop is incredible in its own right.

There are parks (state and national) already heavily commercialized. Spanning Tennessee and North Carolina, Great Smoky Mountains National Park is the most heavily trafficked park in the nation and has the amenities to support that, but it's still natural; there is still a wildness to it.

By contrast, Missouri's Gateway Arch National Park is artificial, smack-dab in the middle of the city and not at all intended to be wild. They each offer something all their own, and mass commercialization should not be on the table because the park is the draw, not its amenities.

So I warn you: just because you agree with some of your party's politics doesn't mean you have to accept them all. That goes for both sides of the aisle. Speak up and speak out against this bald-faced greed and save our national parks from becoming theme parks that fund private interests and not the public coffers out of which they were created — before it's too late.

steps down from soapbox

Gulf State Park was polished. Roads were paved, manicured, and access to almost every part of the park was quick and easy. This was advantageous for the hundreds of people I saw fishing and walking and taking pictures on the drive in, where the speed limit is an alien 26 miles per hour.

Yes, 26.

An article on alabama.com made note of the strangeness, saying "The thought behind the change, according to Gulf Shores Police Chief Edward Delmore: 'We believe the unusual speed limit on the signs will help drivers take note and slow down. The new limit of 26 miles an hour emphasizes that something is different.'" It was weird, but with people stacked in the park like sardines, it was probably essential to safety.

There was a lagoon, a brackish canal system, and a public beach with a fishing pier. Naturally, I fished all three. The canals were mostly full of Bluegill and Pinfish, but I did see a few snook. I'd hoped for a Marsh Killifish in the lagoon, but no dice. I didn't even see the ubiquitous Sheepshead Minnow, so I wrote the canals off and headed to the pier.

It was a public pier on a public beach, and it was loaded with people. As with most piers, few of the anglers knew what they were doing, and when I walked up, I made quick note of the kingcroaker and small, silvery fish I couldn't identify in the shallows, just feet from the surf breaking on the white sand beach.

On light tackle, the little croakers made for great fun, and I caught a dozen fishes in 15 minutes or so, mostly Gulf Kingcroaker and Southern Kingcroaker, but I did add two new species: the Atlantic Bumper and half a dozen tiny Florida Pompano.

Species #354 — Atlantic Bumper (*Chloroscombrus chrysurus*).
Species #355 — Florida Pompano (*Trachinotus carolinus*).

I wish I could tell you it all improved from there, but it didn't. I spent the next few hours catching nothing of import further down the pier. On several occasions, I did see what were either large remoras or sharksuckers of some kind, and I eventually sightfished a bite. The fight was the most intense I've ever had on a light rod from a pier, and it took a lot of skill to keep the fish from breaking off if I do say so myself. After 15 minutes or so, I'd managed to keep the double-digit fish of nearly 36 inches and maybe 11 or 12 pounds, out of the pilings, and I was ready to land it. Well, sort of. It was some 30 feet down, and I didn't have a drop net. I didn't have a crab trap. That's not ideal when it comes to pier fishing, especially when your light rod is fishing an ultralight sabiki with maybe eight-pound-test. SMH.

A small crowd had gathered, and I asked if anyone had a drop net or ideas on how to land it. Since this pier had a pay station and a bar at its entrance, I couldn't just walk down the pier like I'd done before in California. I asked someone to grab my heavy rod and considered snagging the fish with a jig. I had a kid hold my rod briefly before giving up. Another guy came up and said he'd try and hook it for me. I said to hold the fish, and I'd try to jig it up, but "I already have a rod right here!" he exclaimed.

Yes, yes he did. And in one heartbreaking instant he snagged and snapped my line with his heavy jig when it swung into my taut line and snapped it like twine, allowing what would've been a world record fish — regardless of whether it was a remora or sharksucker — to swim free.

I turned red and just about beat the Roll Tide out of him, but I stopped myself and decided to leave before I ended up in an Alabama jail cell. Cooling off was difficult in 90-degree weather, but the Bayfront Park Pier did it for me since the fishing was anything but hot.

That evening, I returned to Gulf State Park just before dark as the sky soured, and rain began to fall in droves. Once I'd caught a few fishes for live bait off the pier and realized I was the last of the 200-plus people who'd been there just an hour before, I passed through a crowded karaoke session in the restaurant/bar at the end of the pier and braved the treacherous wetness for the 10 seconds it took me to wrap all the way around the walkway and take shelter under the pier.

I've been in lots of thunderstorms in Texas, Alabama, and Florida, and this was perhaps the best. The rain was pouring so hard that rivers of rainwater were cascading down the sloped beach, carving little canyons in the sand and desalinating the water in the immediate vicinity of the surface. Thunder pounded overhead, and a dazzling lightning show illuminated the sky beyond the pier. Overhead, alcohol-emboldened people took turns butchering classic songs, including one I formerly considered a favorite, Alannah Miles' "Black Velvet" that might be ruined for me forever.

After an hour, I figured the sharks and rays weren't coming up to the surf to feed, but I'd tossed the last few rancid pieces of shrimp left over from the hot day's efforts, and I was parked *a long way* from the pier. So I could get miserably wet, or I could try to wait it out. I propped up my rod using the strap from my gear bag to create a sort of sling around the piling and set to work trying to catch lightning on film. I'd tried it numerous times before, failing miserably every time. I had nothing but time, and the lightning was frequent and very close, at least once per minute. So I waited.

My reflexes, as it turns out, are cat-like. Dead cat-like.

I missed half a dozen times before I finally did it: I caught lightning on film. Though the moon was drowned in clouds, and the night was as black as Alannah Miles' velvet, the lightning was close enough that it completely lit up the world in clean white light, for just a fleeting moment, and then it was gone in a — you guessed it — flash.

Either by divine intervention or skills I didn't know I possessed, I got three or four pictures of this phenomenon. Two of them even looked halfway decent, and though they say "Lightning never strikes the same place twice," I found myself struck with how beautiful and oddly serene each flash made my little slice of reality. The rain didn't let up, so I made like a librarian and booked it to the car.

Chapter 40
Photos, Pirates, and Pearls

July 20, 2019

Day 36
Origin: Gulf Shores, Alabama
Destination: Hattiesburg, Mississippi

"There's a fine line between fishing and standing
on the shore like an idiot."
Steven Wright || American Comedian

    I woke up early and went to a local coffee shop, as I'd tried to do whenever possible. Behind the counter of the markedly Bohemian spot I chose was an insanely attractive half-hippie blonde in a red shirt and overalls. She had this sweet, country girl next door vibe that I was all about, and I definitely turned on the charm. We chatted briefly, but the line was long, so I could only pine for so long before taking a seat at the gnarled oak bench to sip my coffee and eat the maple pastry that wasn't nearly as sweet as my new crush. I tried repeatedly to steal a lingering glance, but she was either too busy or she wasn't intere— well, for the sake of my ego, let's go with too busy — to notice.
    Sixty years later, I died alone. No, 55 years because single men don't live as long.
    There was no future anyhow. The coffee was foul, so we never would've worked out. I polished off my cup, tried to steal one more

glance, and then allowed my feet to sink into the soft, wet dirt outside to match my sinking heart. I hopped in the car, found the ferry going across the southern part of the Mobile Bay was full and mused "Cool cool cool cool cool" to myself in the car as the aftershocks of the previous night's rainstorm dribbled from the gray sky.

Remember how I stayed in Mobile the first night and drove east to Gulf Shores to fish? Well, I did the opposite the next day. It was inefficient at a near-Federal level. Cute coffee girl or not, I'd basically wasted a lot of drive time for no defensible reason. I could've taken the ferry across, but I hadn't planned ahead, and it was full, so that meant driving around Mobile Bay again. In my arcing trace of the Mobile Bay, however, I passed a strange landmark. Then I passed it again. There was a large building with the words "LIVE BAIT" written in sans serif white lettering. In front of the building was a massive Rainbow Trout next to a sign that read "BLUEGILL RESTAURANT: Famous Flaming Oysters," and I was dead as the cognitive dissonance played out in my head. I needed bait, so that's how I justified stopping to take a picture. Sadly, it wasn't a bait shop, and "LIVE BAIT" was just the name of the restaurant that failed shortly after the "Bluegill" died suddenly of an identity crisis.

Dauphin Island Marina

For years, I wanted to craft my own identity. I had an idea in my head to create a logo for my brand, CaughtOvgard, that stacked the words on top of one another. The "C" in "Caught" was a fishhook baited with a worm that was extending out from an apple that formed the "O" of "Ovgard" because in case you've forgotten, I'm a teacher. Thus the apple. Brilliant, right? Well, I'm creative, and I have a fair bit of artistic ability, but when it comes to drawing or painting, my skills dry up faster than a puddle under the Alabama summer sun.

So instead of making my creative vision a horrendous reality, I hired my friend Stephen Griffin of Griffin Design Company. Yes, I did mention this already, but there's a point to my rabbit trail.

Long story short, the apple and worm and hook logo wasn't great when it came to — wait for it — fruition. So we went back to the drawing board. My second idea for a logo was a guy riding a fish like it was a bucking bronco or rodeo bull. I thought it was creative, but apparently so did someone else because I found a few logos with that general idea, and we ultimately arrived at the "fish that's also a boat" idea Stephen made a reality.

As I drew closer to the Dauphin Island Marina, I could see signs for the Dauphin Island Deep Sea Fishing Rodeo everywhere, and I couldn't help but picture the long-dead second iteration of my logo with a stick figure version of me riding a fish like a bull. Strangely enough, almost nobody was actually at the marina. It left me to fish alone for all the Hardhead Catfish, Atlantic Croaker, and Pinfish I could catch, the former all ranging from one to four pounds and challenging me quite a bit as I tried to keep them out of the dozens of small pilings with light tackle. I lost two of the 10 or so I hooked.

That wasn't why I was there, though, so I went into the tackle shop and asked for advice. The vast majority of my saltwater fishing spots have come this way, and just because Fishbrain, USGS data, Instagram, Facebook, and a host of other platforms now exist to provide information, just visiting the bait shop and jawing is still effective. I was told to try a nearby public beach called Pirate's Cove, and I was optimistic my treasure might be waiting there even if I couldn't find an "X" to mark the spot.

Pirate's Cove

Pirate's Cove is another part of Mobile Bay that has fallen victim to various levels of hurricane ... redecorating. The long pier that extends out half a mile or so is almost completely out of the water, and the once-popular fishing site sits as an eerie reminder of man's ultimate futility in the face of horrible natural forces such as hurricanes or reality TV. The area is now a muddy salt marsh loaded with mosquitoes and popular with swimmers and sunbathers who frequent the cove itself, a rounded, C-shaped beachhead offering miles of sandy surf.

Immediately, I tried my shortened sabiki and caught the sea catfish, Atlantic Croaker, and Pinfish I'd found to be the norm in the Mobile Bay. Then, I caught something else. It was a Florida Pompano. Funny how despite all of the time I'd spent in Florida, all of my Florida Pompano had been caught in Alabama. Maybe not that funny, but I'm easily entertained, probably beneficial because I wasn't catching anything new.

Realizing that sharks and rays were likely close, I impaled the first Pinfish I caught on one of my trusty 7/0 circle hooks and hoped a big shark would take my live bait. The beach was a sand flat, and I didn't have rod holders big or strong enough to support the butt of my shark rod, so I looked around and got creative with driftwood, crossing two large pieces and shoving the butt of my rod into the partially hollowed-out end of one, facing the surf. It was ingenious, but the bloody fish didn't reward my ingenuity. No dice. After an hour, I kept one of the Atlantic Croakers, cut it in half, and used one half as a large chunk of cut bait. That proved to be the ticket. As my shark bait soaked, I added the Northern Kingcroaker, the last fish of the trio found in the Gulf.

Species #356 — Northern Kingcroaker (*Menticirrhus saxatilis*).

I thought I'd seen a hit, but it certainly wasn't a big shark or ray. It was, however, a shark. I fought the little guy in and had my first Blacktip Shark, differentiated from the similar Spinner Shark by a pure white anal fin. Counterintuitive, really, given that the Blacktip Shark has fewer black tips than a Spinner, but I can't tell you why that is. I just work here.

Species #357 — Blacktip Shark (*Carcharhinus limbatus*).

Stoked despite the diminutive size of what would be my last shark of the trip, I took a few pictures before letting the little two-foot-and-change terror of the shallows go. The looks on the faces of the beachgoers were priceless as they asked the usual questions.
"Is that a shark?"
"There are SHARKS here?!"
"How big do they get?"
"You're not gonna kill it, áre you?"
"Have you ever been bitten?"
"We swim here. Will sharks attack us?!"
I assured them the lil pup would be fine, and they probably would be, too, so long as they didn't tape chunks of Atlantic Croaker to their feet. Who knows? It might become a fashion trend if TikTok survives long enough.
Amused, I set to fishing for another hour or so. I'd initially planned to stay in Mobile again, but as the bite died, I opted to make my way to Memphis that night instead of waiting until the next morning. At my "one more fish" ultimatum, my rod tip bounced, and I reeled in another new species: the Sand Seatrout. It was just two ounces shy of the world record (this was my fourth fish of the trip within four ounces of a world record), and that was a little frustrating, but hey, new species!

Species #358 — Sand Seatrout (*Cynoscion arenarius*).

With that, I drove up and out of the Mobile Bay, arcing my way around the large, productive terminus of the Mobile River and towards Louisiana.

Louisiana

I made a quick stop at the Pearl River on the Louisiana-Alabama State Line because I wanted to add Louisiana to the list of states in which I'd caught a fish. I pulled under the highway and set to work. There was a massive pile of dead crabs, and I was a little shell-shocked by this strange sight, but I was clawing to get to my next state. A pair of catfish helped Louisiana become the 24th state in which I'd caught a fish. A few hours later, Mississippi would become No. 25.

Mississippi

I arrived in Hattiesburg, Mississippi. It's not a well-known city, and apart from the University of Southern Mississippi, it doesn't have many points of interest. So I settled for Hattiesburg realizing I probably was not the first person to utter or write "settled for Hattiesburg."

There is a zoo in Hattiesburg with a concrete-lined, channelized portion of creek that runs through town. Sort of like the San Antonio River below the San Antonio Zoo but on a smaller scale and with markedly fewer homeless people and invasive fishes. I figured it was a reasonable way to end my day, so I walked down the concrete chute into the more natural stretch of the creek. I caught sunfish, shiners, topminnows, and mosquitofish but nothing new.

I wasn't impressed with Hattiesburg that night, but that would change dramatically the next day.

Chapter 41
Judge Not, Lest Ye Be Wrong

July 21, 2019

Day 37
Origin: Gulf Shores, Alabama
Destination: Hattiesburg, Mississippi

"Do all that you can to live in peace with everyone."
Romans 12:18 || From *The Bible*, New Living Translation

I grew up in the Pacific Northwest (PNW).
You know, that part of the country that was largely settled after the Civil War and didn't really take part in it. That part of the United States that is more progressive (to the point of being obnoxious) than the rest of the country. That part of the nation with beaches, mountains, trees, the nation's best drinking water, and no hurricanes, tornadoes, or dust storms.
I've now visited almost every state, and the Pacific Northwest has a well-deserved reputation as the best part of the country, but that sort of gives residents a superiority complex. From speaking the purest, least accented English in the English-speaking world to having the best coffee, beer, and food in the New World, we sort of pride ourselves on being a cut above. That sounds cocky and high-handed but that's because it is. Now hear me out: it's also a bit rude.
#ThatPNWLife may be great, but it comes with an insanely high cost of living; San Francisco, Seattle, and Portland (in that order)

have some of the highest cost of living indices in the entire world thanks, in part, to artificially high minimum wage, high taxes, and elevated property values that continue to climb due to the concentration of absurdly high salaries of those working in the tech sector. In Seattle, this phenomenon was eventually christened "The Amazon Effect" by economists.

The whole of the PNW is expensive, and we pay for our creature comforts quite willingly. Growing up in the PNW, you always knew you lived in the best part of the country, and you were sort of raised to avoid the East Coast if possible because of the rude people and frantic lifestyle. You were also raised to avoid the South at all costs. This wasn't my parents; it was just a pervasive notion in our PNW society. After all, the South was supposed to be a hotbed of racism, natural disasters, venomous snakes, and swamps, mud flats, and jungle as far as the eye can see. Why would anyone ever live there?

Now, I realize that is an oversimplification of these two areas, and though the PNW is still markedly better than the South or the East or the Southwest or the Midwest, in my opinion, these regions each have their merits. I could sell my modest, 1000-square-foot house in Oregon, for instance, and live like a king almost anywhere in the South. Though I'd have to give up unmatched coffee and the varied cuisine of the PNW while seeing the lingering racial caste system of the South firsthand, in turn, I could have weather conducive to year-round fishing, a low cost of living, and no shortage of friendly people — a triad not found anywhere in the Pacific Northwest.

Given the strongest resistance to Civil Rights took place in Alabama and Mississippi, I just (unfairly) assumed everyone there was a racist Confederate, silently pining for secession. I mistakenly believed it was a backward place. Hattiesburg, Mississippi, completely destroyed that perception for me.

The small college town looked a lot like Corvallis, Oregon, home of Oregon State University. There was new development alongside rustic brick, rich plant life, and trees everywhere. Not to mention the high-quality and surprisingly varied food. I couldn't believe my eyes. I loved Hattiesburg, Mississippi.

Seriously. I *loved* it there.

I started my day with a respectable breakfast at the Midtowner, a breakfast cafe not far from the college, too many donuts at Midtown Donut, and then some coffee, but I was here to fish, and I figured I'd try to get out on the road while most people were still at church that Sunday morning. I couldn't help but appreciate Hattiesburg for shattering my preconceived notions.

But again, here to fish. My first stop was still technically in town, and I stopped below a culvert. Apart from Spotted Gar that would've given the world record a run for its money, there was nothing worthwhile there. Still, I found myself chasing the gar for longer than an hour. I hooked it three times but given the high banks, landing it proved difficult. If I'm being honest, it was probably only eight pounds or so. That would make it over a pound shy of the world record but still massive for a Spotted Gar.

Eventually, I admitted defeat and walked back to the car. A filthy hitchhiker walked by, reeking of alcohol. His once-pale skin was so caked in filth and sweat that he probably hadn't showered in weeks. He asked for a ride to a diner, and I declined, instead giving him a cold bottle of water, an apple, a granola bar, and a packet of tuna — the same thing I planned to have for lunch. He was grateful, and I felt like it was my own small step toward restitution in my long-time bias toward the South, but I still have a ways to go, just as the South does.

Cherry on Top

On my drive north to Memphis, I was in touch with Juan, my Memphis Couchsurfing host, and he seemed very friendly. I told him I'd be arriving late, and he seemed to be disappointed by the idea that we wouldn't get to hang out. Most Couchsurfing hosts up until this point had been hosts who wanted to share a meal or two, conversation, or coffee, but not much else. Being an introvert, I was totally fine with that arrangement.

Juan was not an introvert, though, and he was reaching out long before I even arrived.

I spent too much time in Hattiesburg, and since I was initially supposed to go from Mobile to Memphis without detouring through Louisiana or Hattiesburg at all, I had mapped out no fishing stops along the way. On my way out of Hattiesburg, I grabbed a can of Cheerwine, a regional soda popular in the South that sort of tastes like Cherry Coke. I'm not much of a soda drinker, but I put it in the cooler and drove north.

When my bladder couldn't take it anymore, I pulled off the highway to a random parking lot with a creek that passed under the highway. I quaffed the icy Cheerwine, relishing the sweet cherry taste as I made my way down to the creek. It was heavily overgrown, so I had to get in the water to fish. Almost immediately, I spooked a hogsucker. Unsure if I was far enough north for it to be a Northern Hogsucker, I hesitated a moment before dropping my micro sabiki upstream of it. I caught it and later, through some detailed range mapping and input from a few experts on NANFA, ruled it to be a Northern Hogsucker — a new species!

Species #359 — Northern Hogsucker (*Hypentelium nigricans*).

It was a fine start to the stop, and I immediately set my timer for one hour. That's about all the time I had to fish even though I knew there would be a score of species in this creek I didn't have given I'd fished this part of the country very little.

Twice, I came across submerged snakes, and though I was terrified at first, I overcame my fears when I realized they were harmless. Unnerving, but harmless. If only my bladder had realized that in time.

I caught a bunch of sunfish, topminnows, and Weed Shiners under the heavy canopy that filtered the heat and light away from the small, sandy stream. The light-colored bottom made it easy to spot fishes but difficult to differentiate one Leucicid from the next. Even still, I could tell when something new came out to play if I really focused. Apparently, the cherry scent on my breath had called in the pretty little fish with bright red fins, and I landed several Cherryfin Shiner, another new species.

Species #360 — Cherryfin Shiner (*Lythrurus roseipinnis*).

My timer went off, and I made my slow way back upstream to the underpass before climbing out of the cool reprieve of the shade and into the stifling heat. I still had a way to drive, but the Cherryfin Shiner had been the perfect topping for my Sunday.

Jackson

Mississippi's capital city is named for Andrew Jackson, hands-down the worst president in U.S. history and one of the worst leaders in history. The man was responsible for furthering the racial divide between Black and White that ultimately led to the Civil War. He owned slaves and treated them poorly. He murdered a political opponent in a dual. Worst of all, he was the man responsible for the Trail of Tears, as well as the continuous genocide of countless millions of Native Americans.

Fortunately, the city seems to have moved past the tragic and unfortunate roots of its name to become a fairly modern city, complete with modern amenities and a seemingly harmonious mix of cultures. The highlight of the city, for me, was the Cultivation Food Hall, an indoor market featuring eight food vendors that offered everything you'd expect from Southern cuisine along with more exotic options such as poke and Ghanaian. I sampled a few places, making sure to try Ghanaian food, one cuisine I hadn't yet tried. It was delightful, and it gave me the energy I desperately needed for the ordeal ahead of me.

I'd marked a spot on the Pearl River, a few miles downstream of a spillway. It looked promising because it was right on my route north, so I figured the detour time would be minimal. Belly full of a veritable United Nations of food, I made my way to the parking lot of a title company or insurance agency or investment firm or something white collar. I loaded up my gear and walked down to what I assumed would be the nearby river.

The Pearl River is quite large, and in the flood stage, it probably would've been close to where I'd parked. Midsummer flows were much lower, though, and I had to slog through several hundred yards of mud and thick vegetation to get to the water. I quickly caught Channel Catfish and sunfish, but I was after Blue Catfish, *Ictalurus furcatus*. I knew they were there, and I figured I'd be able to get a small one with relative ease. I was wrong.

It had rained the night before, and the already-muddy waters were dirty and flowing higher and faster than they had been for most of the summer. I deduced this from the looks of the barely submerged waterline vegetation which had only recently become aquatic vegetation. I just couldn't keep my worm on the bottom out in the deep hole at the center of the river due to the ripping current. Downriver, I could see what had to be buffalo jumping and surfacing, and since I'd never caught any of the three buffalo species, I figured that was a better use of my time.

I waited and waited, plowing through the Bluegill, Channel Cats, and Redbreast Sunfish. When I caught a Freshwater Drum, *Aplodinotus grunniens* I was briefly excited, but that faded. I wanted a buffalo. Though many anglers mistake buffalo (native suckers) for Common Carp, they're not even in the same family. Common Carp are naturalized invasives from Asia in the Cyprinidae or Old World minnow family, while the buffalos represent three of the largest sucker species in the world, all capable of exceeding 60 pounds. Sadly, buffalo are a prime target for wanton bowfishermen who routinely kill and waste multiple specimens in a single outing because buffalo lack the protections of gamefish they so readily deserve. My first buffalo was a Smallmouth Buffalo (despite the name, the Smallmouth is usually the heaviest of the three species, while the Bigmouth Buffalo, *Ictiobus cyprinellus* is usually the longest), and though it was only about five pounds, it was a welcome sight.

Species #361 — Smallmouth Buffalo (*Ictiobus bubalus*).

The fish was beautiful. Each overlapping scale shone iridescent purples and greens and blues depending on the tilt of the fish in the shrouded sunlight. This is called "structural color," a phenomenon composed by small structures within the scale that cause light to refract in different ways, creating a shifting rainbow that most people would recognize in the feathers of songbirds or ducks.

I posed for a quick picture, soaking myself in the muddy water in the process, but it was totes worth it!

Since I'd rushed all day long, I finally had time to relax and fish, waiting out the Blue Catfish or maybe a bigger buffalo. Except that I didn't. The sun was choked with thick, gray clouds that spread ominous gloom over me, and I could actually see the storm moving into the valley. Pushing it to the last minute not for the first time, I finally got a Blue Catfish — then another — in the minutes before the sky opened up, and the Biblical deluge began.

Species #362 — Blue Catfish (*Ictalurus furcatus*).

I sprinted to the car as best as I could, my flip-flops not the best choice of footwear in the rapidly emulsifying soil. I zipped under the highway bridge, up into the parking lot, and piled my gear into the car, once again leaving my tenkara rod on the roof.

This marked the fourth time I'd done this now. Fifth time? I was forgetting the rod, so don't expect me to remember the less important details such as how many times I'd forgotten it. I'd already lost one or two tenkara rods this way, and if I hadn't stopped to gas up just down the road from where I'd been fishing, I would've lost a lot more than the five minutes it took to backtrack. The rod was there, thankfully still retracted into the sturdy metal cylindrical base section. It had wedged against the curb in the parking lot, where the base segment had been chewed up by the gravel as it rolled to a stop against the concrete lip. Leaving that rod on the roof of my car was becoming the bane of my existence, but it was far from my biggest mistake of the day. That title would go to fishing a hatchery pond by mistake.

Lost Puppy

In our youth, my brothers and I used to attend an event at the hatchery where kids could fish the "natural pond" for hatchery Rainbow Trout. In retrospect, gross, but we were kids and didn't know any better. I joke about hatchery trout, but in a closed system like a lake or pond with no outlet that has no native fishes to displace, they're actually a great option to introduce kids to the sport and keep "meat fishermen" from ravaging wild native trout or other game species with too much sport value to be harvested.

Even still, my brothers and I wouldn't just plop a worm in and catch the first fish that swarmed it like all of the plebes did. No, we carefully targeted the largest fish in the pool and worked together to catch the largest pus-gut hatchery fish in the pool. Nine times out of 10, my friend Dominick "Dom" Porcelli's catchphrase "Persistence pays off," would be true, and one of us would catch the largest fish of the day. Dom is third all-time on the species list, so he might be on to something.

Regardless, after junior high, I aged out of that event, but I never forgot the unique experience of fishing at the hatchery. For almost 15 years, I never again fished a hatchery. That is, until July 21, 2019, when I repeated my childish actions — completely by mistake.

I'd marked data from the USGS for a spillway that contained half a dozen large species I'd never caught, and I was optimistic that I might be able to catch one of them if I detoured to the large dam, walked upstream a half mile or so.

My first omen to turn around was the road closure. The road leading up to the dam, the spillway, and a series of buildings I couldn't identify was blocked off. It wasn't signed, but I couldn't get my car through. There was road work of some sort. Not one to give up easily, I parked nearby and began the half-mile slog to the water.

The canyon was steep and didn't even look worth attempting on the near side of the river. The far side? Well, I'm not sure what Gary Larson's iconic comics have to do with it, but the other side of the river looked doable even if access was limited by high fences that blocked off all but a narrow strip of weeds along the canyon wall. The weed patch was chest-high and looked impenetrable, so I wandered over to the buildings to see who was around the seemingly government complex, but it was Sunday evening, so exactly no one was around.

Outside the fence and away from the buildings sat a small pond, maybe half an acre in size. Bored and hoping I could take a Flier or some other random species found in the area. I caught a few small Channel Catfish before realizing I was fishing a hatchery pond. There were no trout or salmon, so I'd failed to realize it was a hatchery. As I sat there with my baited hook in the water, I zoomed in on the map and scrawled to where I was sitting when "Redacted Fish Hatchery" showed up on the map. Okay, it didn't say "Redacted," but I refuse to self-incriminate.

Let's just say I've never reeled in so quickly as the moment I realized what I was doing. Not only could I have potentially gotten in trouble, but the implications of fishing a hatchery pond were too much, so I walked along the fence, hoping I could get to the river and justify my detour to that location. Following the river upstream, I noticed the depth and slope of the canyon diminish, and eventually I made my way down to the water, ambling over loose boulders and nearly dying just a handful of times. Worth it, right?

When I got to the water, the steep slope and loosely seated rocky topography remained, so fishing proved awkward. The water was dirty and slow, and though gar were surfacing here and there, all I caught in an hour of trying were catfish*, Blue and Channel alike.

*Not worth it.

As I climbed back out of the canyon, I half expected a line of cops waiting to imprison me, but apparently there was no harm and no foul, so even though I'd likely been on some security recording and flagged for arrest, I drove on to Memphis, stopping at a nondescript stream along the way where I added two new species, although the latter is still up for debate as to whether it is genetically distinctive enough to be its own species.

Species #363 — No Common Name (*Lepomis solis*).
Species #364 — Finescale Stoneroller (*Campostoma pullum*).

Social Butterfly

That evening, I was staying with Juan. Remember? The guy who'd reached out days before just to chat with an introverted old me. The friendly banker sent me his address, and I parked in the driveway and walked up to the front door.

A panel of security camera feeds showing behind the gathered group of half a dozen as I entered the living room. Cold sweat beaded on my forehead, and I just sort of assumed I'd stepped into some strange cult gathering. Or maybe an orgy?

"Oh no," I thought to myself. "Not again!"

What if it was something even worse?!

"Dear God! Please don't let it be some 'independent sales rep' trying to get me to buy Tupperware or dietary supplements or skin care products. That would be horrible."

Fortunately, it was none of those things.

"I just like to be sure my guests and I don't get robbed," Juan said, smiling to ease my obvious tension and offering to take my luggage while offering me something to drink. "It can be a sketchy neighborhood sometimes."

I settled on one of the couches with a ragtag group of people, each speaking differently accented English. There was a guy from France, one from the United Kingdom, one from Turkey, a guy from somewhere in the Midwest, and a young couple from somewhere on the East Coast. It was so far-flung from all of my Couchsurfing experiences to-date that I was a little on edge. Juan was the consummate host, and offered us all drinks, snacks, and even a massage. Tempting as the latter was after sitting in a car all day, I was still uncertain of the situation and politely declined.

We regaled one another and exchanged stories until well past my bedtime, but it was interesting to have so many different perspectives in a single, shared setting. I relaxed and allowed my introverted self to unwind and appreciate the genuine human interaction after spending so many hours alone with nothing but my thoughts and whatever flavor of the month audiobook I was currently listening to.

Just as I settled in and felt relaxed, the drugs came out. Though he didn't partake, Juan had a stash of weed and the associated paraphernalia in a small box that he kept for guests. At first, I found it odd, but then I remembered the beers in my own fridge. I don't drink, but I keep half a dozen beers in the fridge for guests, so I guess it's not *that* different. Everyone passed the bud around, and several of those present obliged the offer. Neither Juan nor I partook.

Being in the Air Force, I couldn't partake even if I wanted to, but having never done so in the 26 years before I swore in, it wasn't much of a sacrifice to keep that train rolling. Then again, I was a little concerned about the secondary exposure that might have resulted and shown up on a random drug test, so when Juan asked them all to smoke outside, I was visibly relieved.

The evening wound down, and Juan and I exchanged stories as people trickled off to bed. Juan set me up on a mattress in the living room, and I was gone in a matter of moments — though not quite as quickly as I might have been, I suppose, had I smoked the sweet ganj.

Chapter 42
Apple of My Eye

July 22, 2019

Day 38
Origin: Memphis, Tennessee
Destination: St. Louis, Missouri

"I'm in the wetlands. I've got a poker thing, and I'm gonna clean them up. So the next time you want to tell me that I'm uncharitable, why don't you just ask yourself who called you from the wetlands?

minutes later

"Look, I screwed up, okay? I'm lost and I hate them. I hate the wetlands. They're stupid and wet and there are bugs everywhere and I think I maced a crane, Michael. Look, you've got Dad's car, why don't you come pick me up?"
Lindsay Bluth || From *Arrested Development*

I awoke early, exhausted from the late night. I thanked my gracious host, and hit the road.

Two blocks from Juan's house and still in the heart of suburbia, an older bearded Black man jumped into the road and began waving at me to stop. Thanks to the stop sign 20 yards before his move, I was just rolling along, but it was still startling. The spry maneuver had drained him, and he came over to my window slowly.

"You got a cigarette?" he asked.

"I don't smoke," I replied.

"That's the right move," he said with a chuckle that became a, wet, hacking cough.

I offered him something to drink, and he declined.

Huh. Strange interaction.

Three Strikes

My next few stops were also strange.

I hit a big muddy river, a crystal-clear stream, and a small trickle the locals probably called a "crick" or something equally colloquial. I'm not really an asshole; I just play one on TV.

Missouri is incredibly biodiverse, so the stops I made should've resulted in a new species or two, but that wasn't the case. I did manage to catch a few sunfish, Spotted Bass, and my first Emerald Shiner since the Great Lakes the summer before, not to mention a load of Rainbow Darters.

It wasn't the best start to my day, but I'd planned this route on purpose and reached out to Tyler Goodale, a guy I knew from NANFA who was a wizard at identifying fishes. He'd helped me on numerous occasions this trip. As it happened, he was available to meet up for a little while, so I kicked around Poplar Bluff, where he lived, grabbed some coffee and food, and then moved to some nearby wetlands where he said he'd meet me. It took me a few wrong turns before I found the wetlands where we'd agreed to meet, but eventually I made it, and it was one of the best stops of the trip.

Wetlands

For the better part of a decade, I haven't been able to hear or say the word "wetlands" without envisioning the *Arrested Development* episode in which a comedy of errors and mistaken identity leads Michael (Jason Bateman) to accidentally kidnap a woman he believes to be his mother's maid when he thinks she wants a ride to work. En route, his sister calls for help, so he takes the terrified woman to the wetlands with him to save his sister, Lindsay. The hapless woman in his car believes he's going to kill her due to a shovel in the backseat and a few other misnomers I can't spoil for you. The misunderstanding ends with the woman jumping out of the car and running away as Michael tries to find his sister in the marsh.

All's well that ends well in that episode, and despite my struggles earlier in the day, that's exactly how my wetlands experience panned out: with a mistakenly kidnapped woman in my car.

JK.

It ended well. That's where the similarities ended.

I was able to get two of the three targets I'd been given by Tyler, and I briefly hooked and lost the third (Chain Pickerel, *Esox niger*) as well as a large Shortnose Gar, *Lepisosteus platostomus*. Both fishes had smashed lures worked along the bank.

I wasn't too disappointed, though, given that I caught one sunfish species I desperately wanted to catch: Bantam Sunfish.

Species #365 — Bantam Sunfish (*Lepomis symmetricus*).

Both little fish were beautiful and exciting additions to my list, and I was quite pleased. Tyler got caught up and wasn't able to actually fish with me, but he arrived as I was on my way out, and we shook hands and chatted briefly. I gave him some of the CaughtOvgard swag I'd picked up in Orlando and promised I'd be back with more time to fish.

Apples and Oranges
Wetlands behind me, I continued to enjoy the rich biodiversity offered by Missouri.

Almost immediately after I'd joined the NANFA forum on Facebook, someone posted about the Old Appleton Bridge in Missouri. She wrote that it was perhaps the single most biodiverse freshwater site accessible to anglers, so I made sure to make a note of it. With more than 70 species sampled there, I was dead-set on fishing it. Unfortunately, by the time I arrived, I only had a few hours of daylight left.

As always, deciding whether to sight fish micros, fish a set bait, cast lures, work a jig, et cetera was my challenge. I started by sightfishing the micros in the outflow of the pool. It would've been markedly more productive with more daylight, but I still pulled in some sunfish and shiners, including four shiners that were brand new to me. Most shiners aren't terribly distinctive when not in spawning coloration. Unless they have really unique markings (like the Cherryfin Shiners I caught the day before with their vivid pink-red fins), identification can be difficult. Fortunately, these shiners were another easily identifiable minnow. They had massive eyes, disproportionately large on their small, slightly pointed (some might even say boop-able) noses. They were Bigeye Shiners.

Species #366 — Bigeye Shiner (*Notropis boops*).

I gently booped their noses as I released them. No I didn't. That would be ridiculous, but with the Latin name *Notropis boops*, I couldn't help but write that.

It was the beginning of a great evening, and in total, I would catch 12 total species below the Old Appleton Bridge in about two hours' time. The largest was a four-pound Blue Catfish and the smallest was a tiny Blackstripe Topminnow barely longer than the first joint of my pinky finger.

I was entertained with the variety, but I found myself fishing a micro sabiki baited with flecks of worm more often than not. As I ducked under a deadfall to get right up to the base of the water spilling over the top of the dam, I could see schools of Logperch darting under my feet. They could've been new, so I caught a few to check, but they were just plain ole Logperch.

As I got closer to the pseudo-waterfall, I began to notice small silvery fishes jumping from one small catch pool to the next to escape my lumbering presence. Some were shad, I think, while others were either Bighead Carp, *Hypophthalmichthys nobilis* or Silver Carp, *Hypophthalmichthys molitrix*, but I couldn't tell which of the two invasives were present.

They weren't interested in my offerings, but eventually, I pissed off a tiny, palm-sized Silver Carp enough to elicit a strike. One of the hooks was in its mouth, and two others had snagged its body, so untangling the wriggling invasive bugger was a literal pain for both the fish and my fingers.

Species #367 — Silver Carp (*Hypophthalmichthys molitrix*).

Here's where it gets interesting. Silver Carp are filter feeders, so to catch one — especially a juvenile — is a strange development. Most of the Silver and Bighead Carp (collectively labeled "Asian Carp" by the media even though most carps are Asian, so it doesn't really narrow it down) are filter feeders, but large specimens can be caught on bait and lures in rare instances — almost all of which involve fishing below dams with sabikis or jigs because invasive species in waters they're not native to often fill unique, abnormal ecological niches. But juveniles? That was an exciting development.

The night continued to be awesome, and I desperately wished I'd planned more time to fish that spot. I caught loads of Bluegill, Central Stonerollers, Golden Shiners, *Notemigonus crysoleucas,* Largemouth Bass, Logperch, Longear Sunfish, Redbreast Sunfish, more topminnows, and then, when I least expected it, my final new species of the day.

I was fishing below the Old Appleton Bridge, in Apple Creek, in a town called Appleton, so imagine my surprise when I caught an Orange ... spotted Sunfish.

Species #368 — Orangespotted Sunfish (*Lepomis humilis*).

Apples and oranges.
The male was a brilliant cool blue with vertical purple stripes, rich orange fins, namesake orange spots, and faintly green striations serving as a hidden treasure for those willing to fully take in the beauty of the little denizen of the depths.

I had to make my way to St. Louis that night, so I left with the daylight, content with the way my day ended having added three new species of sunfish to my list and officially putting me over the halfway mark to catching all of the currently recognized species of sunfish in North America.

At that point, I'd caught the original Rock Bass, *Ambloplites rupestris,* Sacramento Perch, *Archoplites interruptus,* both species of crappie, Bantam, Bluegill, Pumpkinseed, *Lepomis gibbosus,* Green, Longear, Orangespotted, Redbreast, Redspotted Sunfish, *Lepomis miniatus*, and Spotted Sunfish.

I still needed to catch the recent Rock Bass splits, Flier, Mud Sunfish, *Acantharchus pomotis,* Northern Sunfish, *Lepomis peltastes,* and the famously tough trio of Banded Sunfish, *Enneacanthus obesus,* Blackbanded Sunfish, *Enneacanthus chaetodon,* and Bluespotted Sunfish, *Enneacanthus gloriosus*. So 13 down, nine to go.

Challenge accepted!

Chapter 43
The Ozarks

July 23, 2019

Day 39
Origin: St. Louis, Missouri
Destination: Oklahoma City, Oklahoma

"We do not inherit the earth from our ancestors;
we borrow it from our children."
Native American Proverb

    I'd stayed with a guy named Sunil the night before and arrived late, so we didn't get to talk much, but he told me about his incredible living situation in which he worked from a new city every quarter, relocating for a few months, working remotely, then returning to his St. Louis home where he'd work for a month or so. In a given year, he'd work roughly four months in the office, and eight working remotely from a different city. I was insanely jealous of this arrangement, but his leather couch was nice, so I tried not to drool too much. Still, he had my dream life, and I went to sleep dreaming of the possibilities of a life like his...

    Who knew that less than a year later, in the wake of COVID-19, working remotely would no longer be a pipe dream for many people?

    We parted ways the next morning, and I grabbed some coffee and a cookie at a nearby coffee shop he'd recommended before heading to my first stop. The trek took me off the Interstate to smaller, state highways. Missouri uses numbered *and* lettered highways. Try to envision my disappointment when I came to Highway K. I mean, they could've at least named it "Highway Okay" or "Highway Ok" but just Highway K? Apparently, the road department just wasn't that interested in that highway. I sure hope Highway K took the hint and didn't get its heart broken.

Speaking of heartbreak, I almost experienced that myself.

I fished the confluence of two rivers in hopes of catching one of several buffalo or redhorse species found there. After two hours of striking out, I reeled in my first rod and put it in the car. I returned to reel in the second when it bowed steeply, and I knew I had a fish on. The fish sucked line and ran, ran, ran. It was either a massive buffalo or sturgeon or catfish, but before I could get it out of the rod holder, it broke me off.

Talk about heartbreaking.

I grabbed my other rod back from the car, tossed it out and set to work retying my recently victimized fish-catching implement. I figured as soon as I got it ready, I'd pull stakes and move on. I re-rigged the broken-off rod, put it in the car, and walked back to the rod I'd left in the holder. Again, I got bit. I fought in a small redhorse I would later identify as a Black Redhorse and let it go before heading on into the wilds of Missouri.

Species #369 — Black Redhorse (*Moxostoma duquesnei*).

Ozark

*segues poorly, as *Arrested Development's* George Oscar Bluth (G.O.B.) rides up on a Segway and changes the subject*

The Netflix series, *Ozark,* is riveting. It's similar to *Breaking Bad*, but the main character (portrayed by Jason Bateman of *Arrested Development* fame), launders money for a cartel on the shores of Lake of the Ozarks. It's not for children, but it's very entertaining.

Sidebar: in the inevitable biopic about my life, please cast Will Smith, Will Arnett, or Jason Bateman to play me. Not sure how that would work given they're all quite a bit older than myself, but I'm sure cloning or the Holy Grail's equivalent will have been invented by then.

Anyhow, the show portrays a dark and brooding forest where evil lurks around every corner. That was far from the Ozarks I saw. Though thickly forested, the sunlight filtered through the trees and shone on beautiful, crystal-clear water with cobble and sandy bottoms running lazily through the summer calm. Only twice did I encounter the cartel, and then only in the spoken words of the audiobook I was listening to.

The first place I'd been told to fish was on private land. I'm not sure if that was the case when the person had initially shared it, but it was practically in someone's backyard, so I didn't want to risk it. Instead, I drove on to the next planned stop. When I drove over a shallow draw that rose to a gap between a ridge blanketed in amber sedgegrass, it was enough to make me pull over on the highway shoulder, walk back down the road, and amble down to the promising untested water.

In the pool immediately underneath the bridge, I could see half a dozen redhorses and carpsuckers, but alas, they could see me, too. They had zero interest in my baits, so I gave up and tried instead for the horde of smaller fishes flitting about in a pool diverted from the main channel that served as a respite for the countless sunfish, minnows, and killifish that occupied it. Longear Sunfish battled for my attention, but when I finally caught all of those present in the pool, I was able to add my second new species of the day: Northern Studfish.

Species #370 — Northern Studfish (*Fundulus catenatus*).

These handsome fish earn their title. Not only are they large, vibrant, and aggressive, but they are one of the larger killifish species and seem to know it. Unlike other killifish, which can be a bit tentative, these little guys zipped over to my baited hooks like the scaled-down pike they resemble in profile. Recent research by one of my editors, Zach Alley, shows they are genetically distinct in the Ozarks and will likely be reclassified, but for now, I'll keep calling them Northern Studfish for simplicity.

These studfish tended to reside near the surface in the slower-moving water at the margins of the pool, so once I'd caught a few, I thrust my micro sabiki into the pool. Another Longear Sunfish obliged me. Then, I got something else. A pair of minnows that (and this is rare) were unmistakable to me. They were Bleeding Shiners.

Species #371 — Bleeding Shiner (*Luxilus zonatus*).

The silvery fish weren't in full spawning plumage, but they still had reddish marks on their fins and at the base of the gills with a roseate blush to their cheeks that hinted at the beautifully bold coloration they would take on for the next round of genetic propagation.

Though I was off to a strong start, I could see every fish in the small clear oxbow, and I knew I'd done all I could there. I wasted an indeterminate amount of time playing with the closed-lip suckers before moving upstream to a gently flowing cobbled run.

I could see a large school of fish that were too small to be redhorses but too large to be shiners. It was a mystery easily solved when one of them hit my worm without hesitation. It was a large-mouthed chub with large scales that resembled the Creek Chubs so widespread in the Eastern United States, but it was golden with a small orange dot on its head you could most aptly position by saying it was on its ear. Fishes don't have ears as we do, but they do have internal ear parts capable of detecting sounds, which means the Hornyhead Chub I caught definitely heard the "Hell yes!" I said aloud, really feeling myself after the fourth new species of the day.

Species #372 — Hornyhead Chub (*Nocomis biguttatus*).

I could've left then and there, but the sun had yet to reach its zenith, and I hoped my day was still on its way up, too. Persistence paid off as I began to notice another minnow species similar in size to the Hornyhead Chubs but with slightly different behavior. They didn't eat right away, but before long, I had one.

Species #373 — Central Stoneroller (*Campostoma anomalum*).

Releasing the stoneroller, I noticed small darters just upstream in the run as the baseball-sized rocks became pebbles. Well, it paid off in the sense that I could see them. Those who have ever chased darters know simply seeing the fish means almost nothing — especially in the daylight.

A solid half hour passed, and I was soaked with sweat from hunching over trying to get the finicky little bastards to nibble my worm, then the piece of a dead crawfish I'd found, then the worm again. Nada. Perturbed, I began changing tactics to see if I could catch one of the madtoms or sculpins I figured had to be present. I put my bait next to larger rocks, hoping to entice one of the primarily nocturnal predators out. It didn't work, so I tried flipping rocks to see if there were any sculpins or madtoms around, or if I was just wasting my time. A small black form darted out from a rock and was such a shock that I didn't know how to react. I'd never seen a madtom (a family of small catfish) before, and now I had the chance to catch one.

I could tell you the long story that involved chasing that little guy for half an hour from rock to rock, describing the emotional toll it had on me (and probably the fish, too), but rather than diving too deeply, I'll cover it at the depth where that bloody madtom resided.

Fishing, for me, is such a holistic spiritual experience that it's hard for me to describe what all I love about it. It's also hard for me to describe the pain of disappointment when you put so much stock in a single, recreational activity that doesn't always pan out how you hope. When I succeed and catch a new species, that dopamine hit is substantial. When I catch any old fish — even one that's not new — it's still something. But when I fail, as I did in that moment, there is a temptation to sit and let darkness take over. Those who have never experienced depression might think this is overly dramatic or perhaps even pitiful, and through objective eyes lived outside of the experience, it kind of is. Yet, when it wracks your brain and narrows your life into a tiny tunnel, it doesn't feel overly dramatic or pitiful.

Fishing, I've found, doesn't just put light at the end of the tunnel; it operates as a light switch that brightens up the tunnel itself. It guides you out of it and through it and helps you find your way. I know other people view it this way, too. One of my favorite musical artists, Brandi Carlile, once wrote "fishing is really just an attempt to connect with something that you know is there, but that you can't see." I love this quote so much, I actually open a later chapter with it.

Now, I'm not saying fishing is God or even a cheap substitute for God, but I genuinely believe fishing is one of those unique human experiences that comes as close to a reproducible divine experience as human beings can get. Swiss naturalist Louis Agassiz once defined each individual species as "a thought of God," and the more species I catch and hold and photograph, the more I tend to agree.

Fishing drives out the darkness in a way that nothing I've ever found does, and the power for good it has in my life is truly a blessing. The flipside is that sometimes, when fishing isn't going well, or I can't fish, or I get too wrapped up in a myopic hunt for one individual species instead of enjoying the experience, it can bring the darkness right back.

Sometimes, the switch flips on and then back off, sending me back into the dark tunnel as it did that morning — albeit briefly. Since that tunnel is purely metaphorical, though, I didn't have to grope blindly in the dark for a way forward. Especially not in that precious moment where I was already within arm's length of the switch, ankle deep in clean, cold water.

Though I felt the immense pressure of depression pushing down on me, and the moment of darkness could have been two minutes or 20, after sitting there paralyzed with rage and hopelessness and disappointment in myself, I was finally able to expel a long sigh, check my bait and keep going. Not in the sense of a motivational poster that reads "Just keep going," and demands we muster internal resolve to defeat our internal demons but in a literal sense: I kept fishing.

I walked away and tried for darters again. The water was clear enough that I could easily see the darters (again, not always the case) contrasted against the bottom. While bouncing my bait in the face of one wary little tease, I noticed what looked like a large Logperch come up, curiously inching toward my bait and just like that, any hint of darkness fled, and wonder replaced despair.

Naturally, I let the fish bite and pulled in what I assumed was an Ozark Logperch, *Percina fulvitaenia*. As always, I gently pinched one pectoral fin in between two fingers so it would lay flat along the length of my hand as I submerged it ever-so-slightly for a picture. Its fins erect, I snapped a quick picture and let the beautifully striped fish with red freckling go. I wouldn't discover its identity until I posted it with all of my other catches from the day on NANFA's Facebook forum, and someone messaged me, saying it was an endangered Niangua Darter. Thankfully, I'd let it go immediately and kept it underwater to take a quick photo for identification. I'd never even heard of the darter, which proved to be the largest darter (including logperch species) I've yet caught.

Species #374 — Niangua Darter (*Etheostoma nianguae*).

Five species by noon? Heck yes, I was feeling pretty confident. I returned to my darter and madtom nemeses (yes, the plural of nemesis is nemeses — I Googled it, and the Internet never lies) in hopes my luck would continue. At first, I was a bit irritated when I caught what I thought was a female Rainbow Darter, one I'd caught in more places than you can eat green eggs and ham, but Tyler Goodale later identified it for me as a female Orangethroat Darter. Self five.

Species #375 — Orangethroat Darter (*Etheostoma spectabile*).

In retrospect, I should've set aside a week for the Ozarks, but I'd set aside just a day and a half. I was supposed to be in Oklahoma City that evening, so I made the responsible choice and moved on.

My second stop was uniquely beautiful, as well.

It was planned, and I drove across the paved creek crossing and found parking nearby. The pavement had slowly been falling away from the lip, and the jagged edge created a pseudo-waterfall that had caused fishes to congregate in some numbers at its roiling base. I started there, nabbing a few more Bleeding Shiners right away before getting another, slightly more streamlined minnow that Tyler once again identified for me: Ozark Minnow.

Species #376 — Ozark Minnow (*Notropis nubilus*).

The forest canopy shaded patches of the water even with the sun high in the sky, and the thickly layered river rock streambed looked promising. This time, I didn't waste time and got right to looking for sculpins and madtoms, my efforts were rewarded with almost immediate movement against the textured bottom.

Rather than the madtoms I was expecting, it was a sculpin. Now, I've caught a lot of sculpins — as many as any other Species Hunter, so the last thing I expected was a new one, but both of the sculpins I caught turned out to be Ozark Sculpins. Not only a fish I didn't have, but a fairly localized endemic. One of my goals is to be the first person to catch all of the North American Cottidae species, and this made 22, so I was off to a strong start. Spoiler alert: I'd be well over 30 by the time I wrote this chapter.

Species #377 — Ozark Sculpin (*Cottus hypselurus*).

Again, I've caught a lot of sculpins. Hundreds of them. Almost all of the freshwater sculpins have been sightfished at night using a headlamp, and though a few have been caught during the day, never so soon or so easily after I started trying for them. Curious what else was under the rocks, I flipped a few more and found one of the madtoms that had eluded me at the last stop.

Target acquired.

It didn't take long, and I caught the first one so quickly that I couldn't believe I'd wasted so much time chasing them at the previous stop, so I hit my forehead repeatedly with the heel of my hand repeating "Stupid, stupid, stupid" over and over again.

Species #378 — Slender Madtom (*Noturus exilis*).

It was crazy I'd just caught my first madtom. The craziest part? I caught four more of them in about 15 minutes. I took plenty of pictures and videos and only got "stung" by impaling myself on their pectoral spines twice. The cold water helped stem the bleeding and pain.

Tyler had given me one spot to try for Ozark Bass, *Ambloplites constellatus*, a Rock Bass split, and I was very much interested, so I packed up and headed that way. Here's where all of my good luck evaporated faster than the cold stream water on my legs as soon as I'd finished wet-wading.

The Ozark Bass didn't bite, and as I tried to catch one of the schooling redhorses as a consolation prize, they also ignored me. I caught Smallmouth Bass, *Micropterus dolomieu* and the obligatory Longear Sunfish in droves, but no Ozark Bass and no redhorses. Wistful sigh.

Fortunately, a school of micros in a too-shallow-to-fish fork of the river justified my efforts, and I landed two new species in rapid succession: Carmine Shiner and Duskystripe Shiner.

Species #379 — Carmine Shiner (*Notropis percobromus*).
Species #380 — Duskystripe Shiner (*Luxilus pilsbryi*).

It was still fairly early in the afternoon, but I had a long drive ahead. Still, the Ozarks had been otherworldly, well-preserved and though latticed with human presence, not compromised by it. It made me smile despite the long drive ahead.

After all, St. Louis to OKC meant about nine hours of driving. This meant I had to get going or risk arriving late. My host messaged me as I crossed into Oklahoma, saying he was too sick to greet me, but he'd set out a sleeping pad and encouraged me to make myself at home. It was different from what I was used to, but the dirty floor upon which my makeshift bed lay and the potential for spider bites didn't scare me away, and I slept soundly.

Chapter 44
40 Days and 40 Nights

July 24, 2019

Day 40
Origin: Oklahoma City, Oklahoma
Destination: Santa Fe, New Mexico

"Oh, what a beautiful mornin'!
Oh, what a beautiful day!
I've got a beautiful feelin'
Ev'rythin's goin' my way."
Rodgers and Hammerstein || American Playwrights
From *Oklahoma!*

Despite a night on the hard ground, I woke up feeling great, honestly. Like the song from the musical/movie *Oklahoma* (one of only a handful of movies I've ever fallen asleep during in my 30-plus-years of life), I had a beautiful feeling. A quick cup of coffee paired with a light breakfast of cheese sticks, some fruit, and a peanut butter sandwich was enough. I had a long day ahead, with almost eight hours of driving and not a lot of fishing, but that didn't stop me from having a positive outlook.
    Until it did.
    Forty days has significance on a Biblical scale. Noah and his family floated atop a flooded world for 40 days and 40 nights. Moses waited and prayed on Mt. Sinai for 40 days and 40 nights while the Israelites rebelled against God and built a golden calf. Jesus fasted in the desert for 40 days.

So, when my trip rolled into its 40th day, it felt significant. Whether it actually was significant, I'm not sure. I just work here. What I can tell you is that on Day 40, I got swallowed by a fish, stuck on a mountain, victimized by pestilence, and spent time fasting in the desert.

Ooooh! Ominous foreshadowing.

Since I had another long drive (OKC to Santa Fe) planned out that day, I knew fishing would be incidental in the vast dry grasslands and desertscape that make up this portion of the country. I'd been given a few pins in New Mexico, but I had nothing in Oklahoma, so I was forced to do my own research. I considered hiring a grad student or recent PhD to do the work for me at abysmal wages, but I'm not a heartless university, so I had to do it myself.

As it happens, there are almost no streams or rivers crossing Interstate 40 in this stretch, so I was forced to go off the interstate. Admittedly, driving through the vast emptiness made scrolling through my phone tempting, but that would be dangerous, so I didn't do it as frequently as I could have. Besides, for a flat and featureless landscape, there were a surprising number of dead spots that Verizon's network just hadn't gotten around to engulfing yet.

So I drove.

Jonah

I'd never been to Oklahoma before, let alone caught a fish there, so that was priority No. 1. The tiny creek I marked was remote, under a small bridge, and far enough away from the highway that I figured I could get in and out relatively easily. What a sweet, naive boy I was.

Naturally, the walk to the creek was difficult given the thick, soupy mud. There were fishes in the creek, but they proved challenging to catch. I was hoping for something else, but after almost half an hour of chasing the skittish little fellas, I finally caught my fish in Oklahoma. It was just a mosquitofish. Western Mosquitofish are pretty unglamorous, though in flowing water environments, they're about 100 times more difficult to catch than their Eastern cousins. Small consolation.

Judgment largely unimpaired, I decided to get one more fish before calling it quits, given all of the potential micros that could be swimming in that ditch. I got another fish, and somehow the little mosquitofish surprised me enough that I lost my footing, broke a flip-flop in the soft muddy bottom of the creek and took a spill into the alkaline water. So even though the fish swallowed my bait and not me, I related to Jonah because I found myself on my hands and knees at the edge of the water, soaking wet, dirty, and knowing full-well the basic alkaline water would irritate the heck out of my skin — probably not as much as stomach acid, but still.

If you're wondering whether I went to Nineveh, Indiana, or Nineveh, Pennsylvania, the answer is neither. I did, however, detour for lunch at a restaurant in Amarillo, Texas, that served alligator. Gator happens to be one of my favorite foods, and I hadn't eaten it since south Florida, so that was my excuse for killing an hour to power down a plate of fried gator and okra before pressing further into the desert.

Moses

My second pit stop was just off the main drag. I could see a small stream crossing under a paved road and what appeared to be a vacant lot on my maps so I planned to stop there.

Perfect.

Upon my arrival, I could see the stream was mostly dried up. It was not the Promised Land, but rather a stagnant cesspool with several homeless camps nearby, so I turned right back around and sort of wandered aimlessly through the desert, hoping to find another source of water.

I didn't have a staff to crack open any rocks, so it was fortunate that I found a larger river crossing the highway a short distance down the road. My trials weren't quite over, though. It was a river that routinely floods, and as I walked the long slog below the highway bridge through thick, sucking mud, I came to a range fence meant to keep cattle from getting into the roadway.

Rather than being stuck just outside the Promised Land, I climbed it with remarkable dexterity and made my way to the clouded waters of not the Red Sea, but the Red River.

Leaving my sandals — okay, flip-flops — on the bank, I wet-waded upstream in search of my principal target: the Red River Pupfish.

"It was the Promised Land," I realized aloud as I waded up the milky river to a honey hole where I'd catch my first species. Milk and honey? How 'bout that.

Species #381 — Red River Pupfish (*Cyprinodon rubrofluviatilis*).

Though they have one of the longer Latin names around, the Red River Pupfish is a short and stocky little critter that I find absolutely adorable. I wasn't able to find any of them until I located a small, clear trickle flowing into the mainstem of the river, where a small school of what *haaad* to be pupfish were feeding actively. By staying far away from the little school, I was able to cast upstream and allow my micro rig to drive down into their midst. My worm chunk must have looked like manna from heaven because the little bulldog of a fish hit it with fury.

My pilgrimage to the Red River was already working out for me, but I had to really work for the next fish I'd catch. Though it felt like wandering 40 more years through the desert in the thick mud and fighting the current, I probably only walked about a mile all told, going up and up and upstream looking for the little pockets and margins clear and slow-moving enough to fish. My diligence paid off, and I thanked God with each additional, hard-won Lifer that day.

Species #382 — Plains Minnow (*Hybognathus placitus*).

I also caught a beautiful spawning male Red Shiner. Not a new fish, but always a welcome visitor in my life with its vibrant purple-pink-blue triadic color scheme and the pink-and-blue markings used to inspire the pastel color choices for bachelorette party decorations.

Then I saw the killifish. I knew both Plains Topminnow and Plains Killifish were in range, and killifish happen to be some of my favorite species, so I had a new mission, a new obsession. Unfortunately, the tiny little edge water behind a stick impaled vertically in the mud that created a current break wasn't enough to make the little killis feel comfortable, and I struggled trying to get them to bite. Several times I left and came back, and it was only after maybe 50 drifts or so that I finally got one. It wasn't a topminnow; it was a Plains Killifish.

Species #383 — Plains Killifish (*Fundulus zebrinus*).

Satisfied that one of my unresearched, completely whimsical "that looks fishy" stops had resulted in four new species, I decided to count my blessings and move on. This is where I got stuck on a mountain — just like Moses.

Sort of.

It was a planned stop I'd fished once before when a friend had told me to try it out. On my first trip, I'd been sorely disappointed in the rusty red water with thick, red mud so sticky that it was virtually impossible to get off my shoes. Since there were several species there I hadn't caught, I figured it was worth another shot. It wasn't.

I drove to the remote slot canyon and walked to the bridge cut into the mountainside then down the steep slope to the bridge. Pestilence ensued, as I was swarmed by biting flies, buried in the water that looked as though it'd been turned to blood and mixed with mud.

Naturally, the fishing was terrible again, and I was unable to even find water more than two or three inches deep. I grew tired of swatting the flies, and they bit hard enough to draw blood, which just attracted more of the filthy buggers, and I was trapped in a vicious cycle of misery. I peeled my feet from the incredibly sticky streambed and ambled up to the steep rocks below the bridge that I'd climbed down.

I'd been on the road fishing for 40 days at this point, sleeping primarily on couches and floors and cheap mattresses, and I was exhausted. I'm not sure what possessed me to try going back up that way instead of taking the longer, more gently sloping route out the other side, but I'm sure I figured short-term extreme pain was better than drawn out moderate pain.

Well, short term extreme pain is exactly what I got.

My flip-flops were so muddy and slippery that I had to decide whether to go barefoot and risk slicing my feet open or keep them on and risk slipping and falling to my death. I went barefoot and dodged the scorpions one by one as I climbed to the top.

About halfway up, I was so dead tired, my feet aching, my bloody bug wounds so unpleasant, my back so stiff, that I had this moment of cold clarity in which I saw myself for the insane-looking creature I was. I was covered in mud, sweating profusely, bleeding from small bite marks all over my face, neck, legs, and arms, and I'm sure the wild and frantic look in my eyes was absolutely horrifying.

So I stood there for a moment, feeling irreversibly wild and admittedly afraid of that side of myself, that indomitable, press-on-at-all costs piece of Luke unafraid of pain or suffering so long as I reached my end goals, which, in this instance, involved chasing a fish and failing miserably. The craziest part is that it was far from the last time I'd find myself fishing barefoot in harsh conditions on this trip, and I had less than a week to go.

Jesus

After wandering around the deserts of Oklahoma, Texas, and New Mexico that day, I was beat. I'd eaten twice, but I'd still fasted 10 hours or so after lunch, and the strain that simple act put on my body while I carried out my daily routine made me realize what a feat fasting for 40 days was.

I also found myself praying a desperate prayer of "Jesus, please don't let me be maimed, bitten, scraped, or otherwise injured at my final stop. And please help me to catch a Rio Grande Chub, *Gila pandora*." What a spiritually profound prayer. Goodness.

Okay, I didn't include the Latin name in the prayer — that might've opened Pandora's Box. Also, I'm a little disappointed in the scientist who described the Rio Grande Chub, gave it the scientific name of *Gila pandora* and then didn't call it Pandora's Chub. I digress.

As I pulled up to the little stretch of the Pecos River another Lifelister, Ben Cantrell, had provided for me and wet a line, I nearly stepped on a rattlesnake. Prior to this trip, I'd seen exactly one living rattlesnake. This marked the third of the trip, and without that prayer, I might not have noticed it soon enough, and it could've been my last.

Thank you, Jesus.

I caught a pair of chubs to finish my day with five new species. Not bad for a place largely devoid of water.

Species #384 — Rio Grande Chub (*Gila pandora*).

From there, I drove the rest of the way to Santa Fe, hit up my favorite African/Caribbean restaurant, Jambo Cafe, before arriving at a Quality Inn with an overhang next to the front door. I was hit with déjà vu, but I couldn't quite place it until I got to my room.

I'd stayed at that same motel on one of my previous road trips, but that time, the overhang had collapsed the day I was there when someone crashed into the support pillar. I awoke to see the devastated entryway and felt blessed to have avoided being crushed by just a manner of hours.

Not everything had gone my way, but it had been a beautiful day. Perspective hits differently.

Thank you, Jesus.

Chapter 45
Time as a Force of Change

July 25, 2019

Day 41
Origin: Santa Fe, New Mexico
Destination: Flagstaff, Arizona

"'I think balance is for people who don't know why they're here, who haven't found their passion yet.'"
Marcus Slade || From Blake Crouch's *Recursion*

How people traveled before smartphones, I honestly have no idea. Don't get me wrong, I grew up hunting, and the dog-eared Rand McNally map book was an essential part of the experience of wending through backwoods Forest Service roads, but there was always someone to navigate and someone to drive, and we were moving slowly.

Though I've done it, reading behind the wheel isn't quite so ideal — especially at highway speeds.

That's why the smartphone was the single greatest invention for the solo traveler. Not only do Apple or Google Maps change the game, but being able to look up restaurants, make calls from the road, take notes, save data points, take pictures, flex on social media, listen to audiobooks, and play music truly make the experience bearable.

I shudder to think of a road trip in which I had to meticulously scour a mapbook before every turn while following exit signs to food and gas and listening only to whatever station was available on the radio as I made my way to catch a fish I had to photograph with a conventional camera and record it on a notepad.

Can you imagine the horror? Well, if you're over 25, you didn't have to imagine it; you lived it. As a result, I have tremendous respect for those who managed before the smartphone. I only had to endure childhood and my teens without one.

Despite my meticulous planning, I'm very easily distracted on the road. Between the scenery, songs on repeat, and whatever audiobook I'm currently listening to, I often lose focus. At this point in the trip, I was listening to Blake Crouch's *Recursion* when two of the main characters have a discussion about passion and the central role it can play in the lives of those who've found it, about whether it's a blessing or a curse.

"'I think balance is for people who don't know why they're here, who haven't found their passion yet,'" Marcus says.

His friend, Gwen, counters in her mind without actually saying anything.

"In high school, in college, she was encouraged again and again to find her passion — a reason to get out of bed and breathe. In her experience, few people ever found that raison d'etre.

"What teachers and professors never told her was about the dark side of finding your purpose. The part where it consumes you. Where it becomes a destroyer of relationships and happiness. And still, she wouldn't trade it. This is the only person she knows how to be."

Bruh. That felt like it was written for me.

In the waning days of my trip, I thought about how much my absence this summer had kept me away from my friends and family, and even though it was an essential, beautiful experience, I'd certainly made tradeoffs.

My own obsession with fishing, the 150 or 200 days a year I indulge in it, represents the single largest commitment of my time outside of work, and even that is too close to call some years.

If you think for a moment that the apropos interchange from *Recursion* shook my resolve to be insanely passionate, you're sorely mistaken, but it certainly helped me take stock of my life on my quest to an ever-clearer self-concept.

On this day of my trip, my obsession would send me barefoot through a high mountain forest in a flash-flood caliber rainstorm on a quest for a rare fish preserved almost exclusively on the Fort

Apache Indian Reservation in Northern Arizona but not without a few detours along the way.

Ode to Siri

Before I got there, I missed a turn. Normally, I used Siri, but I'd failed to activate my Maps app, and I just kept listening to that same enthralling book. A sign for a city I shouldn't have been heading toward tipped me off, but I'd driven 20 minutes in the wrong direction before realizing my mistake. Again, how did people manage to travel before the modern convenience of a smartphone? How did people navigate without Siri?

Siri, Alexa, Cortana, and whatever other pseudo-AIs have been created since I wrote this are truly incredible. Though technically Cortana existed in the *Halo* video games long before Siri uttered her first syllable, Siri certainly set the mood for the entire industry, and I can see why. Though Siri is imperfect (if I had a dollar for every time she mispronounced "Orlando" or "battleship" I could've financed my trip), but other than that, she's a modern miracle.

In my rarely humble opinion, Siri is so named for a character from the *Hyperion Cantos* books, a science fiction series by Dan Simmons about a futuristic intergalactic society ruled by the Hegemony. Some of the worlds found within the Hegemony have warp portals called "Farcasters" capable of transporting people instantaneously from one place to the next. As the Hegemony grows, it tries to place Farcasters on every world, but not every world is amenable to it due to the massive increase in tourism the Farcasters bring. One such world is a planet called Maui Covenant, an aquatic world in tune with the oceans and nature. On Maui Covenant there lives a girl named Siri.

When a representative of the Hegemony named Merin Aspic comes to visit and explore the idea of Farcaster development on Maui Covenant, the pair fall in love despite the girl's resistance to the idea of the portal. Since there is not yet a portal, Merin must travel by spaceship from the planet and go on his merry (Merin?) way. Parting is sweet sorrow for the young lovers, and each time Merin leaves, he invites Siri to go with him, but she is unwilling to leave her home. Seven times over the course of her life, Merin comes to visit. Due to the effects of relativistic travel, Merin ages just months between visits, while Siri ages years.

In their first meeting, Siri is a teenager. By their seventh and final meeting, Siri is an old woman while Merin has aged less than a decade. It's a beautiful and tragic love story in which Siri slowly battles the construction of the Farcaster. Ultimately, it is built, and the subsequent millions of tourists destroy the fragile ecosystem of the planet. As one of her final acts, she destroys the Farcaster and returns Maui Covenant to its independent state after much damage has already been done by the influx of millions of tourists and the resulting ecological destruction they bring with them.

Siri never leaves the planet. She never gets a formal education. She never marries. She never experiences anything beyond what she grew up knowing. And she never stops loving Merin Aspic. Siri of Apple fame knows darn near everything. So why, you may be wondering, would Siri be named for this girl who never saw the larger world?

Because Siri (*Hyperion's* Siri) proves that a single person — a single voice — can make a profound and lasting difference just by speaking up.

Siri (Apple's Siri) absolutely made a difference in my life. This trip, and subsequently *this book*, wouldn't have been possible without her. So thank you, Siri, from the bottom of my heart.

The Rez

Seeing how maps became apps is a stark contrast I lived through. How the wild, untamed lands inhabited from time immemorial by Native peoples became riddled with pavement and thrust into modernity is not. Still, I tried my best to respect those changes when I visited.

Northern Arizona's Fort Apache Indian Reservation is home to some incredible fishing. It's also home to the Arizona State Record Brook, Brown, and Apache Trout, *Oncorhynchus apache,* the latter of which is also the world record. Apache Trout are in the same genus as Rainbow and Cutthroat Trout, *Oncorhynchus clarkii,* and these beautiful fish native to a small range in the American Southwest are a treasure that has been painstakingly preserved by the diligent efforts of dozens of interest groups, including the Apache Tribe, the State of Arizona, the United States Fish and Wildlife Service (USFWS), the Western Native Trout Initiative, and many more. In conjunction, these groups have not only saved an isolated endemic from going extinct but have led restoration efforts to keep it strong enough to support a small recreational fishery. There's a fascinating podcast produced by the USFWS called "Apache Trout - From near Extinction to EcoTourism" available on YouTube if you care to learn more about the history of this incredible species, and my own contribution to that ecotourism had me detouring through Northern Arizona.

Despite my trout obsession, I hadn't caught a single Salmonid on my trip. Never in my life had I gone on so many consecutive fishing trips without catching a single trout, so it was long overdue.

I arrived at the stretch of river I planned to fish only to find a small group of people hammering the hole closest to the parking area. The ground was wet and muddy, and while it was too hot for rubber boots, it wasn't ideal for flip-flops, either, with all of the broken terrain.

So I did what I'm sure countless other anglers had done in generations long past: I went barefoot, carrying my flip-flops with me in case I needed them. Walking the soft forest loam and grassy meadows that framed the clear, cold creek was an almost spiritual experience, allowing me to commune with God and His creation in a more personal and intimate way than I ever could in the concrete canals of Miami, under a well-traveled highway in the Midwest, or in the constantly swarming humanity of the Mobile Bay.

Once I got a few hundred yards from the pavement, I escaped the other swimmers, hikers, and anglers, and I felt completely at peace with my reality — so much so that I failed to realize the sky overhead was souring.

In this part of the country, storms arrive in a hurry. The sky darkened and opened up in a matter of minutes. The pouring rain soaked the surrounding area, and I took shelter under a pair of evergreens. I sat there on the forest floor as the world around me shrunk to the individual blades of grass, the dry pine needles greedily sopping up the precious moisture, the sound of a torrential summer rainstorm muffled and canned by the trees upon which it fell. I watched the tiny forbs and wildflowers drink up the rainfall as the microcosm of the world stood still around me, timeless in its wholesome embrace of the moment.

I'm not overly emotional, but that moment was so perfect that it made me tear up. I relished every second of it until the storm passed. That moment consumed me so completely that I didn't want it to end or even consider the possibility until it had passed. Returning to the creek, I felt restored. I wet-waded up the stream barefoot, one pool at a time, and finally caught a fish.

Species #385 — Apache Trout (*Oncorhynchus apache*).

In short order, I caught two more, all between 10 and 15 inches in length and decided they justified my barefoot walkabout. Heading back to the car, I came across an angler carrying a dead trout on a stringer. I couldn't believe he was keeping such a rare fish (and a small one at that), but the restoration efforts of the interest groups maintaining the Apache Trout have been so successful that apparently harvest is sustainable — if still a little cringeworthy.

Though I've never found a wild trout tasty enough to make the case that its food value is higher than its sport value, I don't begrudge the sustainable harvest of trout. I certainly wouldn't trust the culinary judgment of anyone who likes trout; literally every single saltwater fish I've ever eaten (and I've tried dozens and dozens of species on four continents) tastes markedly better than anything caught in freshwater — especially trout — but not everyone has access to palatable fishes, I suppose.

Grayling

Speaking of fishes too perfect to eat, my next target was the Arctic Grayling, *Thymallus arcticus*. The Arctic Grayling is a majestic and iconic fish synonymous with the cold, clear waters of the North. It can be found throughout Canada, Alaska, and the mountainous reaches of several other northern states. You know where it can also be found? Arizona.

Mind-blowing feels too tame a descriptor for this revelation made to me by my friend Chris Moore, but a fish native to the arctic circle does, in fact, swim in a state that borders Mexico. After I'd walked the entire span of the small lake for more than an hour, struck out on every lure and fly I had with me, I was ready to call it a day. As I made my way back to the car, I noticed something sip a hapless insect off the surface. I had no 3-weight or even 5-weight fly rod with me. Nothing light enough to dance a mosquito on the surface and wait for a take.

On a whim, I tied on the Bergie Worm Jr., that tiny ice fishing jig, and cast it out with my spinning rod, slowly stripping it just under the surface. I hooked up briefly, but lost what I just assumed was a trout.

Two or three more casts had hits, and I kept missing, but I finally hooked up and landed the first of what would be several grayling that afternoon.

Species #386 — Arctic Grayling (*Thymallus arcticus*).

I know what you're thinking. An Arctic Grayling in Arizona? This guy must be full of it. You're more likely to stumble across a nude beach in Utah. But it is absolutely true, and I have the photos to prove it! I have photos of the fish, too.

That pretty much wrapped up the day. I hopped into my car and drove into Flagstaff, a cool little city lacking only in fishable water and hipster-free bars. I inhaled a delicious pizza and rented a motel room in which I could bleed myself to sleep.

Chapter 46
Five Decades of Cultural References

July 26, 2019

Day 42
Origin: Flagstaff, Arizona
Destination: St. George, Utah

"All these years have taught me that fishing is really
just an attempt to connect to something that you
know is there,
but that you can't see."
Brandi Carlile || American Musician || From *Broken Horses*

    I awoke in Flagstaff, once again lamenting the fact that the otherwise wonderful little city is virtually devoid of fishing opportunities. There would be no quick stops at streams, rivers, or culverts today. Instead, I'd be driving for hours to a series of remote hot springs in the middle of Utah. It was a beautiful day, and as the summer sun climbed the sky, I could feel the desert soaking up the warmth with eager delight. The wispy strips of cloud draped across the vivid blue horizon provided a breathtaking contrast to the red rocks of the desert and the dingy green and gray of the mountains beyond.
    As of 2023, I've been to every state except Alaska, Montana, and the Dakotas. Apart from California, Utah is the only part of the United States that really holds a candle to Oregon's diverse,

unmolested beauty. If Utah had a coastline, it just might overtake Oregon as the most beautiful state. Still, I enjoy every visit to the heart of what was once known as Deseret.

All the romanticized appreciation of the Western landscape distracted me long enough that I failed to realize I'd lost service. Having turned off my Maps app to save battery, I wasn't sure how far I'd driven, so I checked my trip meter. At first, it took a moment to realize what I was seeing. I'd set the trip meter at the onset of my trip, and I'd driven thousands of miles, but now it was sitting at 107.

"Oh no!" I said aloud, accenting the statement of shock with profanity.

I'd cleared my trip meter by mistake, I thought, and I was upset about it until I realized there were only four number slots, and I'd last seen it as 9,700-something the day before. It had hit 10,000 miles and reset. I had left home 42 days earlier, and I'd driven more than 10,000 miles since. That's not nothing. Relieved that I hadn't lost my precious mileage calculation, I continued on for four or five more hours to the first hot spring.

Meadow Hot Springs

There was what appeared to be a single, massive cloud up ahead, but not the type you pay to access and store data in. No, what had been a bluebird day for hours and hundreds of miles rapidly became ominous and brooding. Though I'm sure it was my imagination, it appeared to be a single swirling nautilus of gaseous condensation circling around a fixed point, sort of like Mt. Doom (*The Lord of the Rings*, 2000s) or like Death Mountain from *The Legend of Zelda: Ocarina of Time*'s (1990s). I was about 30 miles away from my destination, and I prayed desperately that the isolated storm system was not looming over my intended stop, but as I left the pavement under angry skies darkened mightily by the swirling forms above, the rain began pummeling my car. I couldn't help but bitterly note that it was just my luck.

By the time I made it to the first turn in the sopping gravel, I had to turn off my audiobook because the torrential deluge was *that loud*. To make matters worse, I'd stopped just once on the six-hour drive (I know, I was proud of my bladder, too), but that meant I'd had to pee for roughly 100 miles or so. The rainfall certainly wasn't helping that, but the standing water on the packed gravel-and-dirt roads told me I'd be soaked if I left my car. I made it up to the unimproved parking area and found the little pool that housed all manner of exotic species released from aquaria into the small, slightly off-smelling petri dish called Meadow Hot Springs.

There were two other cars there, but as I arrived, they both left. I decided not to think about what sort of strange drug- or sex-related debauchery I'd just broken up with my mere presence and searched my car for a water bottle with a wide enough mouth for me to relieve myself. All I had were water bottles, and not to brag, but even in the slightly colder weather brought on by the rain, the half-inch opening of a standard water bottle wouldn't suffice. Mercifully, I found an empty coffee cup in the trash can and set to work. The first thing I thought to myself was "Glad I didn't get a large coffee," but then, as the cup filled a little faster than anticipated, I wished I had gotten a large.

I turned off the faucet mid-stream, quickly opened the door and emptied the cup, hoping the fluid in which my left arm was immediately soaked was just rainwater (or at least mostly rainwater) before proceeding to fill up the cup again. Repeating the process a second time, I tossed 12 more ounces of used coffee and water out of the cup. After Round 3, the tank was empty.

To my horror, a car full of at least two younger women had shown up just as I'd gotten started, and I'd failed to notice. They were smiling and waving, and I was lowkey mortified. The lightning wasn't the only thing flashing at Meadow Hot Springs that day, apparently. Realizing I had nothing left to lose, I took a gamble that the lightning wouldn't find me, and I quickly threw on rain gear and started fishing.

The water was murky, and the unrelenting barrage of raindrops made sightfishing impossible, but I'm just that good. I caught half a dozen Convict Cichlids, *Amatitlania nigrofasciata* as my new fan club loudly hooted and hollered out the crack in their window.

Before long, I got something else, and I was stoked to pull in my first-ever molly. Coincidentally, I was not the first person in that parking lot to hold molly in-hand; I thought the carload of girls was simply drunk, but they were high on Utah's finest MDMA. This became clearer when they hopped out of the car in skimpy bathing suits and began "swimming" where I was trying to fish. It was still raining lightly, but this only encouraged them, as they reveled in the feeling of the raindrops that cascaded down their bodies. It was clearly pleasant because one of them just sat there, mouth open and arms akimbo as she spun slowly with her head leaned back. Had she not tripped on her feet and fallen over, it might've been slightly endearing.

There were two younger women, both twentysomethings, and an older woman maybe in her forties.

They put on a show for me, rubbing up against each other, lounging seductively on the rocks at the water's edge, and splashing and giggling for almost half an hour. Some of you might be thinking "What a lucky guy," but if their gaunt faces, sunken eyes, and rotten teeth were any indication, molly was one of the safer drugs they'd used.

One of them called for me, saying "Why don't you join us?" with a rancid chortle only a meth-addled mind could find attractive. It just made me sad, so I was friendly but tried to keep my eyes down and stay focused on fishing — easier said than done at a pond maybe a quarter acre in size.

It was still raining hard enough that sightfishing remained impossible, but that didn't stop me from catching an absurd number of Convict Cichlids, various jewelfish, a pair of Jack Dempsey Cichlids, *Amatitlania nigrofasciata,* and a pair of cichlids I identified as Oaxaca x Redhead hybrids. A friend (Steve Wozniak) would later catch one from that same spot and register it as the IGFA All-Tackle World Record Oaxaca Cichlid, *Vieja zonata,* but don't worry; I'm not bitter. I caught it in July of 2019 and didn't submit a record. Steve got it in November of 2019 and submitted his record. A year later, I came back and reset the record in August of 2020.

Begrudgingly, I didn't call it a new species given the unique conditions of the little pond. Maybe I should have? I did manage to catch a new species in the Shortfin Molly.

Species #387 — Shortfin Molly (*Poecilia mexicana*).

Though I caught 37 fishes in just a few hours, without being able to see deeper than a foot to target specific fish, I knew it was a fool's errand. My fan club left, and I hoped they wouldn't get in a wreck. The downpour started up again, and I decided to move on, mollified.

Like a Virgin

Virgin, Utah, is the gateway to Zion National Park. In retrospect, I probably should've just visited the park while I was here, but I was on a mission from God, so the park named for God Himself was unavoidable. Okay, I wasn't technically on a mission from God, but apart from walking, fishing is the only recreational activity we know Jesus Christ himself participated in, so it falls into line.

Well, net, given the gear they used at the time.

After leaving Meadow Hot Springs wet and fairly disappointed with the lack of new species, I headed toward St. George, where I'd planned to stay that night. En route to St. George, I had a stop to fish the Virgin River in hopes of catching one of several sucker species I've never caught (namely the allegedly common Utah Sucker,

Catostomus ardens, which I'd struck out on in Northern Utah on my drive down earlier in the summer). The spot itself was a bit of a hike from the pavement. Had I known I'd be walking almost three miles round-trip down and then back up a small mountain to the river carving out the small canyon, I wouldn't have worn flip-flops. Likewise, if I'd known the water was so cold that it was like reliving the Ice Bucket Challenge (2010s), I probably wouldn't have opted to wear flip-flops for that reason alone. Then again, if I'm sticking with the Virgin theme, the Holy Virgin herself likely wore sandals every day, so it fit. Unfortunately, I didn't catch a sucker, but I did catch a fish I didn't even know existed until I looked it up. As it happens, it was an endangered species, so I'm glad I quickly released it.

Species #388 — Redacted Leucicid (*Leucicidae redactus*).

It's virtually impossible to control what will hit a worm (unless, of course, it's me trying to catch any species of Western sucker, in which case it won't happen), so I didn't feel too bad about catching that fish, as I kept my hands wet, unhooked it immediately and let it go. I'll leave it as "Redacted Leucicid" because again, it's protected, and I don't want to encourage people to chase sensitive species.

Fortunately, apart from the pestilent (and highly invasive) Smallmouth Bass, I managed to catch one other species that was not endangered. Not wanting to get another Redacted Leucicid or one of the stunted smallies, I left the rod with half a worm on shore and decided to microfish for the school of tiny fish feeding near the bottom. I wasn't sure, but I half-suspected they might be dace. Probably Speckled Dace, *Rhinichthys osculus,* a fish I'd already caught, but a species I knew was being considered for splitting into several different species, so it might be one I could bank for a future taxonomic shift. Unlike the Speckled Dace I'd caught before, though, these were a pain to get to bite. Eventually I caught one, and I was shocked to see it was not a mottled brown, white, and tan Speckled Dace, but an entirely silver little fish.

At first, horrified I'd just captured a Federally Endangered Woundfin, *Plagopterus argentissimus,* I quickly noticed it didn't have vestigial barbels at the corners of its mouth, so it wasn't that. Phew. What it was, I had no idea. I snapped a quick picture of the mystery fish in my cold, wet hand and let it go. It rejoined the school, and I figured I was playing with fire given the presence of two endangered species in this stretch. In retrospect, why is this river open to fishing at all? To keep the invasive smallies in check?

I'd later identify that fish as a Virgin Spinedace, *Lepidomeda mollispinis*, a fish with a limited range but an almost entirely protected habitat that kept it out of serious danger and kept it off the Endangered Species List.

Species #389 — Virgin Spinedace (*Lepidomeda mollispinis*).

Though not endangered, I would later learn the fish is on Utah's "Prohibited Fish" list, with the regulation stating: "Possession of the following nongame fish is prohibited. If you catch any of these fish, you must release them immediately." Since I released the fish immediately and didn't kill it, I had broken no laws, but it still felt sort of morally gray, so I'm glad I stopped at that point. As I waded back to the shore, I went to grab the rod I'd left on the bank and reached within a foot of a rattlesnake coiled in the shape of the streamside vegetation. I jumped up and backward, nearly losing my footing on the loose river rocks and tumbling backward into the river. As I climbed back up to my car, air drying in the stifling heat I was reassured of my decision to leave.

I prayed a quick prayer of absolution for catching the Redacted Leucicid, which I did release immediately and again, broke no laws in catching, but it wasn't a fish I was proud to have caught even if I'd done so incidentally. Just "Like a Virgin" (1980s), the Utah Suckers would have to wait for the right time.

Pacu

Going from a filthy hot spring to a pristine (some might even say Virgin) river flowing through a rocky canyon was quite a contrast. My third and final stop of the day was much more like the former than the latter, but given that it was in the middle of a city across from a shopping center, it felt even less pristine than Meadow Hot Springs had been.

There were allegedly half a dozen species of exotic fish in this pond, called "The Boilers" by locals for the hot springs that fed it, but when I arrived, I saw just three species. First, I found a massive double-digit pacu (a group of giant, vegetarian piranha-like fishes from South America), half a dozen Red Devil Cichlids, and a single respectable (maybe four- or five-pound) Largemouth Bass. I was heartbroken. This place was supposed to be very productive, but it was virtually devoid of life.

I would later learn someone put in a dozen Largemouth Bass that ate most of the smaller fishes before being caught and harvested. A single bass had survived and continued thinning out the remaining handful of unfortunate cichlids.

The last fishes swimming were more paranoid than a lifelong stoner in a tin foil hat. I couldn't even get close enough to cast a small bait, but I could stand on the surrounding slope and tell what they were nonetheless. Having caught enough Largemouth Bass and Red Devil Cichlids to not waste my time with those two, I focused on the pacu.

It wouldn't touch worms, lures, or jigs, so I thought and thought. I had been eating peanut butter sandwiches almost every day for the whole summer, so I kept bread and peanut butter in the car. With waning daylight, I figured it was worth a shot.

I pulled out a small doughbait hook, tied it to a long, 10-pound fluorocarbon leader and mashed a bread ball on the hook before coating it with peanut butter.

I had to walk around the pond half a dozen times before the pacu stopped moving and stayed in a place where I could cast the lightweight rig to it. Three times, it came up on the breadball and swung but failed to bite. Then it wised up and just hid up against the bank on the opposite side of me. I moved and snuck around but failed to get another cast in.

"Nate"

Resigned, I left to grab dinner and lament my disappointment while the autobiographical and deeply personal song "Nate" (2020s) by one of my favorite artists, NF, came up on the shuffle. The lyrics near the end of the track hit me, hard:

"It sounds awesome, at the same time, it doesn't matter
At twenty-seven [I was 28 at the time], we'll make millions, but it's really sad 'cause
You'll learn to realize that none of this will make you happy."

This hit me not because I was even remotely as successful as the popular artist, but because this trip had been the best experience of my life, and almost every day had been great. I'd made and set goals, caught all of these fishes, and ultimately caught more fish species in the United States than (probably) anyone else before me in such a short time period. I'd caught almost 200 species in six weeks. That should've been enough. That should've made me happy, confident and put me on top of the world, but it didn't. Maybe because few people actually cared or found any significance in what I'd done, but more likely just because accomplishment doesn't directly equate to happiness.

I just felt like it had been distracting me from the dissatisfaction I'd felt for so long. There were just a few days left in my trip, so I wouldn't have this incredible distraction for much longer. How, I began to wonder, could I go back to a life I wasn't satisfied with?

Shoving it down, I decided to enjoy the rest of my time and deal with those emotions later.

Whenever "later" was.

Chapter 47
Heaven and Hell

July 27, 2019

Day 43
Origin: St. George, Utah
Destination: Barstow, California

"Men of the present time testify of heaven and hell,
and have never seen either."
Joseph Smith || Founder
Church of Jesus Christ of Latter-day Saints

St. George, Utah, is named for the St. George of legend. There is some debate about which of two versions (Greek or Latin) the St. George acknowledged by the Catholic Diocese is based upon, but the sainted martyr's exact exploits were relatively unknown to the Catholic Church of the day that sainted him. At the end of the 5th century A.D., Pope Gelasius (the pope who canonized St. George) is noted to have said that St. George was one of the saints "whose names are justly (revered) among men, but whose actions are known only to God," so what he actually did remains lost to the ages.

Did his torture and eventual martyrdom really lead to the salvation of more than 40,000 people as the Latin version insists? Was his father a martyr for Christianity before him as the Greek version claims? Was he actually slain and resurrected numerous times as a prophet for the Islamic faith as several Arabic legends suggest? Did he slay a dragon as a later English addendum in the 11th century argues?

Many of these questions cannot be answered, but his name is widely known, a historical figure whose exploits have been embellished to the point of legend.

St. George, Utah, is named for the man, the myth, the legend, St. George, which makes it fitting that a man considered to be so close to God is also close to the national park named for God Himself.

I drove the hour from my motel to Zion National Park, and I was instantly impressed. Zion was certainly impressive and a testament to an insightful and powerful Creator worthy of the praise of St. George and the other great men and women who have walked this earth.

In addition to a very pleasant drive from one end of the relatively new park to the other, there are also countless hiking trails, vistas, and canyonlands to explore. I didn't spend much time outside of the car, but I did pause to appreciate the beauty of the Virgin River and a small herd of Bighorn Sheep standing watch on a distant ridge.

The park entrance fee is $35 per vehicle, but as a member of the military, I get a free America the Beautiful Pass, which allows free access to almost all Federal lands, including national parks. Had I paid $35, I would've happily spent a full day there, but I was trying to get to Las Vegas by that evening, hoping to fish along the way. After driving through the 1.1-mile-long tunnel twice, I returned to Interstate 15 and started heading in what was both figuratively and literally the opposite direction from Zion: Sin City.

The allusion was not lost on me.

Nevada

Not long after crossing over the Nevada-Utah border, I decided to stop at a place I'd marked for Guppies. You may remember I attempted to catch one on the first day of my trip (in Northern Nevada) and failed miserably. Well, I'm a glutton for punishment.

The Guppy is a livebearer native to South America that has long been popular in aquaria. As a result, the fish has been bred and altered to the point where hundreds of variations exist. Though the fish is not as cold-tolerant as other livebearers (such as the closely related Eastern and Western Mosquitofish), it has become established in warmer waters across the American South, and Nevada is no exception. The state with the least water is also the state with the most widespread Guppy population. Guppies can be found from the northern reaches of the state (where I fished at the start of my trip) all the way down to Las Vegas in every spring, heated drainage ditch, and warm water river and stream and effluent across the state.

My stop took me off the pavement along a serpentine dirt road with powdery soil so soft and dry that I had to sit in my car for 10 minutes after parking before the dust finally settled. Upon exiting my vehicle, I quickly realized that it was not conducive to walking in flip-flops or shoes, but it was so hot that walking barefoot wasn't great, either, so I hurriedly ambled down to the river, my tenkara rod in hand.

I descended the steep bank, only slipping a lot as the bank collapsed beneath me, and I half jumped, half fell into the river. I landed with both feet planted in the deep mud of the riverbed, eternally thankful there had been no broken glass underfoot and relishing the cool water. Sadly, my indelicate landing had scared every fish from within easy reach, and the outside bend of the river I had landed in was the only fishable spot for hundreds of yards in either direction given the high, clouded water absent only in this shallow bend.

Patiently, I awaited the return of the fish, and it paid off. I could see the distinctive yellow-orange tails of Mexican Molly, *Poecilia sphenops* and what appeared to be Western Mosquitofish at first glance curiously return to the shallows. Though I got the mollies to nibble a few times, I failed to hook one.

Stubborn in my resolve, I kept trying until, finally, I got one of the not-mollies to bite. I was disappointed, thinking it was a Western Mosquitofish, but as I looked for the telltale black "teardrop" below its eye that just wasn't there, the light reflected off the blue flanks, and I knew I'd caught a Guppy that had reverted to natural coloration. After striking out for this species on my very first day of the trip, I'd made up for it at the very end. If you love those feel-good, full-circle moments straight out of a Hallmark movie, then you're welcome.

Species #390 — Guppy (*Poecilia reticulata*).

I caught a few more Guppies, taking careful photos in the (for once) almost perfect lighting conditions. The mollies vanished entirely after my third or fourth Guppy, so I cleaned off as best as I could and climbed the high steep bank with all the grace of a bear awakened part way through its hibernation to find itself on a sheet of ice.

Somehow, I made it to the top without breaking my tenkara rod and then (here's the more impressive part), I remembered to load my tenkara rod into the back of my car before driving away.

I know. I was proud of myself, too.

Vegas Springs

Though none of the half dozen springs within an hour of Las Vegas are called Vegas Springs, I'm sure there's a casino or hotel or roadside dive with that name.

I fished two springs not far apart from one another, but the first was tiny and devoid of fish. I'm sure it had held fishes in the past, but given its small size, I imagine it's quite susceptible to wayward raccoons coming in and cleaning it out from time to time. At its largest point, the spring is no bigger than a luxury bathtub.

The second spring, though, proved a lot more productive. This one included a small cave that appeared to house the source of the crystal-clear water. It butted up against the side of a barren, rocky mountainside with another cave up top. I quickly climbed it and surveyed the area before climbing back down and fishing.

This spring was probably awesome at some point, but with people swimming (questionable given its smell and small size) and taking out the most valuable exotics, it had been overrun by stunted, inbred Pearlscale Cichlids and mollies. I could've caught 100 or more of the cichlids, and in the gin-clear water, it was easy to see that cichlids and mollies dominated the fish assemblage. I worked hard for the mollies, catching four Shortfin Molly but seeing a handful of Mexican and Sailfin Molly mixed in.

It took more effort than I thought, but I finally got the Mexican Molly I was after. Huh. I'm probably not the first Vegas visitor to utter those words, am I?

Species #391 — Mexican Molly (*Poecilia sphenops*).

The Mexican Molly, also called the Common Molly, is differentiated by the yellow-orange bands on its caudal (tail) and sometimes dorsal fins. The males, in particular, are especially beautiful little fish. I saw just one or two Sailfin Mollies but failed to gain their attention, so I circled the pond several times, looking for the other species I knew had been recorded in that spring in the recent past.

Though I caught two Oscars I could see hiding up against the bank, the Green Swordtail, *Xiphophorus hellerii*, Red Zebra Cichlid, *Maylandia estherae*, and other exotics once present were nowhere to be seen. This was feeling remarkably similar to Blue Lake, and I just knew someone would show up in a week and catch something I hadn't that would pop up on my Insta feed shortly thereafter, but I still had to admit defeat. I left the spring pool and fished the outflow until it became too narrow and overgrown to wet a line in. I caught more mollies and a lot more Pearlscale Cichlids, each one looking more ragged and deformed than the last.

Indian Springs

The third and final spring I'd mapped out was in a town called Indian Springs. Green Swordtail and Southern Platy, *Xiphophorus maculatus* had been recorded there by USGS surveys, and I was optimistic I could catch one or both of them.

I probably could have if, after driving 45 minutes out of my way, I hadn't learned the spring was surrounded on all sides by fenced private residences. Normally, I would've knocked on a door and asked permission to walk in and fish, but the high fences didn't exactly resemble a white picket fence with a sidewalk and mailbox. I circled the compound three times, probably looking like a criminal scouting the place, but I was unable to find a single door to knock on that wasn't blocked by a high fence, and I wasn't about to climb a fence into someone's backyard.

This is part of the gamble of fishing, and given I was in Vegas, it made sense that the House (or in this case, houses) had won out.

Las Vegas

I'd never been to Vegas before, and I really had no desire to visit. For a guy who doesn't drink, smoke, or sleep around, Vegas doesn't have a lot of appeal. I've bought my share of lottery tickets throughout the years and twice I spent an hour or two in other casinos while traveling to say I'd done it, but when the time came, I decided not to go to the Vegas Strip. It was Saturday night, and I knew it would be a shitshow, so I never set foot in a casino or made it to the Strip. That didn't keep me from gambling, though.

No, I never played roulette, blackjack, or sat in front of a slot machine, but I did eat at a place that sold "sushi burritos," so I can definitely say I gambled in Vegas. Unlike with Indian Springs, I won that bet. The sushi burrito was uniquely tasty, and it satiated me all the way to my final stop for the night: Barstow, California.

Hell on Earth

If you've never been to Barstow, California, let me save you a trip and just encourage you to visit North Korea instead. Or maybe go back in time and visit a war-torn Kosovo, any part of Europe during the Dark Ages, or perhaps a nicely appointed Soviet gulag.

Barstow is where all the worst elements from Southern California and Las Vegas converge.

As America's fifth-most dangerous city and the most dangerous city in California, Barstow has 1.5 violent crimes per 100 residents every year and boasts a veritable smorgasbord of other felonies and misdemeanors.

Of course, I had absolutely no idea that was the case when I stopped at Walmart that evening to stock up on bait and food for the last leg of my journey. I'm sure there are parts of Barstow that are only sort of terrible, but the Barstow Walmart is the single worst place I've ever been.

Walmart became my friend on this trip because every few days I'd stop in and buy ice, bait (worms and/or shrimp), fruit (to keep scurvy away), vegetables, and whatever other random product I needed to keep my trip moving forward. I hate to disparage Walmart after it was such an essential part of my trip, but this Walmart? It was something else. I would later learn that the Barstow Walmart is where they hold auditions for Hell, but given my experience there, I shouldn't have been surprised.

For starters, parking took forever because of the three — yes three — marked cars with their lights on slowing traffic in and out of the parking lot. I could see one of them had an officer clearly arresting someone but didn't get close enough to the other two to understand their respective presences.

My first few attempts to find spaces were thwarted by broken glass, and when I did finally park, I immediately stepped out of the car onto something soft and squishy. I lifted my flip-flop to see a used condom. Gagging, I made sure to lock the door before walking inside. A man on foot exchanged a paper bag for a wad of cash with a man in a brown Astro van. Then the van sped off. Trying not to make eye contact, I hastened my pace to the safety of the store.

Inside wasn't much better. The entryway to the store was littered with cigarette butts courtesy of the pasty dude in sweatpants and a graphic tee bearing a pentagram drawn in blood who stood out front with glassy eyes and an "I'd kill you for $6 and change" expression that sent a shiver down my spine.

I made my way up and down the aisles, picking up what I needed, and saw the most unwashed and scary collection of humanity assembled since the last Insane Clown Posse concert. I saw horrors I can't even describe in that store. When I finally checked out, I could feel a contact high coming on.

Cautiously, I walked to the opposite end of the store — in full view of the cameras and artificial lighting — before going through the exit. In addition to the employee scanning receipts at the exit, there was also a security guard who was staring daggers at the people all around me. I shuddered.

When the automatic doors closed behind me, I walked quickly to my car, fired up the engine and got out of there as fast as I could.

Had I known what this place was like, I never would've booked a cheap motel here, but we all make mistakes. As I settled into a room where the best feature was the faint cigarette smell, I just hoped this wouldn't be my last mistake. I deadbolted the door, used the chain, and slid the furniture up against the door. Dead serious.

I've never done that before or since, but I did it that night.

I also carried most of my fishing gear into my room (something I hadn't done at all on my trip) and covered everything I had to leave in the car with the dingy towels (complete with cigarette burns) that I borrowed from the motel bathroom for the evening. My car was dirty and didn't look like it had anything of value from the outside, and I hoped that was enough.

Miraculously, I made it through the night, and so did the windows of my car, but I learned one thing: Barstow is a place you should never go. It's like the Farm Team for Hell, where they send people when the prisons are too crowded, or where people who can't afford to fly to Amsterdam go to try all of the hard drugs.

Never, ever go there.

Chapter 48
Bad Decisions

July 28, 2019

Day 44
Origin: Barstow, California
Destination: Alamo, California

"There is no ceiling on stupidity, but you can never separate a man from his dream."
Joe Mauck || American Teacher
2019 Oregon ACTE Conference

I made it almost the entire summer without getting poison oak, poison ivy, or poison sumac, but with three days left in my trip, that streak ended. I got poison oak on my legs, my feet, and my hands when I brushed up against a plant. Because, of course. I realized my mistake, lost my balance, and slowly began sliding down the steep canyon wall grabbing the only plant I could see to stop myself from certain death and/or dismemberment.

You're probably wondering how I got there, so let me backup.

Everyone has those hurdles in their life that they struggle to get over, those simple tasks or problems and/or goals that don't seem so hard but take on an existential difficulty as the time it takes to complete them steadily mounts.

For me, catching Western suckers was, well *is*, one such hurdle.

Growing up, I lived in a state with more than a dozen sucker species, but I was in my mid-20s before I ever caught one. On numerous occasions I'd fished waters that *allegedly* contained suckers but failed to hook into one. Granted, I'd caught three sucker species in Oregon by the start of 2019, including the Klamath Largescale Sucker, *Catostomus snyderi* that earned me my first world record, but that was it. One fish.

On different occasions, I'd struck out for suckers across my home state of Oregon, as well as California, Nevada, Utah, New Mexico, Arizona, and Texas. In fact, apart from a few species of redhorse (all caught east of the Mississippi), a lone Smallmouth Buffalo, and a pair of Largescale Suckers, *Catostomus macrocheilus* I finally caught in Portland a few months before this big trip, any time I spent chasing these fish, I was the only sucker you'd encounter. Yet for some strange reason, I was convinced I could catch a Sacramento Sucker, *Catostomus occidentalis* — one of the most widespread and least imperiled sucker species in the West — by fishing the Kern River Canyon in Southern California.

This river is most popular with trout anglers who chase the Kern River Rainbow, a subspecies of Rainbow Trout found only here and in the river's tributaries, as well as anglers who fish the deeper holes and impoundments for invasive catfish and bass. Nobody fishes it for suckers. Except this sucker. (Points thumbs at self).

Getting there was a trek. Not only did I have to leave civilization and travel through a town so small and quaint that it still had the old-timey gas pumps that used spinning numbers reminiscent of a slot machine, but I had to detour on slow-moving two-lane highways for more than a hundred miles behind tractors, horse trailers, and more trucks with boats in-tow than you'd expect in the middle of the desert.

Eventually, I made it to the campsite I'd been tipped off about (thanks, Chris Moore) and parked. I grabbed a few rods and began walking down to the river. Sadly, the steep stone walls worn smooth by centuries of rain and windblown sand made for tough walking, and I was restricted to the trail.

The first "hole" that might have held a sucker was populated with half a dozen swimmers, so finding a place to cast was difficult. Eventually, I got my line in the water, but all I managed to catch were Smallmouth Bass. When another group showed up and jumped into the water, I opted to take the canyon trail further away from the ruckus.

At a particularly steep point, the smooth rock on the downhill side of the trail cut away from the path, while the uphill side was hedged by a tree trunk. Growing in the gap between was a single poison oak plant that I was careful to slowly step over. I made my way down the trail to see if I could fish in another hole, only to be disappointed by the insane bouldering I'd have to do to get down there.

Walking on, I finally saw a place I could climb down, but rather than starting my descent then and there, I decided to walk further down the trail, not realizing there was more poison oak in the path. I brushed up against it, and lost my balance after flinching at my error, my flip-flops failing to maintain purchase with the slick rock, and I smashed one rod against the rock as I righted myself, falling to a knee but no further.

By the grace of God, the rod didn't break, but I'd used my free hand to grab the only thing I could find: another poison oak plant growing in the solitary patch of dirt on the rock wall. I hadn't touched the leaves, but I knew that didn't matter. I sprinted back to the car, tucked away my gear, and grabbed a little bar of motel soap. Immediately, I cut back to the swimming hole and began furiously scrubbing my hands, legs, and feet, first with soap, then with mud. I rubbed my rough, weathered skin nearly raw — a feat given how thick the calluses were after a month and a half of fishing all day, every day, barefoot or in flip-flops under the summer sun. I was satisfied I'd done all I could do and hoped I wouldn't be itching all over in a few days.

After walking back up to the car, I put the soap away, loaded up my gear once again and walked back down to the hole I'd nearly fallen into, rod in my teeth to account for the steep slope with two free hands. I set up there and quickly got a bite. To my dismay, it wasn't a sucker; it was a catfish. I landed several White Catfish and a Channel Cat before thinking I should call it. There was still time to chase the storied Kern River Rainbow. Though it wasn't a separate species, I do love native Rainbows, and it was one subspecies I hadn't caught.

Then, my rod bounced again. I was at once thrilled and shocked to see the golden flanks of a sucker come to my net. It was an elusive Western sucker! I couldn't believe it. I'd actually targeted a sucker and caught one on my first attempt!

Species #392 — Sacramento Sucker (*Catostomus occidentalis*).

I knew it was a longshot, but I'd done it, and though I'd like to call it a happy accident (well, *occident*, given its Latin name), I think my sucker-chasing skills finally developed to the point where I could catch them on purpose. At least, that's what I told myself as a sweat-soaked Luke climbed the canyon wall shirtless that hot July day.

I wish the story ended there, on that happy note, but it doesn't.

While walking back to the car, someone was on the trail coming the opposite direction. That someone was an attractive woman in a Lara Croft-esque hiking outfit that looked great on her, and as I smiled, said "How's it going?" and moved off to the side of the trail, I failed to realize I was standing in a plant. I also failed to realize there were several other people, including a dude that she appeared to be with, walking in a tight line behind her.

She smiled back and continued on, as I nodded to the others, trying to hide my disappointment.

Then I looked down.

"Ahh (eff word)!"

"Come on!"

"You've got to be kidding me."

One long, exasperated sigh and a few hundred yards of sprinting later, I was back at my car, again trading fishing gear for soap. This time, it had only brushed up against my lower legs, but once again, I scrubbed alternately with soap and sandy mud until I was satisfied I'd removed all of the harmful urushiol oil.

I hopped behind the wheel with a mix of emotions, and I drove back to the main road traversing the canyon, California State Route 178.

After 10 miles, traffic began slowing until it came to a complete stop. Given this was the only artery that flows through the entire canyon, I figured it was just piled up due to traffic. As more and more cars ahead of me began to turn around and drive back the other way, I quickly learned it was piled up because of "a three-car pileup," "a mudslide," "a major washout," and "a fallen tree."

Obviously, I didn't know what to believe, save for the fact they all seemed to agree upon: everyone says it will be hours.

I was then faced with a decision: take another route or wait. I decided to stop and fish for trout for an hour and see if the traffic cleared.

First of all, it didn't.

Second, I didn't catch any trout — just Sacramento Pikeminnow, *Ptychocheilus grandis*. Almost an hour had passed, and there was no sign of progress, so I decided to turn around and take another route.

Had the road not been closed, I would've been able to make it to Kettleman City (just under 100 miles away) in about an hour and a half. Instead, my roundabout detour took me back to Lake Isabella, across the winding (mostly 35- or 45-miles-per-hour State Route 155) some 150 miles to Kettleman City.

It took longer than three hours, which meant I had to cut out my final stop on my drive north to the San Francisco Bay. I'd hoped to meet up with Facebook friend Phil Farrell for some massive

Sacramento Pikeminnow, but didn't have time now, so I pressed on to the Bay Area, where I was staying with my friends Steve Wozniak and Marta Bulaich. I called and told them I'd be later than expected and then drove another four hours in heavy traffic to their home in Alamo.

My only stop came at a roadside culvert when I needed to stretch my legs where I climbed down and caught and released a Coastal Roach, a close relative of the Northern Roach I'd caught to start my trip.

Species #393 — Coastal Roach (*Hesperoleucus venustus*).

After I stretched, the road stretched out in front of me, and I drove the rest of the way to Alamo.

I vented my frustrations of the day to Steve and Marta, but the frustrations melted away as we caught up and planned for the next day's fishing. I realized the tacos represented the first home-cooked meal I'd eaten since I'd stayed with Marcus and his family almost two weeks before. I ravenously scarfed down several plates of food before we wound down for the evening, and I showered, hoping to rinse off any residual urushiol oil from my skin.

Chapter 49
The Elephant in the Room

July 29, 2019

Day 45
Origin: Alamo, California
Destination: Tiburon, California

"Inconveniently, books are all the pages in them,
not just the ones you choose to read."
Don Paterson || Scottish Poet || From *The Book of Shadows*

    Marta went to work, but Steve had taken a day off to fish with me. Steve decided pier fishing would be our best bet, and being his understudy in the eternal #SpeciesQuest, I deferred to his judgment.
    Rather than just grabbing any old red worms or nightcrawlers and some shrimp as I almost always do when fishing the salt, Steve wanted to get pile worms. Now, I'd used artificial sandworms before, and they look remarkably similar, but I'd never even seen live pile worms. How on earth we could get them was beyond me, but Steve had a guy for that.
    From a lifetime of fishing all over the world, Steve has a guy for pretty much everything. I've used his guys (and gals) myself for everything from tracking down imported Japanese fishing tackle to chasing Bluefin Tuna, *Thunnus thynnus,* in Croatia. Add finding niche baits in the San Francisco Bay to that list.

To earn his place at the top of the Lifelist Fishing leaderboard with well over 2,000 species at the time I wrote this (eclipsing second place by more than 500 species), Steve had to be a competitor. He was the first person to hit 1,000 species of fish, the first to 2,000 and will be potentially the only to ever hit 2,500 or 3,000 if he can kick his Red Bull habit and live to 80 or 90.

For someone who effectively wrote the book (well, the blog) on an entire subset of fishing, he's remarkably down to earth. He's just as likely to fish with someone yet to hit 100 species as he is with someone over 1,000. After all, when I first emailed him back in 2016 to ask questions about submitting my first world record, he replied to my email. Not many big names in the fishing world would do that. From there, it grew into a friendship and mentorship that helped me rapidly climb from just 80 species when I first reached out to him in late 2016 to almost 400 when we fished together less than three years later during this, the final leg of my epic road trip.

Steve is one of those people who sort of casually drops knowledge at intervals. Some of the revelations are dynamic and earth-shattering, and he constantly proves why he's a person you should know.

Even still, I'd argue his sense of humor is his greatest strength. After all, without the subtle witticisms on Steve's own fishing blog, 1000fish.wordpress.com, I might never have begun my very own #SpeciesQuest in earnest.

Needless to say, I owe a lot to Steve.

So after years of reading his blog posts about fishing the piers in his area, I was stoked to learn I'd get a chance to fish those same piers with him. There were at least half a dozen very viable species I could catch, and I chomped at the bit as we detoured to get bait. Once we did, it was game on.

Well, it would have been had Steve not seen a Burger King. The man is an incredible angler with a lot of talents. Did you know he plays ice hockey without a face mask? When Marta isn't looking, he's just as reckless with his food choices.

I'm of the mind that you only eat fast food if you have to, and even then, I'll usually just skip a meal before eating fast food. Steve uses fishing as his chance to get away with eating fast food, much to Marta's (and probably his doctor's) dismay.

So there we were at Burger King. I hadn't eaten at Burger King in years. Five? Seven? Ten years? Certainly not since my undergrad days in 2013.

I almost never eat fast food, and when I do, I tend to only eat at a handful of fast food restaurants. This list is short and typically includes Chik-Fil-A and just a handful of others like Panda Express because nobody cooks pandas quite like they do. I'm kidding, people. Everyone knows that panda tastes better raw.

I sort of argued against fast food with Steve, but the man was letting me stay with him and taking me fishing, so I figured the least I could do was join him for this passive suicide attempt at — gags — Burger King.

We didn't die on the spot, and since Steve paid, I only felt slightly guilty for eating there. Sated and experiencing the meat sweats, we moved on to fishing, and I just hoped Burger King wouldn't decide to expand its kingdom beyond the walls of my stomach.

Elephant Rock

Steve has held records for several surfperch and seaperch species throughout the years because these are the primary winter targets near his house. Several of these records have come from Elephant Rock Pier in Tiburon. The pier itself is tiny by the standards of most piers. It has room for maybe six or seven anglers if they stand shoulder-to-shoulder, and in a post-COVID-19 world, that seems unrealistic. The fishing platform extends out maybe 25 feet or so over the water, and a giant rock the seagulls use for target practice juts up from the middle of the platform and apparently looked like an elephant once.

I was optimistic, even though the seas were rough, and the wind was high. Really high, actually. For the first time all summer, I had to don a sweatshirt. I threw some pile worm chunks on the three hooks of my truncated sabiki, careful not to get pinched by the nightmarish little monsters.

My hooks were stripped clean half a dozen times with nothing to show for it, until I remembered that you often have to set the hook on the slightest bite with a perch. That was the ticket, and I pulled up my first fish of the day, a Black Surfperch.

Species #394 — Black Surfperch (*Embiotoca jacksoni*).

The name "Black" is sort of a misnomer because while the fish was dark, it had varied levels of darkness across its thick body that shone green and purple and blue and red in the sunlight. It was a remarkably beautiful fish, and I snapped several pictures before jettisoning it off the pier and back to nature. Steve and I caught a few more Black Surfperch before anything else exciting happened.

The next fish to show up was a Dwarf Surfperch, a striking little fish with a white gold base color mottled by irregular coppery patches and both yellow and black striations elsewhere on its little body.

Species #395 — Dwarf Surfperch (*Micrometrus minimus*).

I'd tried for this fish in Southern California but struck out faster than I typically did with the women down there, so I was especially pleased to catch it. Given the small mouths and generally frustrating bait-stealing antics of every surfperch species, the dwarf version proved to be especially infuriating, and I'm blindly accusing these little guys of stealing my pile worms time and again that day until I finally hooked up once more.

This fish was clearly different, and I thought it was a blenny or sculpin when it broke the surface tension with its flopping body, but Steve quickly pointed out that it was a kelpfish. He gave me some pointers on this famously difficult-to-identify fish which I later confirmed with several, more formal sources. It was a Striped Kelpfish, a species famous for hiding in thick vegetation where the sun doesn't shine.

Species #396 — Striped Kelpfish (*Gibbonsia metzi*).

On several occasions, I'd seen these uniquely beautiful fish lurking in thick vegetation in the tidepools of Southern California, but I'd never been able to entice a strike at night — despite my best efforts.

Steve and I exchanged stories about life and just enjoyed the breezy day on the water while he told me what else I might expect to catch. Though I was hoping for a White Surfperch, *Phanerodon furcatus* or Barred Surfperch, *Amphistichus argenteus*, a Black and Yellow Rockfish, *Sebastes chrysomelas*, or a handful of other species, we came to the subject of Jacksmelt, *Atherinopsis californiensis*, and Topsmelt, *Atherinops affinis*.

"Those are here. Just take the weight off your sabiki and drift it," Steve said.

I tried it, but naturally, that's when the wind picked up even more. I gave this method about half an hour before returning to bottom fishing. It was fate because I caught not one but two fairly rare species in the span of about half an hour that neither of us even considered as viable possibilities: Bonehead Sculpin and Bluebanded Ronquil (the former is also called Bonyhead Sculpin; the latter is also called Stripedfin Ronquil).

Species #397 — Bonehead Sculpin (*Artedius notospilotus*).
Species #398 — Bluebanded Ronquil (*Rathbunella hypoplecta*).

Both of these species are so uncommon that Steve couldn't recall seeing a large Bonehead Sculpin (sadly not quite a pound to qualify for a world record) caught and could count just a handful of ronquils caught in the Bay. He'd caught both species, of course, but I was certainly somewhat lucky to get both in a single day.

The wind worsened as the day wore on, and we caught sporadic surfperch and kelpfish but failed to find anything new. With traffic, we weren't in a rush to get home, but neither were we desperate to stay there and have our gear pushed into the rocks every few minutes by the now roiling surf, so we decided to call it a day.

I was quite happy with five species, particularly the last two. At the time, I hadn't finished identifying all of my fishes from the trip, so I then thought I was sitting at around 395 species. In reality, I didn't correctly identify several more species from the trip until after writing this book, but even if I hit 400, it was still a far cry from Steve's staggering tally of more than 2000 (then 1800 or so), but I felt like I'd spent the day with a giant.

Chapter 50
The Last Day

July 30, 2019

Day 46
Origin: Alamo, California
Destination: Klamath Falls, Oregon

"Why do all good things come to an end?"
Nelly Furtado || Canadian Musician
From the Song "All Good Things"

This was it, the very last day of my trip.
I would've stayed in the Bay Area a few more days, but I got roped into a last-minute education meeting I was supposed to attend for my day job. I desperately wanted to keep fishing, and I begrudged the fact, but I had to be back in a few days for Drill anyhow, and I'd already been gone for 46 days. How many people get to drop work and responsibility and fish for 46 straight (well, 43-of-46) days? I counted my blessings.
I awoke early, thanked Steve and Marta and promised to keep Steve posted. He'd given me a couple spots, and I opted to fish two of them: Suisun Marsh and the Russian River. I was after any of almost 10 species I didn't have in the Suisun Marsh and just one in the Russian River, a small Leucicid called a Hitch, *Lavinia exilicauda*.
After a quick breakfast in the Bay Area that wasn't Burger King, I drove north to Suisun City. The Suisun Marsh is a unique place. The water is brackish enough to allow dozens of saltwater species to call it home but fresh enough to allow native and invasive freshwater

species alike to flourish. According to the USGS data, Fishbrain catch reports and Steve's personal experience, at least 20 species could be found there at various times of the year, including:

American Shad, *Alosa sapidissima*
Bigscale Logperch, *Percina macrolepida*
Bluegill, *Lepomis macrochirus*
Chameleon Goby, *Tridentiger trigonocephalus*
Channel Catfish, *Ictalurus punctatus*
Jacksmelt, *Atherinopsis californiensis*
Largemouth Bass, *Micropterus salmoides*
Leopard Shark, *Triakis semifasciata*
Longjaw Mudsucker, *Gillichthys mirabilis*
Prickly Sculpin, *Cottus asper*
Rainbow Trout/Steelhead, *Oncorhynchus mykiss*
Sacramento Pikeminnow, *Ptychocheilus grandis*
Shimofuri Goby, *Tridentiger bifasciatus*
Shokihaze Goby, *Tridentiger barbatus*
Splittail, *Pogonichthys macrolepidotus*
Starry Flounder, *Platichthys stellatus*
Striped Bass, *Morone saxatilis*
Topsmelt, *Atherinops affinis*
Tule Perch, *Hysterocarpus traskii*
White Sturgeon, *Acipenser transmontanus*
Yellowfin Goby, *Acanthogobius flavimanus*

Crazy, right? Talk about diversity. Even though nearly half of those species are invasive or at least naturalized non-natives, there were still a lot of native species to account for, chief among them were the Tule Perch and Splittail. I wanted to catch a Tule Perch so desperately that I was willing to fish there all day if it came to that. Steve assured me it wouldn't come to that.

I paid the $5 for parking and set out one rod while I prepared another. It took about 20 minutes, but I finally got a bite. The first species was the one I most expected to catch: the Yellowfin Goby.

Species #399 — Yellowfin Goby (*Acanthogobius flavimanus*).

As I waited on the dock, I noticed two teenage girls emerge from the water nearby. They'd been swimming in it.
Wait. Really?!
I'd fished nastier water but not many times, and I'd never swim *there*. They sat on the dock across from me, giggling and kicking their feet in the water. When a police officer arrived and got out of his car, I was afraid I was about to be kicked out. To my surprise, he approached the girls and told them they needed to leave.

"I've told you two you can't swim here several times before. The water isn't safe [it wasn't], and there are boats everywhere [I didn't see a boat all day, but sure]. Do I need to call your parents?"

Begrudgingly, with a pair of eye rolls, the girls left. The cop nodded to me and drove away. I took that as my cue to move somewhere else because I clearly wasn't catching anything else in the featureless silt- and mud-covered flat. I moved to a rocky shoreline nearby and snagged one of the hooks into my leg not for the first time this trip. As I struggled to free the hook with some pliers, a couple of the hooks fell into the water right at my feet. When I got the hook out, I lifted the rod to cast and was surprised to find three gobies clinging to the small hooks.

One was a Yellowfin, but the other two were dark — almost black — with white striations across their faces and bodies. More uniquely, they had brightly edged fins, the dorsals edged with a vivid orange and the anal fins edged in bright yellow. These were Shimofuri Gobies, yet another invasive species released into the waters of California that had absolutely thrived in the region.

Species #400 —Shimofuri Goby (*Tridentiger bifasciatus*).

I'd fished less than two feet from where I was standing and caught fish. Not one to give up on a good thing, I dropped in again. I caught half a dozen more gobies before I got something else. First came the tiny silver fish I recognized as a juvenile American Shad. I'd caught juvenile shad in the Willamette River before fishing right up against the shore like this, but it was still unexpected.

Also unexpected? The Prickly Sculpins that came out of the woodwork, well rockwork, shortly thereafter. I tried using a slightly larger rig for Splittail and Tule Perch, but again, no dice. Just as I prepared to call it and drive several hours out of my way to the Russian River, I caught a tiny Tule Perch, also in the rocks at my feet. It was about four inches long, but a fish is a fish.

Species #401 —Tule Perch (*Hysterocarpus traskii*).

If I'd known the Tule Perch would be my last new species of the trip — Lifer No. 147 since I left home in June — I probably would've set up my self-timer and taken a picture of me holding it for posterity, but my blind optimism was firing on all cylinders, and I didn't even consider that possibility. I hammered the gobies for another 30 minutes, finishing with just shy of 20 of them before realizing I probably wasn't going to catch anything else unless I spent the whole day there. I debated it, but decided I'd rather fish one more spot before making my way back home, so I hopped into my car and headed to my final destination: the Russian River.

Hitch

Narrow, winding roads made the drive feel longer than it was, but compared to my ordeal in the Kern River Canyon a few days prior, it was a cakewalk.

I arrived at the river to find a busy, pea gravel shoreline awash with sunbathers and swimmers aplenty but not one other angler. The fishing was slow, and apart from a pair of Sacramento Pikeminnows that kept the skunk off, I had nothing to show for my hours-long detour.

I tried fishing under a float, with bottom rigs, with micro gear, and even with tiny jigs, but those Hitch were nowhere to be seen. Eventually, I had to accept that it was time to leave, and with five or six hours of driving ahead of me, I looked at the river with a morose sense of appreciation. It was strange, I know, but I felt like that final moment in the California sun marked the death of a part of me, the last line in one of the best chapters of my life.

As awesome as it would've been to be able to say I finished my trip with one more fish, my final target, and went out on top, that's not fishing. That's not reality.

I'd caught literally thousands of fishes in six weeks, representing more than 200 species. As far as I know, nobody had ever caught that many species in such a short window entirely within the United States. If you have, you're just as crazy as I am, and we need to be friends. Hit me up.

That's my claim to fame, my chance at years' worth of bragging rights in very, very specific circles. So I couldn't justifiably complain because as I drove back and reflected on my journey, my adventure (note the correct use of the word "adventure" by a Millennial for a change), I realized how relatively smooth the trip had been.

I hadn't been murdered by a Couchsurfing host.

I hadn't had major car trouble.

I hadn't been seriously injured.

I hadn't gotten arrested, involved in any fights, shot for trespassing or just being in the wrong place at the wrong time, or even been victimized by Florida Man.

Sure, I'd been scraped, cut, and bruised.

I had been eaten alive by ants and mosquitos, and the spider bite I'd gotten on the top of my foot while traipsing through the wilds of Missouri a week or so prior would take weeks to heal fully, but I'd accomplished an incredible feat (haha feet) with relatively few problems along the way.

That's why, when I struck out trying for my final target, the Hitch. I was okay with that. Most anglers in my shoes would've been glad to accomplish all I had accomplished without a Hitch.

Of the 122 spots I fished on my trip, I caught at least one fish at 115 of them. That means at just seven venues, I was skunked. Four of the seven were either blown out or dried up, while two just didn't produce fish, despite looking like they should have, and one was entirely private and fenced off with no access to speak of. I just happened to strike out at the end of my trip.

I headed home.

Months before, I might have been downtrodden by the last-minute failure, but I'd grown and changed during my time on the road, and I wasn't saddened by the less-than-stellar finish; I was just sad my trip had come to an end.

My house was still rented out for a few more days, so I greeted my parents that night with a hug before retreating to the bath. My body ached after more than a month on the road, and I could think of nothing I wanted, needed, more than a nice hot bath pushed to the limit of solubility with bath salts.

That's exactly how I ended my trip, soaking there as all manner of emotions washed over me.

PART 4
THE RETURN

Chapter 51
Coping

August 2019

"Perhaps happiness is to be found in the journey uphill and not in the fleeting sense of satisfaction awaiting at the next peak. Much of happiness is hope, no matter how deep the underworld in which that hope was conceived."
Jordan B. Peterson || Canadian Author
From *12 Rules for Life: An Antidote to Chaos*

The reality of being home was hard for me to swallow. The morning after I woke up from my trip, I was as depressed as I'd been in a long, long time. Perhaps having accomplished so much and knowing it was the end was enough. Perhaps I'd just become accustomed to constant stimulation, sunlight, variety, and the chance to fish every waking moment of my existence. Or perhaps I got a bigger taste of the wider world than ever before and appreciated the self-reliance and independence I'd had the luxury of riding for weeks on end.

I honestly don't know if it was a single thing, but everything coalesced and cascaded me down to a dark place, where I lived for several days.

Interspersed in my wallowing and depression were flickers of productivity in which I began to tally up the results of my trip, quantify and qualify my experiences, and flesh out the book I intended to write — this book — as I coped with my new/old reality.

There was cleaning that needed to be done. Laundry was piled high. A stack of bills and freelancing checks screamed for my attention; I'll let you guess which ones I attended to first.

Everything was just so distastefully ... normal.

Fortunately, I'd scheduled my annual teaching conference for about 10 days after my return, which would take place in Asheville, North Carolina, so I had something else to look forward to.

The days dragged on but sped up as I approached my departure date. I spent some time working on base, finished up my Drill, then drove over to Medford (the nearest town with an airport offering commercial service), and I spent my evening catching up with my Aunt Mary and Uncle Sam, who lived near MFR and offered to let me stay with them whenever I had a flight out. They often open their home to me when I travel. This saves me a lot of time and hassle, for which I am eternally grateful.

The trip to North Carolina was incredible. The conference itself, Lilly-Asheville, was very worthwhile, and I was even able to meet and fish with Tim Aldridge of NANFA fame.

This final trip lasted about a week, and it helped wean me off of a "fish every day, all day in some incredible new place mindset" to which I'd become accustomed. Alcoholics have to be tapered off alcohol to avoid going into systemic shock, and this trip sort of did that for me. It forced me to wait a week between coming home from my road trip and flying out for this one. It muffled that hunger in me to go out and fish all day, as I sat through three days' worth of conference sessions, released to fish only in the evenings.

North Carolina helped me readjust to normalcy, and though it was a struggle, I was able to temper the aching loss of life on the road with one final taste of the unknown.

I'll address it in more detail in another book, *Fishing for Happiness*, which focuses on a period much longer than the six glorious weeks hogging the spotlight herein.

Though *Fishing for Happiness* spans years, the chapters on that North Carolina trip include the intrigue of fishing in two states, catching more than 20 new species, getting a concussion by walking into a doorframe, being marooned with Tim during a raging storm, and even real romance (yes, with a real woman).

Apart from easing into normal life once again, I had another big move in August. Remember Dan Knorr, the guy I spoke with on the last day of ICAST? Well, after some follow-up, he signed me as the first Pro Staffer for Reef Safe Sun (now Tropical Seas, Inc.), a family of environmentally-friendly sunscreens and skincare products that (unlike most sunscreens out there) are safe for the environment and clinically proven to not harm sea life. In addition to doing my part for the environment and gaining access to free sunscreen, shampoo, and skincare products, I get a joke out of it: How White am I? So White that I'm sponsored by sunscreen.

Chapter 52
The Bitter(sweet) End

September 2019 - April 2020

"Kids, sometimes you realize the journey you've been taking has reached its final stop. So the question becomes:
'Where do you go next?'"
Narrator || From *How I Met Your Mother*

A lot happened after my trip. Really too much to try and share in the chronological, episodic style I maintained throughout this book. What I can tell you is that this trip was certainly the highlight of my year — arguably the highlight of my life up to that point.

Okay, definitely the highlight of my life.

Throughout the summer, I drove 13,668.8 miles, and that sounds as insane as it was, but it doesn't capture the fact that I drove 30,477 total miles in 2019. This book represented less than half of my experiences that year, and I think that the mileage of the trip, when viewed as a piece of the whole, helped me stop pining for the past and instead realize the value of each and every day.

This realization wasn't immediate. It didn't even happen overnight, and even though it was tough coming back to the real world after my trip, a part of me was able to accept it as the blessing and once-in-a-lifetime experience, the once-in-a-thousand-lifetimes experience it was.

I caught hundreds of fish, drank in the beauty of thousands of miles, gained the material for this book and came back a changed man. I wasn't fixed, per se, but I was pointed toward contentment, and after getting to taste so much of what the world had to offer, living in the same town I'd spent my entire life wasn't quite so bitter. The world left a sweet taste that overpowered a lot of the bitterness but didn't necessarily eradicate it. Life is bittersweet, after all.

Others have had incredible road trips, but the marriage of advancing a dream career, spending time with family, fishing, and experiencing so much travel over such a long time is pretty unique. Unique enough that I wrote a book about it, and you sacrificed hours to read it. It was worth it to me. I hope you feel the same.

Sure, the North Carolina conference helped me ease into a more realistic schedule and understand that fishing all day, every day probably isn't realistic or sustainable in most contexts, but it couldn't pull away my wanderlust, the desire pulling at the edge of my consciousness that makes me want to repeat the experience — not in the same way with the same venues — but with the same untamed spirit and freedom and that feeling of truly living the life I'd never even dreamed of before it caught me Ovgard.

AFTERWORD

I finished the last chapter in May of 2020. The nation and the world were gripped by COVID-19. In just a few weeks' time, thousands had died, and the economy was in shambles. Thankfully, I'd lost no loved ones, but I had lost almost half of my income.

Schools in Oregon were shut down through the rest of the school year. I still got paid my base salary but lost a lot of additional pay, and I no longer got to teach. Not really, at least, since everything was online. I've always enjoyed my job and liked teaching, but I never considered education my passion like I did fishing and writing. Nonetheless, I missed teaching. As Ted Mosby said in *How I Met Your Mother*: "All that stupid crap they tell you about how fulfilling teaching is? It's all true." It was hard not being around my students. I also missed the interactions with my work friends, which, at the time, amounted to virtually all of my social interaction with adults.

Being stuck at home had an upside, though. I had time to work on this book I'd been unable to finish. I was able to complete all kinds of home improvements. Unfortunately, all of my other income streams began to dry up. I lost two months' worth of Airbnb bookings, and if the company hadn't changed its cancellation policy in light of the pandemic to punish the hosts that pay its stockholders, perhaps the loss would've been less painful. Alas, they didn't.

My military obligations were canceled for two months, and though I put my name on the voluntary deployment list to help face the crisis, my name wasn't called until the fall of 2021, when I spent more than six months serving in hospitals around the state of Oregon.

More than half of the newspapers that paid me for my column every week were forced to downsize, cutting full-time staff members, entire pages, and freelancers such as myself. I lost newspapers across three states at this time. This caused me to launch a Patreon to replace my writing income, which helped recapture a very small fraction of what I'd lost.

If you've enjoyed reading this book and found my writing style bearable, check out www.patreon.com/CaughtOvgard and become a Patron for as little as $1 per month to start reading the hundreds of columns I've posted there over the years. Patreon has an app, so you can even read from your phone if you're not one to read on a computer screen. Patreon is basically crowdsourcing for writers and other creatives, and it's a cool concept. End shameless self-promotion.

That major shakeup in my life happened in a span of two weeks.

Suddenly, I was making about half of my normal income, but I went from about 50-55 hours per week of work obligations down to maybe 5. The time gain was incredible, but now I didn't earn enough to use it. As I learned to live more frugally, the trade-off seemed to have an upside: freedom to travel very inexpensively. That is, until the Department of Defense instituted a Stop Movement Order to all military personnel, which not only put my 2020 trip in jeopardy, but also meant I wasn't allowed to leave town for months during the height of COVID-19 — even though I was penned at home with work put on hold.

I wasn't able to take advantage of those $79 round-trip fares to Miami that some of my friends, pulled from the classroom and living on savings, were able to pull. I knew there was risk and uncertainty, but as a single man who lived alone and was relatively healthy, I figured it would've been worth the risk. Alas, I never got the chance to find out that spring.

With travel off the table, I was able to put the finishing touches on this book, which had been sitting about 90% complete for more than a month when COVID-19 ground the world to a halt.

Honestly, the timing couldn't have been better. March is still too frozen for the local fishing options, so I finished writing in March. By the time those April showers (locally, just as often April snowstorms) came around, I was able to start fishing my local waters almost every day.

Upon returning from my road trip and then my work trip to the Carolinas, I found myself able to chase trophy, pre-spawn trout for a month or two before winter hit. We get snow and ice, but most rivers close to protect spawning fishes and most lakes freeze but not thickly enough for ice fishing. So when I finished writing, I hit the water in April with an almost desperate sense of urgency.

With nothing else to do, I went trout fishing locally almost every day at the start of the Coronapocalypse, and the trout fishing was incredible. I caught more than 100 wild native rainbow trout over

20 inches that spring, but I couldn't chase new species, spend much time with friends or family, or get a break from my little corner of reality.

I know people had it a lot worse than I did, but it was still an adjustment. With the uncertainty, there was a time when I thought the trip covered in this book might have truly been the last big trip of my lifetime. It made me thank God for the opportunities I was given and remember them fondly as often as I could in those dark times.

As months passed and the disruptor that was COVID-19 began to become a new reality, I began to be happy — or at least content — with the boring and everyday once again. Dating, exercising, traveling, and species fishing were on hold long enough to make me return to them in earnest.

I spent a lot of time looking at old fishing videos and pictures, but when pictures didn't work, I could always open the pages of this book and relive it. The exchange rate is still 1,000 words per picture, right? Time will tell.

Time is such a powerful entity. Whether you're at the highest peak life has to offer or the lowest valley, it's imperative to appreciate the in-between. If I learned anything on my trip and in writing this book, it's that life is inherently precious. Time is the only resource we can never acquire more of, so use what you've been granted wisely.

Speculation is rarely productive in a crisis, but I want to be optimistic. I want to believe this crisis will end, and I will once again be able to find myself experiencing the new and unknown every day, thriving on the kindness of strangers, and *Fishing Across America*.

ACKNOWLEDGEMENTS

In August 2019, just a few days after I returned from a life-altering trip and just weeks before my 29th birthday, I began this book. Thirty was just around the corner, and like many people nearing the next age milestone, be it 30, 40, 50, 60, whatever, it caused me to take a long, hard look at my life and evaluate all of my decisions, all of my accomplishments (or lack thereof), and determine if I was on the right path.

That number ultimately meaningless to everyone but me — 30 — motivated me to do what I'd long wanted to do and what I'd tried and failed at several times: Write a book.

When I decided to write this book, I wasn't really sure how to start. Though I'd been writing professionally for almost seven years when these events found the page, my writing experience had been limited to newspapers and magazines and my blog (www.caughtovgard.com). I'd never published any one story longer than 2,500 words, so scaling up to a book was ambitious.

I sat in front of a blinking cursor for a few minutes before the story began to take shape in my mind. With shocking speed and clarity, the story flew from my fingers, gaining momentum and allowing me to write, to really share what I'd lived.

I gave myself six months at home to write, a self-imposed deadline I met by writing for an average of 30 minutes per day, in that narrow window of productivity before work, after work, and on any weekend I could will myself to give up fishing or travel or trying to find love. Some days, I wrote three or four hours per day, but generally, I ate the elephant in smaller bites.

Before I knew it, it was early February 2020, and I was done. Or so I thought. I'd written more than 170,000 words — more than 280 single-spaced 8 ½ x 11-inch manuscript pages — when I came to the horrible realization that the book was just far too long. I wasn't Tom Clancy. I had to split it up, or I'd be charged with assault upon handing it to my readers. But cutting it apart would be messy. This gory, inconvenient truth clawed at my mind for weeks before an acquaintance from my fishing circles, Matthew L. Miller, author of *Fishing Through the Apocalypse: An Angler's Adventures in the 21st Century*, gave me some advice. Matt was the only author of a fishing book I knew, and in the year that would follow, he went from acquaintance to friend.

In an email chain that gave me so much insight into the publishing process, Matt wrote this: "You may well have (two) fishing books pretty much done already. You can run the idea (of my absurdly long book) by the publisher, but they are going to tell you what they want. And they know the industry best, so do pay heed. And if they specify 80,000 words max ... don't send them a word more."

In an effort to get ahead of the publisher-directed surgery, I began to pare down my work. It's difficult to cut away at something you've spent so much time on. I'd read stories about this before, and I know writers and authors struggle when told their perfect vision is, in fact, less than perfect. But I accepted it, intellectually, even as it broke my heart and separated the massively unfocused book into this book, the story of an adventure, and another book about living with depression and using fishing to manage it.

With a book closer to 120,000 words, I figured I was ready to begin submitting to publishers.

In the end, it wasn't the length of my books that publishers took issue with but the book itself. If you ever want to sacrifice your self-worth on an altar of effort, try to find a publisher for a fishing book. I queried more than a dozen publishers, writing hundreds of pages for each query. I ended up writing nearly twice as much trying to sell my book as I wrote to create it in the first place. Most publishers just ignored my work. Only three even responded to say no and of those, only two responded to my emails asking what I could do better next time. Perhaps the most useful (and darkly hilarious) response was this: "Luke, you are a good writer. That's not in question. What I do question is whether we could sell a book about fishing written by someone who isn't already famous. The hard truth is that a fishing book just won't sell unless you're already a fishing celebrity."

That was hard to hear. If my prose was weak, my story incomplete, my jokes half-baked, I could fix all of those things by working harder, taking a class, getting a mentor, or something else that was tangible. But hearing "You're just not famous enough," is not a problem with a solution. At least, not really.

Not ready to give up just yet, I tried finding a literary agent. I found a comprehensive directory and began contacting every agent listed therein. Unsure of a better way, I went down the list alphabetically. By the time I hit the last names beginning with "H" in the directory, I'd prepared more than three dozen queries for agents — all of which were ignored or shot down.

At this point, it was winter of 2021 — nearly two years since I finished writing, and I'd seen nothing but closed doors.

In a last-ditch effort to avoid self-publishing, I tried using Inkshares, a traditional publisher that will publish your book if you can pre-sell 750 copies in a narrow window of time. I figured this window was my last chance.

My regionally syndicated column and more than a quarter million monthly readers validated me and made me confident I wouldn't have a problem selling 750 books, since 750 was less than 1 percent of my readers. If I wanted to make a career out of writing — which I did (and still do) — I had to try everything at my disposal. So I prepared for my campaign.

After some legwork, I amped up to a May 2022 start date. If I could sell 750 books by October 2022, I would have a publisher. I spent a sizable chunk of that summer fishing in Southeast Asia with my friend Dom Porcelli, so from roughly July 1 through August 15, I made zero efforts to sell because I was off on another life-changing adventure. Perhaps, that cost me the sales I needed, but I doubt it. I finished with just under 200 presales. Not even close to my goal. If it's any consolation, the fishing was great.

After every single door and window closed on me, I decided to just bash a hole in the drywall and go through that. So I did. In the fall of 2022, more than three years after returning from the trip that became this book, I decided to self-publish. It was an unpleasant decision for me, and I felt like I'd settled, but ultimately, I decided I'd rather be self-published than not published at all.

Emily Hanson (who edited this book and made my writing much, much better) and Zach Alley (who edited for technical and scientific accuracy herein) helped a ton. I also have to think my friend and graphic design teacher, Jon Rudnicki, for allowing me to hire out the cover design to his advanced digital art class. A senior I'd had in several of my business classes before, Ella Bocchi, ultimately created the winning cover design. Yes, this incredible cover was made by a high school student!

Now that this book is done — really done — it feels so weird. Whether it's a hit or not, it is a relief to have it behind me. Another part already feels a sense of loss, so I guess I'll have to being working on my next book. Who knows what that will teach me?

I learned some things during my trip and during this book. Sure, the perseverance and pain of getting it published proved much more formative than the trip itself, but that trip and the subsequent shakeup of society made me value others so much more. If traveling across the country for the better part of two months taught me anything, it's that truer words than American poet Muriel Rukeyser's have never been spoken: "The universe is made of stories, not atoms."

Everything and everyone has a story. I've been blessed to live a life that has let me share my story here and through dozens of publications throughout the years, but never over such a long period, never in so many words, and never sandwiched between two covers. I hope this story made you laugh (with me and at me), cry, reflect, and find yourself appreciating what really matters in life with the understanding that everyone's driving force is different. Not only that, but that a person's driving force can change and grow and even be temporary, evaporating and changing forms like a morning mist. Mine, for now, remains fishing and then writing about it.

AUTHOR BIO

Luke Ovgard is a lifelong angler and vocal advocate for conservation, outdoor education, and outdoor participation. One of his earliest memories is trout fishing at a small, Southern Oregon lake with his father at age 3. From there, fishing grew into an all-consuming passion that shaped the course of his life. At the time of publication, he has fished in 44 U.S. states and 17 countries. He holds the worldwide Fishing Big Year Record, having caught 416 species in 2021. He has more than a dozen IGFA All-Tackle World Records and currently ranks fifth in history for the total number of fish species caught, with 1,152 (about 3.5 percent of all fishes on Earth) at the time of publication. He is a high school business teacher and Air Force medical officer who loves puns and dad jokes — much to the chagrin of his students and coworkers but hopefully not his readers. Though he enjoys both careers, as well as real estate, his driving passion is writing about fishing, and he has written a regionally syndicated travel and outdoors column called "CaughtOvgard" for a host of newspapers since January of 2015. His primary goal in life is to travel, fish, and write about his experiences full-time, despite being born a few decades too late for this path to be easily realized. Regardless, it is a goal for which this book is a step in the right direction so long as you enjoyed it and tell all of your friends about it, so they can share in the journey. If you did enjoy it, the author appreciates your kind words. If not, he will cry himself to sleep later.

www.ingramcontent.com/pod-product-compliance
Lightning Source LLC
LaVergne TN
LVHW011414080426
835512LV00005B/58